POPPER'S *OPEN SOCIETY*
AFTER FIFTY YEARS

POPPER'S *OPEN SOCIETY* AFTER FIFTY YEARS

The continuing relevance of
Karl Popper

*Edited by Ian Jarvie
and Sandra Pralong*

London and New York

First published 1999
by Routledge
11 New Fetter Lane, London EC4P 4EE

Simultaneously published in the USA and Canada
by Routledge
29 West 35th Street, New York, NY 10001

Routledge is an imprint of the Taylor & Francis Group

Typeset in Garamond by
Ponting–Green Publishing Services, Chesham, Buckinghamshire
Printed and bound in Great Britain by
TJ International, Padstow, Cornwall

British Library Cataloguing in Publication Data
A catalogue record for this book is available from the British Library

Library of Congress Cataloging-in-Publication Data
Popper's Open Society after fifty years: the continuing relevance
of Karl Popper/edited by Ian Jarvie and Sandra Pralong.
p.   cm.
Includes bibliographcal references and index.
Revised papers presented at a conference held in 1995 at the Central
European University, Prague in commemoration of the 50th anniversary
of the publication of Karl Popper's *The Open Society and Its Enemies*.
1. Popper, Karl Raimund, Sir, 1902–94   Open society and its
enemies–Congresses.   2. Philosophy–Congresses.
3. Social sciences–Philosophy–Congresses.
I. Jarvie, I. C. (Ian Charles).   II. Pralong, Sandra.
B63.P6   1999   98–47993
301–dc21   CIP

ISBN 0–415–16502–4

TO ERNEST GELLNER
(1925–1995)

CONTENTS

CONTRIBUTORS

Joseph Agassi is a former Professor of Philosophy at Tel Aviv University, Israel, and York University, Toronto, Canada.

Adam J. Chmielewski is Professor of Philosophy, University of Wrocław, Poland.

Fred Eidlin is Professor of Political Science, University of Guelph, Ontario, Canada.

Andrzej Flis is Professor at the Institute of Sociology, Jagiellonian University, Cracow, Poland.

Sir Ernst H. Gombrich is the former Director of the Warburg Institute and Professor of the History of the Classical Tradition, University of London, UK.

John A. Hall is Professor of Sociology, McGill University, Montreal, Canada.

Cyril Höschl is Professor of Psychiatry, Director of the Prague Psychiatric Centre, and Dean of the Third School of Medicine at Charles University, Prague, Czech Republic.

Ian Jarvie is Professor of Philosophy, York University, Toronto, Canada.

Bryan Magee is a former British MP and Professor of Philosophy, Oxford University, UK.

Christoph von Mettenheim is an Attorney with the Rechtsanwalt beim Bundesgerichtshof in Karlsruhe, Germany.

David Miller is a Reader in Philosophy, University of Warwick, Coventry, UK.

Mark A. Notturno is the Director of the Popper Project at the CEU Foundation, Vienna, Austria.

Sandra Pralong is a Doctoral candidate in Political Science, Columbia University, New York, and the former Director of the Open Society Foundation, Bucharest, Romania.

John Watkins is a former Professor of Philosophy at the London School of Economics, London, UK.

ACKNOWLEDGMENTS

It takes many hands, heads, and hearts to put togeter a volume, and it is always difficult to give each a fair share. However, there are some people without whom this book would not have existed, and whom we take this opportunity to thank: Gaye Woolven, Ernest Gellner's personal assistant, who helped organize the 1995 Prague Conference and energetically started the process of publishing a volume in its wake; John Hall, who succeeded Ernest Gellner as the head of the Center for the Study of Nationalism at the Central European University in Prague, and who kindly secured a small grant to get the project underway; Susan Gellner, Ernest Gellner's wife, who graciously offered the use of Gellner's correspondence; and Raymond and Melitta Mew, Karl Popper's close collaborators and now the executors of the Popper estate, who generously offered the use of archival material, correspondence, and other documents. Also, our thanks go to Richard Stoneman, senior editor at Routledge, for his unfailing support and interest in the project, to Coco Stevenson, his senior assistant, and to Sarah Hall, in charge of production.

Ian Jarvie, Toronto, 1999
Sandra Pralong, New York, 1999

Part I

PRELIMINARIES

INTRODUCTION

Ian Jarvie and Sandra Pralong

Fifty years ago, Routledge & Kegan Paul took a chance on a bulky manuscript by an unknown thinker, that, it turned out, made a decisive contribution to liberal thought. That book was *The Open Society and Its Enemies.*

Karl Popper, who wrote it while he was teaching in New Zealand, called the book his "war effort." As he observed from afar the threat that fascism posed to freedom and rationalism, he sought to encourage reflection about those aspirations and institutions which can help prevent societies from falling prey to totalitarian ideologies.

Perhaps due to the distance separating him from the theater of events, Popper was among the first political philosophers to put totalitarianism in perspective and to conceive of a framework for the study of society that could identify the parallels between all forms of closed society – tribalist, fascist, communist, religious-fundamentalist, etc.

In a way, the book seems a response to Kant's call in "What is Enlightenment?", "Sapere Aude!" – Dare to know! For Kant, "The Enlightenment is the emancipation of man from a state of self-imposed tutellage ... of incapacity to use his own intelligence without external guidance" (Popper 1992: 128). Knowledge, thinking for oneself, questioning authority, criticism and self-criticism are, for Popper as for Kant, the tools of one's freedom. The preface to *The Open Society*'s first edition makes this idea clear: "we must break with the habit of deference to great men. Great men make great mistakes ..." Popper writes, referring to Plato, Hegel, and Marx.

Three views of history: pessimistic, optimistic, indeterministic

The Open Society and Its Enemies was published in London in late 1945, in two volumes. The first, entitled "The Spell of Plato," was a sustained attempt to trace the history and doctrines of historicism to their Ancient Greek origins, especially Plato. "Historicism" was the name Popper coined for the view

3

that there are inevitable laws of historical development.[1] Plato was a pessimist: the laws of development govern a tendency to deterioration. The best we can do is to slow the process, and that requires tyrannical measures (detailed in *The Republic* and *The Laws*).

Although closely focused on Plato, the first volume was wide-ranging. Popper analyzed and criticized the Greek idea that science was the search for essences, that is, for that in virtue of which a thing is what it is. As an alternative, he offered his own view of how modern science proceeds without any theory of essences. Plato had a carefully worked out view of how education and training should prepare persons for the role they will play in society. Popper, by contrast, argued that education should empower one to be autonomous, able to cope with situations and make choices. Above all, Plato was presented as the archetype utopianist, the thinker who, in the name of virtue, considers coercion appropriate. Plato's utopia is backward-looking, a quest to halt the decay of civilization. For Popper, Plato is a great thinker who made great mistakes. This, Popper says, teaches us that we should not defer to great men, but think for ourselves. As an alternative to Plato's influential ideal society, Popper offers the open society, one which attempts to maximize freedom of choice, and which is democratic in the sense that the citizens can overthrow the government without violence.

The second volume, entitled "The High Tide of Prophecy: Hegel, Marx and the Aftermath," looked principally at the optimist historicist Karl Marx, who held that the laws of history governed an inexorable progress, which could be assisted or smoothed in its passage, but not staunched. By contrast with Plato, Marx was optimistic. He offered hope to humankind. One day the exploitation and oppression would come to an end, even if it should need a paroxysm of violence. Marx's ideas about society are dissected exactly as Plato's were in the first volume. Both are accused of mixing brilliant scientific ideas about society and politics with other claims that are merely prophetic: claims about the future course of things that cannot be known in advance. Great men make great mistakes; great men as prophets can be the deliverers of disaster.

The text of each volume was supported by dense endnotes, in which Popper explored ramifications and sidelights, sometimes to the extent of writing complete essays on a topic (e.g. the dating of Plato's dialogues and Popper's new, bold, and straightforward solution to the Socratic problem; they also contain a detailed and breathtaking review of Wittgenstein's *Tractatus*).

Although it attacked the Platonism rampant in British educational philosophy, as well as the Marxism so pervasive among intellectuals then and now, the book was widely discussed in the intellectual press. When it was taken to task

---

1 This was not its established use in historiography, a cause of some quite indefensible misunderstanding and controversy.

by Platonists and Marxists, this was usually done in a full and careful way that made it clear this was a book that deserved to be taken seriously. Popper entered British academe as someone who deserved to be listened to. John Watkins has vividly described the intellectual atmosphere in London after the war, and its manifestation at the London School of Economics, where Popper taught alongside Laski, Hayek, and Robbins (Watkins 1977, 1997).

Modestly self-described as a critical introduction to the philosophy of history and of politics, *The Open Society* was more ambitious than that. It argued that historicism was able to gain its ascendancy largely because the struggle for freedom and democracy had been misformulated by their advocates. There were insoluble paradoxes in the standard discussions of sovereignty and democracy which doomed them. What was needed, Popper suggested, was a recasting of the ideas of the whole tradition. Demands for equality needed to be rooted in the universal human capacity for critical, rational inquiry. Demands for freedom and openness were not about the particular system of government, but about ensuring that in all systems the government be changeable without violence.

The book set a pattern for the reception of Popper's ideas: it tended to polarize serious readers. Although a success with the reading public, its academic reception was mixed. The essentialists, Platonists, historicists, Marxists, and positivists who were attacked in the book adopted various defensive tactics, including distortion and vilification. But the most successful and widely used tactic was to ignore Popper. This could proceed by actual silence; by simply not mentioning him or his ideas no matter how germane; or by quickly knocking down a straw man in his place, such as citing him on some minor point rather than the main point, or giving his name to someone else's ideas or vice versa.

London versus Oxford

In 1946, when the book shot Popper to fame, the dominant school of logical positivism, according to which most philosophy consists of pseudo-problems, was giving way to its analytic descendant, ordinary language philosophy, according to which the analysis of the ordinary uses of words was more than sufficient to dissolve traditional philosophical problems (Gellner 1959). This new philosophy was centered at Oxford University, where Ernest Gellner was on the way to earning First Class Honours and winning the John Locke Prize. Gellner, whose instincts were against language philosophy, was hired to teach philosophy to sociology degree students at the London School of Economics (LSE), possibly as an alternative to allowing them to attend Popper's lectures. It was at the School that Gellner encountered congenial social scientists who showed him how to look sociologically and anthropologically at philosophy. The eventual result was his devastating book, *Words and Things* (Gellner 1959). It consisted of an account of the history, doctrines, practices, and defensive maneuvers of language philosophy, written in a tart and satirical style. Gellner's innovation consisted in arguing that the history of ideas was insufficient to understand why language philosophy was a movement. To understand that, a sociology of its practitioners and of the institutions in which they practiced was required. Gellner duly supplied one. From the dreaming spires of Oxford, the London School of Economics must have seemed like a nest of heterodoxy and intellectual pollution.

Gellner and Popper had little informal contact during their twenty years as colleagues (the latter retired in 1969), but Popper's colleagues John Watkins and Imre Lakatos were firm friends with Gellner. After Lakatos' premature death, Gellner moved sideways into the philosophy department, prior to his election to the Chair of Social Anthropology at Cambridge in 1984.

Towards the end of his life, Gellner (1925–1995) published several pieces (Gellner 1992, 1993, 1996) on the thought of Popper (d. 1994). In one (Gellner 1993), he made it clear that Popper's influence on him was second to none. Popper told Jarvie that after the first meeting between the two (narrated in Gellner 1993), Gellner had written to Popper about *The Open Society and Its Enemies*. Popper averred that it was one of the best critical comments he had ever received (see Appendix B).[2] That spirit of critical exchange was continued by Gellner into his posthumously published work, and in his design and organization of the conference upon the papers of which this volume is based.

Popper in the public forum

The career of Popper's ideas was different inside the academy from what it was outside. In intellectual circles Popper was very much admired. But because *The Open Society and Its Enemies* was hostile to so much academic pretension it was treated less than respectfully by those in the various specialties upon whose turf it trod. An extreme illustration of this is found in the correspondence of two fellow-European exiles of Popper's, Leo Strauss and Eric Voegelin, who lived in the USA. Both considered themselves political philosophers, both were deeply immersed in the Greek classics, and both considered that modern thought had to start with careful consideration of Hegel. Strauss is explicitly opposed to Enlightenment rationalism (Emberly and Cooper 1993: 66). Both also thought that contemporary social science, hollow of philosophical substance, could not explain the rise of National Socialism, indeed might, in some way, be part of the problem. According to Popper's philosophy, *per contra*, the Hegelian irrationalism and esotericism espoused by Strauss and Voegelin were part of the problem, inimical to the open society.

2 Gellner's letter to Popper has yet to be found in Popper's archive. Popper's holograph reply has, however, been found in the archive of Gellner's papers at the British Library of Political and Economic Science. It is reproduced at the end of this Introduction by kind permission of the executors of Popper's estate, Raymond and Melitta Mew.

There was a lot of tension round these issues. In 1950, Popper went to Harvard to deliver the prestigious William James lectures. During his time in the States he appears to have given a talk at the University of Chicago, where Strauss taught. Strauss told Voegelin that the talk "was very bad," "the most washed-out, lifeless positivism" (Emberly and Cooper 1993: 67), and inquired of his opinion of Popper. Voegelin replied with a vicious letter. He reports having reluctantly read Popper because so many people insist his *Open Society* is a masterpiece. His judgment is that the book is "impudent, dilettantish crap. Every single sentence is a scandal ..." (ibid.). Noting that Popper takes the concept of open society from Bergson, he comments that Bergson did not develop it "for the sole purpose that the coffeehouse scum might have something to botch." Voegelin believed that Bergson would have thought that "Popper's idea of the open society is ideological rubbish" (ibid.).

Voegelin is only just getting started. He accuses Popper of "impertinent disregard for the achievements in this particular problem area [the history of political thought]" (Emberly and Cooper 1993: 68) and of being unable to reproduce accurately the ideas of Plato and Hegel. Popper is "a primitive ideological brawler." Voegelin then strings more epithets together, "a failed intellectual," "rascally impertinent, loutish; in terms of technical competence as a piece in the history of thought, it is dilettantish, and as a result is worthless" (Emberley and Cooper 1993: 67).

The reader astonished at this undignified diatribe needs to remember that in the book in question Popper is vehement about the duty to think for oneself and not to defer to the authority of experts. Strauss and Voegelin agree on the opposite, and on the duty of the enlightened elite to defend standards. Strauss had said he was willing to keep Voegelin's remarks to himself. Voegelin concludes: "It would not be suitable to show this letter to the unqualified. Where it concerns its factual contents, I would see it as a violation of the vocational duty you identified, to support this scandal through silence" (Emberly and Cooper 1993: 69). Following this invitation, Strauss showed the letter to Kurt Riezler, "who was thereby encouraged to throw his not inconsiderable influence into the balance against Popper's probable appointment here [in the US]. You thereby helped to prevent a scandal."

With hindsight one might think that the scandal is that someone who had dared to challenge the traditional Germanic learning, the worship of the great men, the enemies of science and Enlightenment, is not met out in the open with argument, but is disposed of behind the scenes, as quietly as possible, by the self-righteous use of power.

The intellectual public, however, bought enough copies of *The Open Society* to keep it continuously in print, frequently revised. Moreover, by the 1950s, it was translated into German and other languages, and its ideas came to have an important influence. One gauge of this in Britain is that Popper was read by working politicians such as Richard Crossman and Anthony Crosland on the left. On the right, Sir Keith Joseph donated the book to the

Cabinet library on first being made a minister, and another Conservative minister, Sir Edward, later Lord, Boyle, wrote an appreciative essay in the volume in The Library of Living Philosophers devoted to Popper (Boyle in Schilpp 1994). In Germany and Austria Popper's vocabulary became standard in the attempt to build a philosophy for the democracies of those countries. Some German philosophers (but only some), and influential members of the intellectual and political class, took Popper's ideas for common currency, showering him with public honor and recognition. Translations into all the main European languages ensured a wide currency for the ideas. It might be only a slight exaggeration to say that Popper is a philosophical icon for the European Union's liberals.

Equally important, though less obvious, was Popper's impact in totalitarian areas of Europe. From Spain and Portugal, through Eastern Europe to the USSR and to China, his works were spread in translation and samizdat publication as a fulcrum of intellectual resistance to the official ideology.

After the fall of the Eastern European empire of the USSR in 1989, there was much need to build free and democratic institutions, and to reintroduce notions of freedom of thought, critical thinking, and intellectual inquiry in the former Soviet bloc countries. Popper was one of the few Western philosophers whose ideas were of sufficient scope and depth to be applied to the task of linking free inquiry, free communication, freedom to enter and exit, with openness and freedom in politics. George Soros, the American billionaire of Hungarian origin who had encountered Popper's ideas during studies at the LSE, set up a network of philanthropic institutions in the region – aptly called "Open Society Foundations" – to put into practice Popper's ideas, by encouraging critical thinking in education, and by contributing to the development of an active, lively, civil society. In addition, Soros set up the Central European University (CEU) in Prague and then Budapest, to provide, among other things, an intellectual training ground for these ideas. One of the CEU's founding Professors was Ernest Gellner, who took special leaves from Cambridge to commute to Prague to set up there his Center for the Study of Nationalism.

Nationalist ideas had been criticized and condemned by Popper as leading inevitably to invidious comparisons and to totalitarianism. Gellner simply dismissed nationalist ideas as uninteresting (Gellner 1983: 124) and insisted that we view nationalism as an historical and a political phenomenon, where he could show it readily lent itself both to oppressive and to liberatory movements. Indeed, in a series of articles and books beginning in the 1970s, Gellner had argued that nationalism was a new form of identity for modernizing societies, and that this made it something we should study and deal with, rather than lament and condemn. When Popper came to Prague, at the very end of his life, to receive an honorary degree at Charles University and to lead a seminar at the Central European University, he chose to speak about the philosopher-president of pre-war democratic Czechoslovakia, Thomas Masaryk.

Masaryk was a liberal nationalist and a philosopher-king.[3] Popper and Gellner, two central Europeans a generation apart, exiled in the 1930s, found themselves in the same city, on the same platform, pondering what needed to be done to bring lasting freedom to the area.

A conference is planned

It was with considerable excitement that those of us involved received Gellner's proposal for a conference at the Central European University, Prague, the year after Popper's death, in order to celebrate the fiftieth anniversary of the publication of *The Open Society and Its Enemies*. The enemies Popper had argued against in 1945, fascism and communism, had been routed from Europe. New enemies were abroad in the world, in the form of military dictatorships, clerico-fascist regimes, corrupt narco-terrorist regimes, and, in the former Iron Curtain countries, militant nationalisms and dictatorial post-communist communist regimes. No one coming to the conference was under any illusion that the open society is an ideal universally endorsed in practice. Still, there was cause for celebration and reflection on a new situation partly brought about by the ideas in Popper's book, yet a situation presenting something of a challenge to its framework. That Popper, one of the great thinkers of the liberal West, should have been memorialized by scholars who, while appreciative, were critical, was no doubt intended by Gellner to be an object lesson.

In the letter of invitation (see Appendix A) Gellner suggested four main themes: the continuing value, in the post-communist Eastern European vacuum, of arguments developed by Popper to undermine victorious or expanding totalitarianism; assessing Popper's parallel between the open society and the organization of scientific inquiry; Popper's intellectual history and the history of liberal thought in Central Eastern Europe and elsewhere; assessing the criticisms of Popper, especially as regards community, and the tenacity of essentialist and historicist thinking.

As indicated at the end of Gellner's letter, his conference plan was to be subject to revision and alteration right up to the time of the meeting. Successive drafts of the program certainly reflect such modification. But, unexpectedly, the decisive influence on the tone and the structure of the meeting was the sudden death of the organizer, Ernest Gellner. He became a structuring absence both at this conference, and at another one a month later, which had been intended to celebrate and discuss his own work, and which became instead a memorial conference (Hall 1998).

3 Popper was quite critical of Masaryk in *The Open Society and Its Enemies*; quite commendatory of him in 1994.

The present volume

These developments and our own editorial judgment, mean that what is before the reader is not exactly the proceedings of the conference, but revised and reconsidered texts prepared in the light of the conference's discussions. Sir Ernst Gombrich, who was unable to come to Prague, consented to have his recollections read. Adam Chmielewski's interview with Popper was offered to us for the present volume. Conducted shortly before Popper's death, and not previously published in English, it forms, in our view, a fitting valedictory into which are woven several of Gellner's themes. Bryan Magee's reflections on Popper and practical politics, when delivered, were already in press elsewhere, and are here published unaltered.

There are three parts to this volume. In the first part, "Preliminaries," *The Open Society and Its Enemies* and its author are introduced. In the second part, "Addressing the text," contributors engage in commentary upon, or criticism of, the ideas in the book. In the third part, "Applying the text," our authors test the current vitality of Popper's ideas by applying them to current social, political, and philosophical concerns.

Preliminaries: Apart from the present Introduction, we have placed here Sir Ernst Gombrich's personal recollections of the tortuous road taken by the publishing process, and Popper's exclusive interview.

By Popper's own account, the original manuscript of *The Open Society and Its Enemies* took almost four years to compose, even in the relative safety and tranquillity of New Zealand (Popper 1976). It took more than a year to find a publisher, and still another year for it to be revised, printed, and bound. Thanks to F. A. von Hayek, Sir Herbert Read, and Sir Ernst Gombrich, the book finally appeared at the very end of 1945. It remains in print, having gone through four editions and numerous printings. Sir Ernst's recollections of its precarious origins have a special poignancy in a volume celebrating its fiftieth anniversary.

In his later years Karl Popper gave many interviews to newspapers and magazines, some reflection of his growing stature in the world, and perhaps also the least difficult means for him to comment on more general matters that did not require intense hours of work at his desk. Adam Chmielewski's interview is one of the latest Popper gave (the English version presented here is exclusive.) In it Popper discusses his latest interests and projects: a study of the Presocratics, his continuing fascination with evolutionary epistemology, his belief about the possible resurgence of Marxism, his concern about the educational impact of television, and others.

Addressing the text: This section brings together five authors who consider problems of interpretation, and offer critical commentary on *The Open Society*.

Mark Notturno, who was personally close to Popper, and who edited his two final books of essays (Popper 1994a, 1994b), takes up Gellner's first theme:

the lasting value of Popper's arguments against totalitarianism. He finds that they need re-stating. He argues that Plato, Hegel, and Marx are stand-ins or particular cases of the main enemies of open society which are: authority (political, social, and intellectual); community (rather than individuality); and bureaucracy. Using Popper's writings as background, Notturno weaves these three themes into current political and intellectual debates.

David Miller, one of Popper's closest collaborators in his last twenty-five years, a co-author, and the editor of a pocket anthology of the writings, *Popper Selections* (Miller 1983), takes up what Gellner referred to as aspects of Popper's intellectual history. Miller discusses the crucial transition in Popper's thought from his original work in the philosophy of science (which used the notion of logical truth, but steered clear of more traditional notions), to his discovery of Tarski's work and its impact on him (a change first advertised in *The Open Society and Its Enemies*).

Ian Jarvie, a student of Popper's since 1955 and his research assistant from 1960 to 1961, also criticizes Popper's formulations before taking up Gellner's themes of the organizational parallel between science and the open society. Jarvie suggests that open and closed are more fruitful if presented as Weberian ideal types. Presented as historical or anthropological descriptions they are controversial in ways irrelevant to the philosophical matters at issue. Jarvie criticizes Popper's ideal-typical view of science, and suggests that real existing science calls into question science as a model of openness.

John A. Hall, an historical sociologist and a colleague of Gellner's, whom Hall succeeded at the helm of the CEU Center on the Study of Nationalism, is a life-long student of Popper's work. He takes up Gellner's invitation to address the themes of criticisms of Popper, especially his historical sociology. While lauding the values of *The Open Society*, Hall criticizes its sociological assumptions, its idealism, and its analysis of what could and should have been done. Admitting that there is a whiff of historicism in all grand interpretations of history, Hall claims his is harmless and offers a "sociologized" alternative to Popper's picture of history as the struggle to implement emerging ideas of freedom and autonomy.

John Watkins, who has been associated with Popper since the 1940s, and who has contributed to both political philosophy and to the philosophy of science, takes a different approach to Gellner's charge: he offers new criticisms of Popper's text. Where Hall wants to defend historical sociology *despite* the whiff of Hegel, Watkins smells a whiff of Hegel in some historical remarks in *The Open Society* itself. He proceeds to expose and castigate this unreconstructed aspect. Watkins agrees with Gellner's view that Popper "is desperately attracted by those things that he also rejects," and shows how certain historicist passages fit this pattern.

Applying the text: The authors of the chapters in the third and final section of the volume look at the implications of *The Open Society and Its Enemies* for law, ethics, practical politics, political developments in Poland, liberalism, nationalism, historical causation, and, finally, at what all this teaches us about the pitfalls of trying to apply Popper's ideas. Each author focuses on different aspects of Gellner's invitational themes.

Christoph von Mettenheim, a distinguished German jurist, evaluates the problem of ethical objectivity by comparing it to the putative objectivity of the law. Although he disagrees with Popper about the relation between facts and norms, he nonetheless finds Popper's work a rich and stimulating source of suggestive ideas. In his chapter, for instance, von Mettenheim attempts to reconcile two of Popper's views which seem in tension: methodological nominalism (and the problem of objectivity) and the theory of piecemeal social engineering as applied to the law.

Sandra Pralong, a former Director of the Open Society Foundation in Romania and a doctoral candidate in political science at Columbia University in New York, tackles the issue of ethical standards. Drawing on her Eastern European background and experience, she argues that in order for open societies to be established in the region, a key condition of the post-communist transition is that individuals be willing to change their ethical paradigm. From Popper's writings, she extracts a minimalist rule that can guide moral decision-making in the open society.

Bryan Magee, philosopher, politician, journalist, personal friend of Popper, and author of the portrait of him in the Modern Masters book series, reflects on how well or ill Popper's ideas fare as guides in the world of practical politics, as well as on some ideas Popper had on current events. His verdict is a mixed one: if followed, Popper's ideas would much improve practical politics; Popper's personal adherence to principle led him, however, to errors of practical judgment.

Andrzej Flis, a Polish social scientist, draws out the grim implications of the attempt to replace communist ideology with Catholicism as the new state ideology in post-Cold War Poland. Powerful elements of orgzanized Christianity are among the new enemies of the open society, now that the older enemies, fascism and communism, have been more or less disposed of. Popper himself did not discuss this danger in *The Open Society and Its Enemies* beyond saying that there are two trends within Christianity, open and closed.

Adam Chmielewski, a Polish philosopher, wonders, more generally, if there can be life after liberalism. By this he means: where do Eastern European intellectuals go after their disillusion with the liberalism so warmly embraced by them in 1989? His argument is that neither Sir Karl Popper nor Sir Isaiah Berlin should be or wanted to be treated as the last word, only perhaps as the first word.

Joseph Agassi, another former student (from 1953) and research assistant to Karl Popper, takes issue with Popper over whether nationalism can be reconciled with liberalism. While sympathetically sketching the problem situation that led to Popper's negative attitude to nationalism, Agassi contests Popper's stand and insists on nationalism's possible compatibility with liberalism.

12

Cyril Höschl, Dean of the Charles University School of Medicine, works out the implications of Popper's falsificationism for historical study, and concludes that primarily because of the limitations that time places on our analysis of relevant data, if there is causality in history we have in principle no tools to discover it.

Finally, Fred Eidlin, a political scientist specializing in Eastern European matters, and founder of the *Popper Newsletter*, attempts a summary of the salient points of Popper's work as applied to scholarly practice. He finds that in spite of the inspiration Popper's ideas represent for both academics and the intellectual public at large, Popperians sometimes are slow to adopt for themselves the principles they teach to others.

It goes without saying that there is one voice missing from the debate conducted in these chapters, the voice that announced the themes that our authors fastened on: Ernest Gellner. Gellner had not scheduled himself to speak at the conference, but he could have been expected to be his usual self and ask pointed questions, express generous appreciation, and to have been the most warm, knowledgeable, and provocative host. No doubt he would have edited and introduced this volume differently. Given his own overwhelmingly busy life, it was typical that he wanted nevertheless to take time to celebrate the political thought of a philosopher from whose ideas he had benefited; discussion of these ideas was a-buzz in newly liberated Eastern Europe.

Popper was an intellectual optimist. One of his most intriguing insights was that ideas, thoughts set down in statements, had an objective existence. What was originally private was now public. Being public meant that it was preserved and it was accessible; thus the fate of ideas could be detached from attitudes toward the thinker. In the upshot, the tension between Popper's reception in the academy and his reception in the broader intellectual world will not matter. It is the broader intellectual community which knew how to recognize his genius and gave Popper his standing as one of the twentieth century's most extraordinary minds. In the end, what matters is that after fifty years his ideas still provoke discussion between all parties, from the most elevated to the most humble, about the vital questions that affect the justice of society and the peace of the world.

APPENDIX A

Gellner's letter of invitation to the Prague conference on the fiftieth Anniversary of *The Open Society*

Central European University, Centre for the Study of Nationalism
Director of Research: Professor E. A. Gellner, F.B.A, M.A.E.

3 July 1995

Dear Colleague

Fiftieth Anniversary of *The Open Society*

This is a follow up letter in connection with the conference, on November 9 and 10, 1995, celebrating the fiftieth anniversary of the publication of Karl Popper's *Open Society and Its Enemies*.

The provisional plan is to have four main themes, namely:

1 The idea of the *Open Society* and the post-Communist East European vacuum. The relevance of the ideas and values of the work to the aftermath of a totalitarian collapse, as opposed to their initial relevance as an attempt to undermine a victorious or expanding totalitarianism.

2 The *Open Society* and the scientific community. The validity or otherwise of the parallel drawn by Popper between the principles of an *Open Society* and of scientific enquiry. This theme of course is particularly suitable for the participants who think of themselves primarily as philosophers of science rather than as students of politics and society.

3 The history of the *Open Society* content. This section could include both papers concerning Popper's own intellectual development, and concerning the history of other liberal formulations in Central Eastern Europe and elsewhere.

4 The *Open Society* and its critics. It is important that the conference should not be simply a celebration carried out by Popper adherents but that it should also discuss the strength of criticisms of the Popperian tradition. For instance, has he underestimated the importance of [sic] or value of communalist thinking? Or, does some of his later work provide evidence of the strength of the appeal of essentialist and/or historicist thinking?

All this of course is just provisional, the details of the programme are open to change right up to the time of the conference itself and will be determined in the light of the contributions offered by the participants. However, for those of you who have not already done so, the sooner we have the title of what you would like to talk about, the better.

With many thanks for your co-operation, and looking forward to meeting you at the conference.

Sincerely yours,

Ernest Gellner

Please excuse that this letter is signed on my behalf.

14

APPENDIX B

Popper's response to Gellner's 1946 criticism

15 August 1946

Dear Mr. Gellner,

I found your long letter not only non-boring but really interesting. Your criticism is going to the roots of the matter, and largely valid, even though I think that there are a number of points – probably less fundamental points – in which I might successfully defend myself.

You have, in your letter, succeeded in looking at my book from an elevated point of view, as it were – looking at my position as a whole, rather than worrying about any details in my reasoning. (You have succeeded, but you should not think that this is the only or the right way of looking at it.) If I may try to do the same in regard to your letter, then I may perhaps say: the fundamental difference between your point of view and that of my book is that you think that I am too optimistic in my belief that we can have (1) "Openness" or "Freedom" and (2) Amelioration. I am just now in a less optimistic mood than when I wrote the book (even though I was not at all sure, when I wrote it, how the war would end), and therefore inclined to sympathise with your point of view.

But you must not forget that the book is, and remains, anti-historicistic. My optimism was not the good news that rationalism will win in the end; it was, rather, a mixture of the following: (1) We have no reason to be frightened out of our wits by the undoubtedly existing difficulties. Although we may never conquer them, this does not show that they are inconquerable. (2) A statement of those values which, in my opinion, makes the conquest worth an effort; and those include "openness" and rationalism. (3) A reasoned argument against what I may loosely call competing solutions, by showing, in the main, that they are not worth while, because they sacrifice certain of these values, either because they think that they are incompatible with others, or without even knowing what they are doing.

Surely, more can and should be said about the "Open Society." Why not? This is not the last word about it, rather the first (although it is not really first, of course). I don't think, however, that this should take the form of a definition of the Open Society (see chapter 11, section II).

I was grieved to read in your letter that you consider the principle of "freedom up to the limit of interfering with others' freedom" as "perfectly useless." Although it is not enough, and although it must be supplemented by other moral ideas, I don't think you are right; and your arguments in this particular point are, I am afraid, reminiscent of Hegel's (who contested the same point against Kant). This is why I am grieved!

You must not forget that, in these matters as in all others, nothing can be said that is completely water-tight and/or completely precise. The art of talking about such matters is the art of talking with that degree of clarity or precision which is appropriate to the subject matter. Nobody who reads what I (or Kant) says on this subject can doubt that we do not consider the murderer's and the victim's freedom as equivalent. Therefore, we must have succeeded, somehow, it [sic] explaining our principle with sufficient precision. Don't forget that I at least (as against Kant) never try to prove such a principle, but that I am content with demanding that certain things should be done, and others not done.

Yours sincerely,

K. R. Popper

REFERENCES

Emberly, Peter and Barry Cooper (eds). 1993. *Faith and Political Philosophy: The Correspondence Between Leo Strauss and Eric Voegelin, 1934–1964*. University Park, PA: The Pennsylvania State University Press.

Gellner, Ernest. 1959. *Words and Things*. London: Gollancz.

—— 1983. *Nations and Nationalism*. Oxford: Blackwell.

—— 1992. *Reason and Culture: The Historic Role of Rationality and Rationalism*, Oxford: Blackwell.

—— 1993. "The Rational Mystic." Review of Karl R. Popper, *In Search of a Better World, The New Republic* 208(16), 19 April, pp. 35–8.

—— 1996. "Karl Popper – The Thinker and the Man." In Stefan Amsterdamski (ed.), *The Significance of Popper's Thought*. Amsterdam: Rodopi, pp. 75–85.

Hall, John A. (ed.). 1998. *The State of the Nation: Ernest Gellner and the Theory of Nationalism*. Cambridge: Cambridge University Press.

Miller, David. 1983. *Popper Selections* [sc. *A Pocket Popper*]. London: Fontana.

Popper, K. R. 1945 (and later editions). *The Open Society and Its Enemies*. London: Routledge.

—— 1976. *Unended Quest: An Intellectual Autobiography*. La Salle: Open Court.

—— 1992. *In Search of a Better World*. London and New York: Routledge.

—— 1994a. *The Myth of the Framework*. London: Routledge.

—— 1994b. *Knowledge and the Body–Mind Problem*. London: Routledge.

Schilpp, P.A. (ed.). 1974. *The Philosophy of Karl Popper*. La Salle, IL: Open Court.

Watkins, John. 1977. "My LSE." In Joan Abse (ed.), *My LSE*. London: Robson Books, pp. 64–82.

—— 1997. "Karl Popper. A Memoir." *American Scholar* 55(2): 205–19.

PERSONAL RECOLLECTIONS
OF THE PUBLICATION OF
THE OPEN SOCIETY [1]

E. H. Gombrich

Karl Popper's two-volume work *The Open Society and Its Enemies* was published fifty years ago. It stands to reason that this happy event was preceded by a long period of preparation and uncertainty. In fact the publication took two-and-a-half years from the moment that he sent the manuscript from New Zealand to wartime England, and by that time, he and his wife were on the boat taking them to London to start a new life here at the LSE.

Though all this is by now very long ago, fortunately I need not rely on my memory of these events, because I was personally much involved, and hence the recipient of any number of letters which I naturally kept. During most of the war such air letters from overseas were miniaturized to save space and weight, and I have no less than ninety-five such aerogramme forms in addition to other communications relating to his job here at the LSE. They make fascinating reading, and all I can try is to give you samples of these surviving documents.

But first a few words about the background. Popper was seven years my senior, and though I had heard of him in my native Vienna, we only met very fleetingly. It so happened that my father, who was a solicitor, had spent the statutory years of his apprenticeship with Karl's father, who was also a lawyer, and they must have kept in touch, for Karl mentioned in one of his letters how helpful my father had been at the time after Karl's father had died.

In any case, our friendship only dates from the spring of 1936 when I was a junior research fellow at the Warburg Institute, and he came to this country at the invitation of Susan Stebbing. One of our joint acquaintances must have given him my address. We both lived in horrible bedsitters in the Paddington area, and we met with increasing frequency. I still remember having been incautious enough to mention that I had read a pamphlet by Rudolf Carnap on the question of other minds, and found it interesting.

1 A Public Lecture at the London School of Economics, 12 June 1995.

Karl was visibly distressed. "I am greatly disappointed that you found that interesting," he said, and from then on I remained a little selective in what I told him.

In 1936 I was twenty-seven and Popper thirty-four. My wife and I visited him and his wife Hennie during a stay in Vienna, and we also saw them during the few days they again spent in London in 1937, before sailing to New Zealand, which was then, as Hennie once wrote "halfway to the moon."

After the outbreak of the war in 1939, I joined the Listening Post, or Monitoring Service, of the BBC. I remember writing to Karl, possibly before that date, but I do not think I received an answer.

Then in May 1943, when the BBC had moved to Reading, I got a letter from him dated 16 April, the first of the ninety-five; it turned out later that Karl had had no idea where I lived, and only got my address almost fortuitously, thanks to a common acquaintance. And so begins the saga of the book, intertwined with that of his Readership here for which Hayek had asked him to apply.

"Dear Ernst" the letter began:

> I have not heard from you for a long time and I was very glad to get your cable. I very much hope that all is well with you and your family. The reason why you have not heard from us is that I have been writing a book. The manuscript is finished; its title is "A Social Philosophy for Everyman." (It has about 700 pages i.e. about 280.000 words.) I believe that the book is topical and its publication urgent – if one can say such a thing at a time when only one thing is really important, the winning of the war. The book is a new philosophy of politics and of history, and an examination of the principles of democratic reconstruction. It also tries to contribute to an understanding of the totalitarian revolt against civilization, and to show that this is as old as our democratic civilization itself.

Let me pause here for a moment to allow Popper's own description of his book to sink in: that the totalitarian revolt against civilization is as old as our democratic civilization itself.

I feel that too many readers of the book were either dazzled or irritated by its lengthy polemics and all but missed the central point of the argument. The book offers an explanatory hypothesis for the persistent hostility to the open society. Totalitarian ideologies are interpreted as reactions to what is described as the strain of civilization, or the sense of drift which is associated with the transition from the closed tribal societies of the past to the individualistic civilization that originated in Athens in the fifth century BC.

You may call it a psychological diagnosis, though Karl might not have accepted this description without qualification. In any case, I must return to his letter:

In view of the immense postal and other difficulties it is absolutely impossible to send the book from here to a publisher and have it sent back if it is rejected; for that would mean anything up to one year's delay in case of one rejection. This is why I need somebody in England who sends the MS to the various publishers ...

On 28 April, having received my consent, he sent me the manuscript, together with a letter and other material.

I am ashamed that I have not written to you for such a long time ... I cannot tell you how much it means to me that you are there and will look after the manuscript. You have no idea how completely hopeless and isolated one often feels in my situation ... But I must tell you what happened so far to the book since I finished it in October [1942]. I had heard that the paper shortage was less pressing in USA; also, the distance is smaller. For these reasons I sent a copy to the USA branch of Macmillan (which, I gather, is quite independent of the English Macmillan). At the same time I wrote to the only friend I had in the USA of whose address I was sure, asking him to act on my behalf. Macmillan turned the book down without even having read it. And this is more or less all I know after 6 months! My friend unfortunately seems to have done absolutely nothing although he had very full instructions. He did not even bother to write before February 16th, acknowledging the receipt of the MS which he got in December! And in this acknowledgment he wrote *nothing* about what he had done (because he had done nothing and obviously he is not going to do anything); he only congratulates me to [sic] my effort in writing such a big book. I don't blame him much, after all, it isn't his book, but you wrn understand what it means to get such a completely empty letter after waiting for six months!

The situation is really rather dreadful. I feel that if one has written a book one ought not to be forced to go begging to have it read, and printed.

From later conversations I know, of course, who that unreliable friend was, but I am not going to reveal his name. It turns out not to have been quite true that he did absolutely nothing. Feeling quite helpless with such a work which was far removed from his field, he sent it to a well-known professor of Political Science, at one of the ivy league universities. After a time the manuscript was returned to him, with a note saying that it was impossible to advocate the publication of a book which speaks so disrespectfully of Plato.

In the parcel which I received I found a carefully drafted letter which Karl wanted me to send to publishers, together with the manuscript. There were another formidable three pages with the heading: "*What I should like you to do*," giving a list of seventeen publishers with their addresses in the order of desirability. There are eighteen points of instructions, some with sub-headings a) b) c), but let me just quote item five: "I enclose two *different* title pages: 'A Social Philosophy For Everyman' and 'A Critique of Political Philosophy' … The reason why I have two different titles is that I am not quite satisfied with either. What would you say to 'A Social Philosophy For Our Time'? (Too pretentious?)"

On 4 May, Karl wrote another lengthy letter revising the order of publishers. Up to that point we had very little idea of how the Poppers were actually living in New Zealand, but on 29 July Hennie sent us a very lively three-page letter from which I want to quote a few passages:

> We live in a suburb on the hills with a very beautiful view across Christchurch and the Canterbury plains. The climate is as nearly perfect as things in this world can be, very long summers with an abundance of sunshine; … It gets frightfully dry … and the raising of vegetables is not quite easy. I try hard in the little time I have and from October till March we eat only "homegrown" vegetables, mainly peas, beans, potatoes, carrots, spinach, silverbeet, lettuce and tomatoes. It is really never quite sufficient, but we have to make the best of it. The rest of the year we live chiefly on a carrot and rice diet, for economy's sake. Karl's salary was never adequate and is now less so than ever … During term-time Karl can only work at the week ends, but during the summer holidays he worked literally 24 hours a day. For the last three or four months he was in a state of almost complete exhaustion; he hardly went to bed because he could not sleep … Karl finished just two days before College started again. On both days which remained from our "holiday" we went to the sea and ate as many icecreams as we could (I had planned it long ago that we would celebrate the end with eating as many icecreams as we wanted).

Poor Hennie! – What she does not say in this letter is how hard *she* had to work on the book and the correspondence, almost day and night. At a much later date [24 October 1944], she wrote to us: "This isn't a proper letter at all, I'm just rattling it off on the typewriter … of course, 'rattling it off' is terribly exaggerated – I'm the worst possible typist, and the more distance I gain from the last nightmare years of typing, the less I can understand how on earth I managed it." Let me add, by way of explanation, that Karl always wrote by hand, in the fluent, lucid script of a former schoolteacher. I could not but smile when I saw an item in Sotheby's catalogue photographed and described as "Popper's typewriter." I very much doubt that Karl ever touched its keyboard. He left it to Hennie, in what she described as the nightmare years, to type and retype countless versions and revisions. Not that Karl was not utterly devoted to her. He suffered agonies when she was ill. But he was convinced that the importance of his work had always to override his own comfort, that of Hennie, and possibly also my own, as the future was to show.

Meanwhile, on 19 August I received a long letter dealing with some critical remarks which he had encouraged me to make on reading the book, for instance: "I fully agree with your remark that the humanitarian democratic creed of the West is historically and emotionally based on Christianity. But this fact has no bearing on my theory, as far as I can see. Or has it?" I must have expostulated to him that he ridiculed Hegel, but did not say a word about Schopenhauer, and he replied:

> Although Schopenhauer was a reactionary, egoistically concerned only with the safety of his investments (he openly acknowledges this), his absolute intellectual integrity is beyond doubt. To be sure, his "Will" is not better than Hegel's "Spirit." But what Schopenhauer says, and how he says it, sufficiently proves that he was an honest thinker; he did all he could to make himself understood. Hegel did not intend to be understood; he wanted to impress, to dazzle his readers. Schopenhauer always wrote sense, and sometimes excellent sense; his Critique of Kant's philosophy is one of the most lucid and worthwhile philosophical writings ever published in the German language. A reactionary may be perfectly honest. But Hegel was dishonest.

I must not give the impression, however, that this correspondence frequently turned on philosophical issues. Perhaps there was only one other occasion, when I sent him Arthur Waley's *Three Ways of Thought in Ancient China*, because I had been struck by certain similarities between his analysis of the Greek situation and that described by Waley. Popper responded by writing that he "had always been much attracted by the Chinese, but always felt diffident concerning the possibility of a proper interpretation, considering how much Plato, for example, has been misinterpreted in spite of the fact that his thought and language has immediately influenced our own." This remained his attitude. It was never easy to interest him in the ideas of other civilizations because he felt he lacked their context.

And now for the other theme of this symphony. On 9 December 1943 he wrote: "A few days ago I got a truly overpowering airgraph from Hayek, whose indefatigable kindness to me promises no less than to change the whole course of my life." Hayek had been asked to find out whether Karl would accept a Readership at the LSE. Since the post had to be advertised, Hayek advised Karl "to instruct your friend who is acting for you over here, to apply in your name when such an advertisement is published, and to supply him for that purpose with all the usual information ... ". "– Now my poor dear friend who is acting for me over there," Karl continued, "you see that I have, indeed, no choice: I *must* trouble you again, much as I should like to spare you." Four days later Karl wrote:

21

We are of course terribly excited, and shaken up in consequence of Hayek's airgraph concerning the LSE readership. I do not think that I shall get it, owing to the fact that I have so few publications; but if I don't get it, we shall be, of course, disappointed, much as we try to fortify ourselves against such a development. I was so nicely working along with a new paper on probability, and now: "My peace is gone, my heart is heavy." Don't think that I am ungrateful. Nobody can feel more strongly than I feel about Hayek. He must have worked for me like anything. And the moral effect of this on me is, of course, tremendous.

In consequence I received more instructions from Karl, his CV, a list of references, and texts and testimonials he had previously had. I also received, then or a little later, two and a half folio pages with comments on the notes of the book. Karl realized, of course, that the notes seemed excessively long and complex, and I had also made certain suggestions. Needless to say he tried to prove that the arrangement he had chosen was the only possible one:

I have most carefully constructed the text in such a way that it is absolutely self-contained for a reader who simply belongs to the educated public, and who has no scientific axe to grind. There is *nothing* in the text that is hard to understand without the notes. I have spent immense labour on this point.

His comments, in fact, revealed, if that is the word, the importance Karl attached to his book:

I am … definitely against cuts. I believe that the book is of sufficient value to be sometimes a trifle less brief than it might be possible to make it. *I do not know any work of which one could not say the same,* often in a much higher degree. The book is written with unusual care; I know hardly anybody who is so scrupulous and conscientious in all details as I am; with the effect that, as everybody admits at once, the book achieves a rare degree of lucidity and simplicity; and this in a book which is, as you will admit, thronged with thoughts on every single page. I entirely reject the contention that there is the slightest intrinsic reason for cuts. The extrinsic reason that the book is a very long book, I admit. But since ordinary intelligent people have read through the text in one week-end, it cannot be too long. And regarding the prospect of selling a long book: the ordinary intelligent man does not like to be treated as illiterate or as an imbecile. He is ready, and even proud, to buy a thick book … I know there is no page in the book which is not full with worthwhile thoughts. This cannot be said of so very many books.

He was surely right. And now the period began when he kept sending me revisions and changes to be made to his manuscript. He was still very uncertain about the best title, and asked, on the 22nd: "What do you think of 'The Open Society and its Enemies' or of 'A Social Philosophy for our Time'? which latter title is of course, very pretentious."

The winter and spring of 1943 and 1944 I had to report to him many disappointments, and a number of publishers who had rejected the book. I believe that is a story that can be told of many important books, but here I can document it. However, in February 1944, I got a letter from Herbert Read, then a director of Routledge, reporting that Hayek had sent him Karl's manuscript. "I am enormously impressed by it, but before presenting a case to my colleagues I should be glad if you would kindly give me a little more information about the author." This I did, and Herbert Read acknowledged it gratefully.

Karl received the contract from Routledge in April 1944, but he instantly began to worry about the US copyright. And now he began to rewrite the book, and I was charged with applying these corrections to the manuscript. It is true that I had his approval to engage somebody to help, an approval which was very necessary, because, after all, I had to do my own work. For instance, on 30 April, he announced that he was sending "by the same mail eleven other airgraphs containing the *corrections*. They look more than they are," writes Karl, but to me they seemed quite sufficient. He expressed the hope that nobody would touch his text, confirming what I have also experienced: "I have only too often found that corrections made matters worse. To be sure, any suggestion for a correction proves that *something* is not quite in order; but only too often the remedy turns out to be worse than the original mistake." On 4 September he announced in addition that he had completely rewritten chapter 17 , which duly arrived. I hope I may quote a fuller sample of the type of letters which arrived so frequently:

> In my typed airgraph of today, I mentioned that, as far as *Ch.12* is concerned, *only* the Section Number Corrections have *first priority*. I now wish to amend this: there is also a false quotation which is important to replace. It is the quotation on MS p.281, from "Hence" in line 5 to the end of paragraph in line 7. – I suggest to correct these lines in accordance with my "Corr. to Ch. 12", Airgraph 4. This however would imply that the passage on p. 281 is replaced by one that is about 2 lines longer. If this creates difficulties, then I suggest to replace the "Hence ... " passage by the following of about equal length: + + States may enter into agreements, but they are superior to agreements (i.e., they may break them).+ + In this case, it would suffice to amend the corresponding Note 72 simply by replacing, in line 3 of this note, "336" by ı ı 330ı ı. If, however, there was room enough for using my original correction to p.281, the "336" should be replaced by + + 330+ + and 333+ +. – Of course,

23

if the full corrections of Airgraphs 1 to 11(?) can be used, then Note 72 should be corrected in accordance with Airgraph 9.

No wonder he wrote: "it will be a colossal job for everybody concerned. It was a colossal job here and I was (and am) very ill while doing it. The doctor has strictly forbidden any work, and I am, of course, now absolutely down again."

.Around that time there occurred an episode which is not recorded in the correspondence, and for which I shall have to rely on my memory. It happened when Routledge decided to publish the book in two volumes, an idea which, of course, much agitated Karl; all the more as it was mooted that paper shortage might necessitate publishing the second volume after a time interval. It was during these discussions that I sent a cable to Karl from our village post office: "Routledges [sic] want division after Chapter 10." A few hours later I was summoned to the post office and asked to explain what it all meant. The word "division" had alerted a censor who thought, of course, of army divisions. Luckily I was believed.

Another complication was that Karl received a number of offers from other universities in New Zealand and Australia, and naturally did not want to give up the chance of London, but needed badly to get a decision. In October he reports on

> two important articles … "Private and Public Values," the other "The Refutation of Determinism." A third one, under the title "The Logic of Freedom" is probably too long for being tackled during the vacations. When these three articles are finished, I intend to give up political philosophy, and to return to practical methodology, especially of the natural sciences. Last year I finished some papers on mathematical logic which I did not try to publish so far because of their length. If possible, I should like to cut them now. This is my working programme. Apart from that, I want to do some music. We have not been able to afford a piano here; I had a beautiful Boesendorfer in Vienna, and I could not bring myself to buying a very bad piano; besides, even the worst ones cost more than we could afford. So I bought a harmonium for £3–10–0; I repaired it, and it is not so bad, but I am getting hungry for a piano. I have had *very* little time for playing.

Meanwhile he was even more impatient to receive a binding promise of a publication date from Routledge. All this was mixed up with the worries about the various offers of a post. In one of his letters he wrote:

> You kindly advise me to prefer Otago to Perth, in spite of the Cangeroos [sic]. But I think you don't really know enough of Australia by far:

the nicest animal there (and perhaps the loveliest animal that exists) is the Koala bear. Cangeroos may be nice, but the opportunity of seeing a Koala bear is worth putting up with anything, and it is without reservation my strongest motive in wishing to go to Australia.

In April 1945 another cloud appeared on the horizon. I had to write to him that Hayek was going to the United States for a period, and Karl wrote, characteristically, "As you say yourself, the whole affair is pretty awful; and so is the fact that 18 days after you sent your letter, the registrar of London University has not yet answered you." He was eager to leave Canterbury, for though he had many admirers and friends among his colleagues, the head of his department had all but persecuted him. It was reported to Karl that he had once said: "We know that he is too good for this place. This we cannot help; and nobody will hold him if he goes elsewhere." "The main fact", Karl explained, in a letter of 9 April,

> is the presence of somebody who works hard and endangers certain accepted standards. I mean standards of relaxation (all chairs are easy chairs). These difficulties have much increased by the writing of a book, and still more, of course, by the delay in its publication. – I am terribly sorry to hear that you feel so exhausted. But I can well understand it. I long to hear you speak of your experiences, and of what you have learned during these years. (Will it ever be? I am nearly 43 now, and if I don't manage to see you before I am 45, I may never have the opportunity: I don't think that anybody would import to England a lecturer over the age of 45 ...).

Though I know the time is getting on, I really must quote for you the whole story of how Karl received the news of his appointment, as he told in his letter of 12 June 1945:

> During the whole of April I was ill again. I am now always getting such terrible colds – starting with a very sore throat, and developing in all directions. I was very weak. My doctor insisted that I should go to the mountains during the May vacations and we went both to the Hermitage, at the foot of Mt Cook (the highest mountain here). I was first pretty miserable there, but after two days I had a marvellous recovery; we went up to a hut (the Ball Hut – see pictures in "Mt Cook and the Glaciers") where we were very happy. On the bus journey back from the Hermitage, on May 21st, in the first village (called Fairlie), the Postmistress came with a cable to the bus. It was addressed to "Karl Popper c/o Bus from Hermitage to Fairlie" and said "Congratulations on London appointment and thanks for excellent article enquiring about permits Frederick Hayek." It was from Cam-

bridge, May 16th. This was the first we heard about it. I had given up the idea of going to London – though subconsciously I still believed in it. – We were both somewhat frightened, mainly in view of my rather bad health, and especially the silly way in which my corpse reacts to bad weather. I am sick of being sick, you will think me a terrible hypochonder [sic]. So do I, but my doctor (a very nice and kind person and an excellent doctor) says that it is unfortunately all true. Anyway, it cannot be helped.

And Hennie added: "I am frightfully scared by the prospect of going to London: I hate meeting new people, and tea parties. I can only hope that tea is so rare and precious that parties have gone out of fashion!"

The new worry arose that Hayek had offered to write a preface to the book. "I need not tell you that I could not accept this under any circumstances (1) because I am too proud to accept such an offer (even if it came from President Truman or John Dewey or Shirley Temple), (2) because it would brand the book and myself." Our correspondence had by then switched to the prospect of their arrival in England, and they kindly inquired how much they should take with them to wartime England, and what presents they might possibly bring. We suggested that it would be lovely if they could bring a cricket bat for our son, and Karl "enlisted the help of the very nice son of a friend of ours and now he knows all about cricket and bats." Not that the complaints stopped. On 25 August he wrote:

> Our departure problems are appalling and (but don't tell that to Routledges!) we probably won't be in England before the beginning of December: we have still no permits to enter Great Britain and I begin to fear that we won't get any. I am, of course, in continuous contact about this with Hayek who says that London University administration has completely broken down.

So let me only quote the last letter of the sequence in full. It came from Auckland, and was dated 16 November:

> Dear Ernst, This time we are really off, I think, We have been allotted berths – in two different four-berths cabins, though – on the M.V. "New Zealand Star", sailing from Auckland between Nov. 28th and December 5th (according to the strike situation). It is a frighter [sic], Blue Star Line, carrying normally 12 passengers, and at present (in the same cabins) 30. We are not terribly pleased to pay £320 for the pleasure of spending 5 or 6 very rough weeks in the company of strangers. I am particularly concerned about the fact that I cannot endure the smell of cigarets [sic] at sea without getting sick – still, I shall have to get used to it. The passage will be very rough since we

sail via Cape Horn – perhaps the roughest spot in all the Seven Seas. Our corpses are expected to arrive, by the New Zealand Star, on January 8th or thereabouts. Please receive them kindly. If there is important news it can, I suppose, be wirelessed to the ship. I shall let you know more precisely when they arrive, and if you *could* find them a room in a Boarding house or Hotel (where they might perhaps be brought to life again), it would be very nice indeed. But I know this is practically impossible: so don't waste your time, if you don't happen to hear about such a room: burry [sic] them. To be serious, I am really cheered up by the prospect of seeing you in less than two months – a very short time (at my age). Yours ever, K.

When they arrived we met them at the docks, and I was happy to be able to bring him the first copy of *The Open Society and Its Enemies*, which he eagerly scrutinized on the train and bus to our little semi-detached house in Brent. Who of us would have dared to hope on that day that despite his fragile health the new life he had just started would extend over nearly half a century, let alone predict how immensely we would all be enriched during these years by his ever active mind?

2

THE FUTURE IS OPEN

A conversation with Sir Karl Popper

Adam J. Chmielewski and Karl R. Popper

ADAM CHMIELEWSKI: *Sir Karl, please accept my best wishes on the occasion of your ninety-second birthday.*[1]

SIR KARL POPPER: Thank you very much.

CHMIELEWSKI: *Sir Karl, despite your quite impressive age, you are a very active philosopher. Could you tell me, what you are working on now in philosophy? Are you still developing your system?*

POPPER: Oh, yes. You see, I always work on several things at the same time. And, of course, my latest publication was a new addition to my book *Logic of Scientific Discovery*, to its German edition. My German publisher always wants me to add something before the new edition comes out, and I usually use the opportunity to add an appendix. So I have quite recently, a fortnight or so ago, published the twentieth appendix, in the tenth German edition of the book, which otherwise appears without any revisions. The appendix contains a new definition of probabilistic independence.

So, I am working on such things all the time. I am working on the Presocratics, in particular on Parmenides, on Aristotle's geometry, as well as on many other things.

CHMIELEWSKI: *So you seem to be continuing your interests which were once expressed in your famous paper "Back to the Presocratics" and in the two volumes of* The Open Society and Its Enemies. *Are you also coming back to your work on Plato, to whom you devoted the first, controversial volume of* The Open Society?

POPPER: Oh yes! I am still interested in Plato. Recently I happened to have become interested in pre-Euclidean geometry, that is to say in geometry without the idea of a closed axiomatic system, as in Aristotle's geometry. I am interested, first of all, in Plato's famous dialogue *Meno*,

---

1 The conversation took place on 29 July 1994, the day after Sir Karl's ninety-second birthday, at his home in Kenley, Surrey. Sir Karl died on 17 September 1994, six weeks after the meeting. This is one of the last interviews he gave. The interview was published in Polish in a monthly journal *Odra*, (Wrocław, Poland), and forms an appendix to a book, also in Polish, by Dr Chmielewski, devoted to Popper's philosophy of critical rationalism.

which is obviously not an axiomatic geometry at all. And there is something in Aristotle which is, in conception, similar to Plato's ideas in *Meno*. The Euclidean idea has been of course immensely important, for example for *Principia Mathematica* by Bertrand Russell and Alfred North Whitehead, and so on. Everything after Euclid is axiomatic, but I think that Plato's proof in *Meno* is, so to speak, an absolute proof, not relative to assumptions. There are no assumptions there. I think these kinds of mathematical proofs which are absolute, without assumptions, have been fatally neglected; it has been a neglected area and it is very interesting for me.

CHMIELEWSKI: *I remember that in your* Open Society, *in the very rich notes to that book, you referred to Plato's mathematical ideas, particularly to his* Timaeus ...

POPPER: Altogether, Ancient Greek philosophy is wonderful. I do not like Plato as an ethicist, his social philosophy is partly extremely clever, but his attitude is authoritarian and dictatorial, and not humanitarian. So I do not like his moral attitude but I admire his cleverness.

CHMIELEWSKI: *Did you ever return to your study of Hegel, another "enemy of the open society"?*

POPPER: No! No! I still hate Hegel! I read Kant instead. I have a number of first editions of Kant's works which I often look into.

CHMIELEWSKI: *Which aspect of Parmenidean philosophy are you working on now?*

POPPER: I believe that Parmenides was a materialist and that he believed that hard non-moving things are real. Now, what was really his attitude? My theory is that he believed that life and light were unreal; but that death was real, so were unmoving tools; a dead body was for him a part of reality. But life is an illusion, light is an illusion, love is an illusion. He speaks of these things but they are treated in the second part of his poem, which is devoted to life, love and light; it is thus about illusions, not about what is real. When something is not movable, it is real, when it is movable, it is not real. That is what I think is his theory. He appreciates beauty, life, but all these things are transient. They are, therefore, illusion. That is what I think is his real philosophy. And I do not think anybody has said so. I think he was a very original and very interesting thinker, and that he was in fact a scientist and an astronomer, a very important discoverer in astronomy.

CHMIELEWSKI: *His interest in astronomy could have been fostered by the Pythagorean influence ...?*

POPPER: Yes, probably. And it was pushing him, as it did Einstein.

CHMIELEWSKI: *Can you elaborate on that?*

POPPER: Yes. Einstein believed that the world was deterministic. That is to say it already pre-existed in a four-dimensional space, with the future and everything contained in it. I tried to show him that he was wrong.[2] Anyway, his system is a four-dimensional block universe, like in Parmenides. That is why I called this view the Parmenides–Einstein view. It is very easy for a scientist to adopt such a view because it is really a form of materialism – a block universe, as a three- or four-dimensional unity.

CHMIELEWSKI: *But you argued against this view. You argued that the universe is open. What kind of arguments did you employ in order to convince Einstein to reject such a view?*

POPPER: First of all, nothing in the whole world suggests it. If you lived in the Antarctic, such a view would perhaps be supported. But the difference between our world and the Antarctic illustrates how wrong the view is. Life is incredibly varied and incredibly productive, it always produces new things. It is like music, the arts, which are incredibly productive and creative. Mozart, Beethoven, or if you like, Chopin – though I must confess I am not myself particularly fond of Chopin – but they were all creative; Chopin has brought something new into the world, a new style, a new way of playing. And the world is, likewise, full of creative things; but the block-universe-deterministic attitude closes one's mind against one of the most encouraging and interesting aspects of the world.

CHMIELEWSKI: *A couple of years ago, in June 1989, I attended your lecture, given before the Alumni of the London School of Economics, on objectivity of knowledge and on evolutionary epistemology. I got the impression that your views on these issues did not change since the publication of* Objective Knowledge: An Evolutionary Approach.

POPPER: I developed them, but I did not change them. For the last fourteen years I have worked very closely with a biochemist, Günther Wächtershäuser, on the problems of the origin of life. He is a professor of evolutionary biochemistry at Regensburg in Germany.

CHMIELEWSKI: *What are your new thoughts on evolutionary epistemology?*

POPPER: First of all, I do believe that the principle of epistemology has to be not about our making observations but about our learning intellectually. That is the topic of epistemology: it is about changing our theories and improving them.

CHMIELEWSKI: *This view is an element of your critique of the empiricist tradition. The rejection of this tradition was the starting-point of your philosophy of science and epistemology, wasn't it?*

POPPER: Yes, of course. Our senses have a biological function to perform and the biological function is not to give us just sensations but to give us knowledge which is important for life. We could not do anything with

---

2 A fuller record of Popper–Einstein debate on the issue of determinism, in which Einstein is nicknamed (by Popper) "Parmenides," can be found in *The Open Universe. An Argument for Indeterminism*, ed. William W. Bartley, III (London and New York: Routledge, 1982), which forms a second part of the *Postscript to the Logic of Scientific Discovery*.

sensations alone. The decisive point is not observation but expectation. Our expectations are biologically important.

CHMIELEWSKI: *Something that is* in *us, not* outside …

POPPER: If you like, but there is not so much difference. The expectation is about what we believe to be outside. Our knowledge is to help us in our actions and in our future. Our knowledge is made of expectations and our life is based on them. You do not expect me to pull a gun out of my pocket and shoot you. The expectation that I shall treat you peacefully is basic for our conversation and it is not based on observation since you have not looked into my pockets. We have to orientate ourselves constantly in all that we are doing or not doing, and all that is based on expectations. We always have expectations that something will happen …

CHMIELEWSKI: … *which are subsequently confirmed or disconfirmed* …

POPPER: These expectations are also the basis for our hypotheses and theories. Obviously that is what our knowledge is all about. Not about whether this is an orange or not, for example. I mean all these experiments whether this egg is open at the back or not. It is perfectly true, that if I show you an egg, you will expect it to be not open at the back, yes, but it is what you *expect*, not what you *see*. Similarly, you expect my head not to be open at the back, and so on. So, we have to look at our knowledge with its function in mind, and the function is fundamentally the same as in animals. Even plants expect things to happen, and they also adjust themselves to future events.

CHMIELEWSKI: *It is natural to ask at this point what are the sources of our expectations?*

POPPER: The source of our expectations is partly our inborn knowledge, that is to say the knowledge which goes back to our Darwinian adjustment to the world. The task of a child is, for example, to adjust itself to the environment using its inborn knowledge.

Incidentally this is the reason why television is so dangerous, because television constitutes a part of the environment of the child and [that child] has [now] the task to adjust itself to it.

CHMIELEWSKI: *Indeed, the child comes to expect the world to be very much like the world-picture presented on television – and is usually disappointed …*

POPPER: Exactly! That is very dangerous. Everything we do is connected with the task of an organism to adjust itself to the environment. Plants adjust themselves, and animals do. Anticipation and expectation are especially important for animals which can move and, in their movements, they must anticipate what will happen, like a car driver. If you drive a car or a bicycle, you anticipate what will happen next. That is what makes up our consciousness.

CHMIELEWSKI: *So one can say that we are just bundles of expectations, drives and wishes, and that in the process of fulfilling our expectations and drives,*

*we are being transformed, together with our expectations and wishes which
are our prime movers ...*

POPPER: Yes, that is a very good point.

CHMIELEWSKI: *Sir Karl, you are one of the most active defenders of contemporary liberalism, a harsh critic of Marxism and of all kinds of historicism,
an unflinching spokesman for democracy. You devoted much of your philosophical activity to combatting communism and totalitarianism, preaching
the idea of the open society. What was your reaction to the democratic revolution in Poland and other countries of Central Europe, which marked the
downfall of the communist system and opened these countries to the Western
world?*

POPPER: Of course I welcomed the changes. But I must say that I do not
think that Marxism has been definitely defeated. I am sure it will come
up again and again and again. Maybe not so much in Poland but surely
in Russia. But perhaps even in Poland, and also in the West. I think
people in general tend to think in historicistic ways. That is to say, if you
look at any newspaper in any language, you will see that the moment
they write about politics, they implicitly believe that the good, right,
wise politician is the one who foresees what will happen next, who has a
gift of prophesy in the realm of politics. But in my opinion this is a
fantastic prejudice, a kind of madness. You cannot predict the future.
The future is not fixed, it is open.[3] All you can do is to try to guess very
vaguely what it is going to be like. You cannot predict when will I die: I
may die today, or I may live for another five years – you just cannot
predict that. No doctor who is really conscientious can predict what will
happen to a patient, except perhaps in extreme cases. If you cannot predict when will I die, how might it be possible to predict anything about
the whole society? So the belief that the future is determined is doubly
mixed and wrong. Even if the future *were* determined, we still might *not*
be able to predict it; but it is *not* determined *and* we cannot predict it!

   To believe otherwise is to fall victim to a superstition, an idiotic superstition which is quite powerful, all over the place. This is the reason why
Marxism will not disappear, for Marxism is not only this superstition – it
is a "scientific" superstition. So it will come up again and again.

CHMIELEWSKI: *In general we are witnessing now, despite your efforts, a strong
revival of historicism in contemporary philosophy. One of many prominent
thinkers of this persuasion is for example Alasdair MacIntyre ...*

POPPER: Oh yes, I knew him when he was very young and a Marxist. I was
invited to a meeting which he also attended. Now he seems to be preaching Thomism ...

---

3 *Zukunft ist offen* [*The Future is Open*], is the title of one of the books written by Sir Karl Popper
together with Konrad Lorenz (Munich and Zürich: Piper, 1995).

CHMIELEWSKI: ... *Moreover, in many philosophical disciplines one can sense a strong influence of the famous* Philosophical Investigations *by Ludwig Wittgenstein, of whom you have always been very critical.*

POPPER: Regrettably, it is true. It is terrible. I really think that contemporary British philosophy is pretty bad ... uninteresting ... boring. It is very boring ... The second book by Wittgenstein is extremely boring. His first book, *Tractatus Logico-Philosophicus*, was very different in character. In general philosophy is dominated by different fashions: historicism, structuralism, new historicism, post-structuralism, post-modernism and others – all these are nothing but philosophical fashions. But a fashion in science or philosophy is something terrible. It is there, it cannot be helped. But it is something that should be despised, not followed.

CHMIELEWSKI: *Do any of the British philosophers continue the philosophy of critical rationalism that you initiated here?*

POPPER: Yes, my former student and assistant, David Miller. He has just published a book on the subject. It is called *Critical Rationalism: A Restatement and Defence*[4]. He brought me this book yesterday as a birthday present ...

CHMIELEWSKI: *When do you expect your book* Conjectures and Refutations *to get published in a German translation?*

POPPER: My *Conjectures*, the first half of the book only, is now coming out in German. The *Refutations* will come out later. Many people have tried to translate it and I found all of the translations bad. Translation needs to be done really conscientiously. And these were not. Now the publisher himself has translated it and sent it to us. Mrs. Mew corrected it, and then I corrected it, and I think in that way it turned out to be quite a good book.

CHMIELEWSKI: *It is in your* Conjectures and Refutations *that you introduced many important philosophical concepts that were subsequently severely criticized by many philosophers of science, e.g. "verisimilitude," "corroboration"* ...

POPPER: Oh yes! Everything in my theory of science was criticized, but all these criticisms were no good. David Miller has answered some criticisms in his book, though I have only glanced through it since yesterday; and I also tried to answer them in my book *In Search of a Better World.*

CHMIELEWSKI: *In the preface which you wrote especially for the Polish edition of* Objective Knowledge, *you mentioned very warmly Alfred Tarski.*[5]

---

4 La Salle, IL: Open Court, 1994.

5 Alfred Tarski (1901–1983), Polish logician and philosopher, member of the Lvov–Warsaw philosophical movement, one of the founders of the Warsaw School of Logic, from 1939 at the University of California, Berkeley; author of the famous work "Pojęcie prawdy w językach nauk dedukcyjnych" (Warsaw, 1933), translated by J. H. Woodger as "The Concept of Truth in Formalized Languages" in Alfred Tarski, *Logic, Semantics, Metamathematics. Papers from 1925 to 1938* (Oxford: Clarendon Press, 1956).

Many readers in Poland are very interested in your personal association with Tarski to whom this book of yours is dedicated, as well as with many other representatives of the Lvov–Warsaw school of logic and philosophy.

POPPER: I met Tarski for the first time in Prague sixty years ago, in August 1934. There I met also Janina [Hossiason-Lindenbaum]. I attended then, for the first time, the International Congress of Philosophy. The Congress was not too interesting, but it was preceded by a Preliminary Conference, organized by Otto Neurath on behalf of the Vienna Circle. After that Tarski went from Prague to Vienna where he stayed for a year and we became friends there. From the philosophical point of view my friendship with Tarski was most important for me. Thanks to Tarski I understood the power of the notion of an absolute, objective truth and how it can be defended.

I do not know how it is today, but at that time people from Poland were more serious than others. I do not mean that they had no sense of humor, that is not it, but that they were more seriously interested in thinking than people from Austria, or Germany, or England, or anywhere. They were very, very good and serious people.

CHMIELEWSKI: *Did you meet another eminent logician of the Lvov–Warsaw school, Jan Łukasiewicz?*

POPPER: Yes. He was a nice man. I liked him very much. We met at the doctoral exams of an another Polish logician, Czesław Lejewski. I was the supervisor of the thesis, and Łukasiewicz was asked to become an external examiner.

CHMIELEWSKI: *As you probably know, he was helped by Heinrich Scholz to escape from Poland during the Nazi occupation and was given, on the recommendation of the Prime Minister of Ireland, De Valera, a mathematician himself, the position of professor in Dublin.*

POPPER: I knew Heinrich Scholz. I met him in the Paris Congress in 1935 which was organized by Otto Neurath. I am glad that he helped Łukasiewicz, he did not mention it to me. Schrödinger was also in Ireland, also taken by De Valera. My teacher in theoretical physics, Hans Türing, when he heard that I was going to visit England, told me to visit Schrödinger in Oxford. That was in 1935.

Recently I was shaken by the death of my friend Jerzy Giedymin, eminent Polish philosopher of science, who had spent many years in England. Not long ago he went to visit Poland and died there.[6]

CHMIELEWSKI: *Many scholars in Poland and other Eastern European Countries – myself included – owe very much to George Soros who founded a number of institutions enabling an exchange of ideas, and fostering contacts between them and people in the West. One of the Soros foundations bears the*

---

6 Professor Jerzy Giedymin, philosopher and historian of science, professor at Sussex University, died in Poland on 24 June 1993.

name of the Open Society Foundation, which is an allusion to your book The Open Society. *How did you both meet?*

POPPER: He was a pupil of mine, very many years ago. But we keep in touch all the time. I met him recently during my visit to Prague.[7] He also visited me twice or three times here. It is always a bit difficult for us; I mean I do not want to continue the teacher–pupil relation. I am very glad you have been helped by him. Soros helps very many people. For example he provided water for besieged Sarajevo …

CHMIELEWSKI: *Among your close friends there was also Nobel Prize laureate, the late Friedrich von Hayek, who wrote voluminously on the theory of liberalism and methodology in the social sciences.*

POPPER: Yes. I knew him for many years. In 1944, when I was still in New Zealand, he sent a telegram to me, offering me the readership in the London School of Economics. I accepted the invitation and I came to London. I left New Zealand before the war with Japan was quite over, but after the war in Europe. The invitation came while the war in Europe was still on. I took the position in 1945, and in 1949 I was given the chair of Professor of Logic and Scientific Method, also in LSE. Friedrich Hayek was three or four years older than I. We have been very close …

CHMIELEWSKI: *Both of you were strongly critical of totalitarian regimes. Friedrich von Hayek is known in the former communist countries as the author of* The Road to Serfdom. *You are most commonly associated with* The Open Society and Its Enemies. *Both of you were defending liberalism which bore, as I see it, evident conservative features. For example, in the book I already mentioned,* Conjectures and Refutations, *you had said that the world of Western liberal democracies, even if it is not the best of all possible worlds, it certainly is the best of all existing worlds. Have you ever been tempted to change that view?*

POPPER: Yes. Yes, but only tempted.

CHMIELEWSKI: *So you did not change your view on that issue?*

POPPER: No. When one wants to be critical, one tries to change one's mind, think matters all over again, but eventually I did not change my opinion.

CHMIELEWSKI: *But as you very well know, the nations of Central Europe, which suffer currently a very painful process of transformation, have repeatedly expressed their disappointment with the policy of the liberal market economy, and in recent elections held in several countries, people unequivocally questioned that policy. One has to stress that they had every reason for their skepticism; newly born liberals in Central Europe did their best to deserve this kind of response. The principle of the free market has become a universal and uncritically accepted recipe or solution to every problem in all walks of social life, a panacea. Currently, many unwelcome results of the*

---

7 Popper visited Central European University in Prague on 26 May 1994.

initial attempts toward reform are only aggravated by the astonishing incompetence of the liberal market politicians. Their corruption has already become legendary. Even though serious limitations of the free market principle have become evident, its liberal champions refuse to face the facts – very much like the communists not so long ago.

POPPER: Well, I still do believe that in a way one has to have a free market, but I also believe that to make a godhead out of the principle of the free market is nonsense. If we do not have a free market, then quite obviously the things that are being produced are not produced for the consumer, really. The consumer can take it or leave it. His needs are not taken into account in the process of production. But all that is not of a fundamental importance. *Humanitarianism*, that is of fundamental importance.

Traditionally, one of the main tasks of economics was to think of the problem of full employment. Since approximately 1965 economists have given up on that; I find it very wrong. It cannot be an insoluble problem. It may be difficult, but surely it is not insoluble!

Our first task is peace; our second task is to see that nobody be hungry; and the third task is fairly full employment. The fourth task is, of course, education.

CHMIELEWSKI: *I thought you would say that. It turns out, however, that in the contemporary world – even in its best part – none of these tasks is easy to achieve. What kind of problems do you see as obstacles in achieving the task of education?*

POPPER: At present the greatest danger to the educational effort is television. Education just cannot go on if you let the television do what it likes. It is impossible for education to work against television unless television recognizes that it also has an educational task which overrules our mere entertainment. Otherwise we cannot have education. From the democratic point of view television must be controlled because of its potential political power which is almost unlimited. If you get hold of television, you can do whatever you like. And such power must be controlled. My proposal is to look at the problem of controlling television as a task similar to that of control of medical people. Medical people have to be controlled too, and they do it very largely themselves. For example, they have to have a certain education. The same applies to the system of control of lawyers, who have their own organization which controls them. Thanks to these systems of control the lawyers do not steal the money from their clients and doctors do not kill their patients. And you have to control all people who work for television in some kind of organization. They would have to be [admitted to] such an organization [only] on the basis of some [special] education, after passing appropriate examinations testing their awareness of the educational tasks, and their sense of responsibility. They would have to learn that their influence is very great and that their responsibility is equally great. It is responsibility for our civilization. Their first aim would be the fight against violence. And on these principles, if some people are found to be irresponsible, their license could be withdrawn. Without such a system of regulation we are running into chaos, violence and crime. The increasing wave of crime is very largely due to television.

CHMIELEWSKI: *How do you perceive the role of churches in contemporary societies?*

POPPER: That is a very important question. The churches have done too much politics, and very little by way of helping people who seek spiritual help. Poland of course is almost completely Roman Catholic. I think that the Catholic Church made many mistakes ... Many serious mistakes. The first great mistake was made in 1890 when the Pope became infallible. It was a very late development – unnecessary, against tradition, history, and common sense. Then of course we have their attitude towards family control and family planning, and so on. The position of the Catholic Church on these issues is very dangerous and irresponsible.

Let us take for example the Church of England. It is almost completely involved in politics, and a very immature politics at that. Traditionally, the church, including the Church of England, has been a carrier and transmitter of education, of literature, of history, good traditions; but now, it is incredible how the people of the church are uneducated; these people are terrible, they know nothing about their own history, their own tradition.

The best religious traditions are in America, although even in America some of the churches and religious institutions can be frightening ...

CHMIELEWSKI: *For example, we should remember here quite recent developments in Waco, Texas, where many people, followers of the cult leader David Koresh, died.*

POPPER: Yes. And in Germany the church during the First and Second World Wars has been absolutely terrible. The leader of the German Protestant Church said such things like the war was the war of God, and they all asserted that they had intimate knowledge of God's political plans. That was terrible ... And all this has its consequences. The churches have really failed. It is very sad.

CHMIELEWSKI: *As the first priority you mentioned peace. But now, just after one part of the world became free, peacefully, from totalitarian oppression, we are witnessing terrible conflict in the south of Europe ...*

POPPER: ... and in Africa, and we will soon have it in other places. Our politicians just do not take their task seriously enough. They do not seem to see how important their task is. The politicians have failed. I think that politically we have missed a great opportunity. The Western countries should have made an offer to the Russians. We should have said to them: "Look at our part of the world. We all live in peace, we are in peace with Japan, China, with everyone. Won't you join us?" We should really have made such an offer at the right time, around 1988. But it was not said. And from the time of the breakdown of the Soviet Union it is *we* who *are* upset.

But philosophers have also failed. They too have shown their irresponsibility. In general, things do not look too good nowadays.

CHMIELEWSKI: *You do not sound too optimistic really. Does this mean that you have abandoned your activist attitude? Are you still an optimist, as you declared many times in your books?*

POPPER: Yes, despite all this I remain an optimist toward the world. It is one's duty to be an optimist. Only from this point of view can one be active and do what one can. If you are a pessimist, you have given up. We must remain optimists, we have to look at the world from the point of view of how beautiful it is, and to try to do what we can to make it better.

Part II

ADDRESSING THE TEXT

3

THE OPEN SOCIETY AND ITS ENEMIES: AUTHORITY, COMMUNITY, AND BUREAUCRACY[1]

Mark A. Notturno

> The more we try to return to the heroic age of tribalism, the more surely do we arrive at the Inquisition, at the Secret Police, and at a romanticized gangsterism. Beginning with the suppression of reason and truth, we must end with the most brutal and violent destruction of all that is human.
>
> (Popper 1945/1993 vol 1: 200)

I had been told that Ernest Gellner was the author of the joke that *The Open Society and Its Enemies* should have been called *The Open Society by One of Its Enemies*. So I was not too surprised to see that the conference that he organized in Prague to celebrate the book's fiftieth anniversary was supposed to have a critical edge. One of the themes that Gellner announced was "the relevance of the ideas and values of [*The Open Society and Its Enemies*] to the aftermath of a totalitarian collapse, as opposed to their initial relevance as an attempt to undermine a victorious or expanding totalitarianism." A second was "the validity or otherwise of the parallel drawn by Popper between the principles of an Open Society and of scientific enquiry." And Gellner, in emphasizing that the conference should discuss *criticisms* of the Popperian tradition, raised the question: "Has [Popper] underestimated the importance and value of communalist thinking?" as a third.

I think it is fairly clear where Gellner stood on these issues. But his unexpected death, just a few days before the conference began, cast a long shadow over them. Some people said that Popper's book *had* helped to introduce open society into Central and Eastern Europe. But others said that Popper's

---

1 This is a revised version of a paper that was published in *Common Knowledge* (December 1997). A Russian translation was published in *Voprosy Filosofii* (November 1996). Unauthorized English, Russian, and Ukrainian versions were published in *Political Thought* 3–4 (1996).

work, and the work of philosophers in general, had had little or no effect upon the collapse of Marxism. And still others said that *The Open Society and Its Enemies*, in any event, was now obsolete – since Popper was not an expert in social theory, since he had seriously underestimated the value of community, and since communalist thinking is necessary to reestablish faith in the legitimacy of government.

All of this may or may not be true.

Marxism, we are told, is dead – despite the elections. And democracy, we are told, is on the rise – along with fascism and nationalism. Indeed, we are told that freedom of speech is now so popular that you can publish almost anything you like in the Russian press – provided you are willing to pay for it.

My own sense is that none of this has much to do with the growth of open society – and that our growing reliance upon the experts of The Scientific Institution who tell us these things may well portend the exact opposite. My own sense is that Plato, Hegel, and Marx were only figureheads for the real enemies of open society, enemies that are still very much with us, and that are now threatening to close our society even in the West. I am talking about authority, community, and bureaucracy. And I think that the question now confronting open society is not whether Popper underestimated the value of community and communalist thinking, but how we can organize society on a large scale without subordinating the freedom of an individual to the authority of his community, and without completely losing it in a labyrinth of bureaucratic structures.

I

Let me begin by saying that Popper believed that science is our best kind of knowledge for the same reasons that he believed that democracy is our best form of government. They have, to date, both shown themselves better than their competitors, and they have done so largely by the ways in which they have dealt with their competitors – or, perhaps more accurately, by the ideals they have articulated and tried to approximate about how to deal with competitors. Both science and democracy try to change their leaders through rational discussion. Both try to learn from their competitors instead of silencing them. Neither has always succeeded in achieving these goals. But each has succeeded with greater frequency than other forms of knowledge and government – though this is an empirical fact that may change with changing conditions in the world.

It is easy to misunderstand this point, and to think that the essence of science and democracy somehow guarantees that they will always be better than their competitors. But Popper taught us to be less concerned with essence than with performance. So if the institutionalists are right that science no longer appeals to rational argument, and if the post-modernists are right that democracy silences those whom it cannot persuade, then we should at least question whether they are still our best available forms of knowledge and government.

It is in the same vein that Popper regarded open society as our best available form of social life – not as a utopia that is inevitably better than its competitors, but as a task at which we must constantly work to avoid falling prey to its competitors. And here, we must bear in mind that success at this task is inevitably and only a matter of degree. For the task itself is nothing less than the battle to preserve our freedom.

The battle to preserve our freedom has always been fought to defend the right of an individual to think and to speak for himself. It has always been fought against our enslavement by ideologies. And it has always been fought with the weapons of truth and rational argument, and with the simple idea that a false statement is objectively false regardless of who says or believes that it is true.

It is, however, one of the great ironies of our time that at the moment when the people of the socialist bloc are struggling to free their minds from ideologies, philosophers in the West are encouraging us to embrace them.

Today, the Wisdom of the West denigrates objectivity, truth, and rationality in favor of subjectivity, irony, and solidarity. It says that a rational comparison of competing ideas is not so much difficult as impossible. It advises us to adopt a paradigm, linguistic framework, or ideology, and to commit ourselves dogmatically to its beliefs. And we now find ourselves, as a result, inundated with linguistic impressions, appeals to authority, veiled threats, and *ad hominem* critiques.

These methods will not help us to discover truth. But they may help to forge solidarity. And while solidarity is admittedly not truth, it is, or so the fashionable philosophers assure us, a reasonable facsimile.

I can imagine how solidarity could be innocuous, if through the free exchange of ideas we all came to agree. But solidarity can be frightening when it is forged through the power politics of community and communalist thinking. For these politics can easily impede the freedom of thought and the growth of knowledge. And if we are truly concerned with the freedom of thought and the growth of knowledge, then it may even be our duty to oppose community and communalist thinking when they threaten to become powerful enough to do so.

I want to emphasize this point – that open society is the task to preserve our freedom – because most of the talk about open society that I hear these days seems to be confused about what it is. I hear, for example, frequent identifications of open society with democracy, and with *laissez faire* capitalism, and even with that "politically correct" ideal of free speech in which everyone can say whatever they like – provided that they do not offend anyone else while saying it.

These are all distortions of Popper's view. Popper contrasted open society with closed society. But he did not identify it with any specific political or economic system. His experiences in Vienna had convinced him that the dangers in socialism were far more threatening than the problems that it was supposed to solve. But he was also aware of the dangers in unrestrained capitalism – dangers that he had learned about, along with the rest of Europe, from the experience of the nineteenth century. So while Popper opposed the means that Marxists advocated to implement their social reforms, he did not oppose those social reforms themselves. And while he thought that democracy was the most likely of all the known political systems to protect an open society, he was also very careful to distinguish between the two.

The fact of the matter is that open society, as Popper understood it, is less concerned with the state and its economy than with the individual and his freedom. "The state," Popper wrote, "should exist for the sake of the human individual – for the sake of its free citizens and their free social life – that is, for the sake of the free society – and not the other way round" (Popper Archives: Box 6, file 6). Popper thus argued that a citizen must combine the duty of loyalty that he owes to his state with:

> ... a certain degree of vigilance and even a certain degree of distrust of the state and its officers: it is his duty to watch and see that the state does not overstep the limits of its legitimate functions. For the institutions of the state are powerful, and where there is power there is always the danger of its misuse – and a danger to freedom. All power has a tendency to entrench itself, and a tendency to corrupt and in the last resort it is only *the traditions of a free society* – which include a tradition of almost jealous watchfulness on the part of its citizens – which can balance the power of the state by providing those checks and controls on which all freedom depends. (ibid.)

Even democracy is to be valued as a means for safeguarding our freedom – by allowing us to get rid of our leaders without blooshed when they turn out to be not as good as we had hoped – and as a means that will not work unless the society that uses it *already* values freedom and tolerance:

> It seems to me of the greatest importance for a free society that democracy should be seen for what it is: that it should be understood without being idealized. And it seems to me especially important to realize that, as a rule, democracy will work fairly well in a society which values freedom and tolerance, but not in a society which does not understand these values. Democracy, that is, the majority vote, may help to preserve freedom, but it can never *create* freedom if the individual citizen does not care for it. (ibid.)

The fact of the matter is that *The Open Society and Its Enemies* is not so much a criticism of a political or economic system as it is a criticism of the idea that there could be anything like a science with theories so well-established that we could safely appeal to its experts, as gods amongst men, for the truth. Popper thought that it was this idea – and, indeed, only their *certainty* in this idea – that gave well-intentioned men and women the courage to undertake, in the name of "scientific socialism" and at the behest of "scientific experts," the drastic social changes that were undertaken by the communists.

But scientific knowledge is simply not like that. And this, in a nutshell, is Popper's critique of scientific socialism. Scientific knowledge is inherently conjectural, and always fallible. There may be experts who know their way around a problem and who have good ideas about why this or that "solution" may or may not work. But none of their advice can be safely regarded as authoritative or final. We should thus be bold in proposing and testing new theories, but not in applying them to the world. We should, instead, practice "piecemeal engineering" – the results of which are more easily reversed than global reforms – just in case the theories that we apply turn out to be false.

But what then is open society, if it is neither market society nor democratic society?

Popper characterized it as a society that "sets free the critical powers of man," and he contrasted it with the "closed" or "tribal" society "with its submission to magical forces" (1945/1993 vol 1: 1).[2]

This is the reason why open society has so little in common with the politically correct version of free speech. I do not think that everyone should be able to say whatever he likes without *reproach*. But rudeness should never be regarded as a *crime*. We should, under normal circumstances, be able to say what we think is true without fear of being punished for it. This applies especially to criticism. Free speech, in an open society, should be an instrument for discovering error, and not a shield behind which to hide it. It is unfortunate that many people regard criticism of their ideas as a personal offense. But free speech must take precedence over our desire not to offend. Open society is not necessarily polite society, and political correctness poses a problem for it. For when avoiding offense becomes our primary concern, it quickly becomes impossible to say anything freely at all.

Here it would be tempting to identify open society with the scientific society, or with the rational society. And Popper was no doubt inclined to do so. But there are dangers of doing so straightaway. For the most popular philosophy of science of our day – I am referring to the institutional theory of Thomas Kuhn – maintains that scientific inquiry begins where criticism leaves off, and that it is not criticism but the abandonment of critical discourse for faith in a paradigm that marks the transition to science (Kuhn 1970: 6). And this, regardless of Kuhn's intentions, is actually a recipe for closed society. It is a philosophy that tries to convince us that no fundamental decision or responsibility on our part is required, that we really should not waste our time on criticism or on trying to understand, and that everything will and must go

---

2 Popper's criticism of Plato, Hegel, and Marx was that they all believed in historicism – the idea that there are laws of history that determine the course of human events – and that historicism is a belief in magic.

well if only we fall into step behind The Scientific Institution and its experts.[3] But when we begin to think of science as incommensurable frameworks, constructed upon paradigms that cannot be rationally criticized either from within or without, when we say that accepting or rejecting those paradigms is like converting to this or that religion,[4] then we are only a stone's throw away from that closed or tribal society and its submission to magical forces.

This idea – that we should not submit to magic and its superstitions – is essential for understanding what open society is all about. There is much in the world that we may regard as magical, and rightly so. We stand in awe of the fact that the world should exist at all. And we are enchanted by feelings of *déjà vu*, telepathic experiences, and improbable synchronicities that we just cannot explain. But regardless of whether or not we can explain these things, the idea that scientists have special powers of understanding and a special kind of authority that others cannot question is an entirely different thing – as is the notion that scientific theories are justified by the consensus of expert opinion. These are mystical ideas that we should recognize as mystical and simply not accept.

Popper understood *The Open Society and Its Enemies* as an assault upon authoritarian science and its superstitions. He wrote that:

> An open society (that is, a society based on the idea of not merely tolerating dissenting opinions but respecting them) and a democracy (that is, a form of government devoted to the protection of an open society) cannot flourish if science becomes the exclusive possession of a closed set of specialists.
>
> (Popper 1994: 110)

And he describes his book in a letter to Frederick Hellin dated 29 June 1943 in precisely these terms, saying that:

> It attacks some of the greatest authorities of all times; and not only a few of them, such as Plato, Aristotle, Hegel, etc., but in fact a great number which are not named in the table of contents. And it does so with a recklessness which is excusable only in view of the fact that *I consider the destruction of the awe of the Great Names, the Great Intellectual Authorities, one of the necessary prerequisites of a recuperation of mankind.*[5]

---

3 Compare this with what Popper says about historicism in *The Open Society* (1945/1993 vol 2: 279).
4 See, for example, Kuhn 1962. Kuhn, I should note, retreated from his original doctrine of incommensurability. But many of his followers in the social sciences have carried it much further.
5 The Karl Popper Archives, Box 28, file 7. Popper went on to say: "This is one of the reasons why it will be difficult to find an authority to recommend it. The established intellectual authorities will not like it, since it fights against the very idea of an established intellectual authority, and since it undermines their glory … Thus my book will not easily find support from those who are 'arrived,' nor from those who hope to 'arrive' one day."

The Open Society – and by this I mean both the society and the book – is opposed not just to this or that authority, and not just to Plato, Hegel, and Marx. It is opposed to the very idea that there can be anything like cognitive authorities whom we can rely upon for the truth.[6]

So if we are going to understand open society as scientific or rational society, then we must also understand science and rationality in Popper's terms. We must think of science not as an institutionalized hierarchy of experts, but as a never-ending process of problem-solving in which we propose tentative solutions to our problems and then try to eliminate the errors in our proposals. We must think of rationality not in terms of justification, but in terms of criticism. And we must think of criticism not as an offense, or as a show of contempt or disdain, but as one of the greatest signs of respect that one mind can show to another.

II

This brings me to Ernest Gellner's question whether Popper underestimated the value of community and communalist thinking. This question strikes at the very heart of Popper's idea of open society. It is as if someone had asked whether Popper underestimated the value of induction. Popper may have underestimated the value of both of these things. But if he did, then a proper estimation will require that we jettison all that is distinctive about open society and critical rationalism. For like it or not, communalist thinking, like inductivist thinking, involves an abandonment of the rationalist attitude. And as Popper put it:

> The abandonment of the rationalist attitude, of the respect for reason and argument and the other fellow's point of view, the stress upon the "deeper" layers of human nature, all this must lead to the view that thought is merely a somewhat superficial manifestation of what lies within these irrational depths. It must nearly always, I believe, produce an attitude which considers the person of the thinker instead of his thought. It must produce the belief that "we think with our blood," or "with our national heritage," or "with our class." This view may be presented in a materialist form or in a highly spiritual fashion; the idea that we "think with our race" may perhaps be replaced by the idea of elect or inspired souls who "think by God's grace." I refuse, on moral grounds, to be impressed by these differences; for the decisive similarity between all these intellectually immodest views is that they do not judge a thought on its own merits. By thus

6 This – as opposed to anything that you might find in the probability calculus – is the big difference between Carnap's idea of confirmation and Popper's notion of corroboration. Simply put, we cannot rely upon the authority of even the best corroborated of our theories.

abandoning reason, they split mankind into friends and foes; into the few who share in reason with the gods, and the many who don't (as Plato says); into the few who stand near and the many who stand far; into those who speak the untranslatable language of our own emotions and passions and those whose tongue is not our tongue. Once we have done this, political equalitarianism becomes practically impossible.

(Popper 1945/1993 vol. 2: 235–6)

These two things – communalist thinking and inductivism – are more closely related than one might think. For it is only communalist thinking that gives the impression that the conclusion of an inductive argument is supported by its premises. This is because there is no contradiction whatever in asserting the premises of an inductive argument while denying its conclusion. So what invariably happens in an inductive argument is what Kierkegaard called "a little leap." This statement is said to be true, and that one too. And this and that are then said to provide justification for a third that, quite simply, does not follow. And this is how little tyrannies begin. First the inductivist takes a little leap and calls it "justified." And then, if nobody objects, he takes a bigger leap and calls that "justified" too. In this way, he finally gets so good at leaping that all hell breaks loose.

Popper appreciated the value of communalist thinking. But he also appreciated its power and its dangers. It is the kind of thinking that led some scientists in the 1920s and 1930s to dismiss Einstein's theory as "Jewish Physics." It is the kind of thinking that led Hitler to national socialism. It is, in fact, the kind of thinking that has usually supported racial, ethnic, and religious prejudices – and it is so regardless of the beneficial ends that can be achieved through it, regardless of who manifests it, and regardless of the individual or group against which it is directed. Someone once said that "prejudice is what holds society together." But if there is just one doctrine that is central to open society, it is that the traits of a thinker have no implications for the truth of his thought.

Some people, nevertheless, think that Popper underestimated the value of community *as a solution to the legitimacy problem*. The legitimacy problem is the problem of what justifies the authority of the state and of why we should accept what our leaders have to say. Some political theorists have argued that a sense of shared community can contribute significantly to the legitimacy of a regime, since people are more willing to accept the authority of a state when they feel that they have a stake in it. But I find this ironic in at least two ways. First, because the legitimacy problem asks for precisely the sort of justification that Popper thought is impossible to give. And second, because communalist thinking is not so much the solution to the legitimacy problem as its cause.

Popper, as we have already seen, believed that we should not simply accept what our leaders say, but should instead combine loyalty to our state with "a certain degree of vigilance and even a certain degree of distrust of the state and its officers." Even a well-designed and well-functioning democracy is not so much justified as the best of a bad lot. And it is our duty as citizens to see that the state does not overstep the limits of its legitimate functions.

Why can the authority of the state not be justified? For the same reason that scientific theories cannot be proven.

Once upon a time, a serious young student asked a wise old sage what supported the earth in its place and prevented it from falling through the heavens. The sage answered that the earth was held in its place because it rested on the shoulders of Atlas. The student was not satisfied and asked the sage what supported Atlas in *his* place and prevented *him* from falling through the heavens. The sage thought for a moment, and then replied that Atlas was held in his place because he stood on the back of a giant turtle. The student was even less satisfied with this answer and asked the sage what supported this giant turtle in *its* place and prevented *it* from falling through the heavens. The sage fixed the student with his eyes, and then said, with deliberate slowness, that the turtle was held in its place because it stood on the back of a giant elephant. When, at this point, the student began to ask the sage what supported the elephant in *its* place and prevented *it* from falling through the heavens, the old man put up his hand and abruptly stopped him. "Won't work," he said, "there are elephants all the way down!"

The reason why we cannot justify the state and cannot justify our theories is that there are not – and, indeed, *cannot* be – elephants all the way down.

The legitimacy of a state becomes problematic when people *cease* to believe in its objectivity. But people cease to believe in the objectivity of a state not because they suddenly realize that the elephants do not go all the way down, but because they begin to believe that it is partial to some sub-community that benefits from it. A legitimacy problem existed in the Soviet Union, because people suspected that some comrades were more equal than others. And a legitimacy problem exists in the United States for much the same reason. But if I am right about this, then communalist thinking – be it the sort of communalist thinking that discriminates or the sort that is sensitive to discrimination – is more likely to be the cause of the legitimacy problem than its solution.

Popper likened the principles of open society to the principles of scientific inquiry. But he held that scientific objectivity has nothing to do with justification, on the one hand, and little to do with the psyche of the individual scientist, on the other. Popper thought that the public character of science and its institutions imposes a mental discipline upon the individual scientist that preserves the objectivity of science and its tradition of critical discussion. This has led many people to talk about the scientific community and The Scientific Institution. But Popper also thought that even the best of institutions can never be foolproof, and that "institutions are always ambivalent in the sense that, in the absence of a strong tradition, they also may serve the opposite purpose to the one intended" (Popper 1963/1991: 351):

"Institutions are like fortresses. They must be well designed *and* properly manned." But we can never make sure that the right man will be attracted by scientific research. Nor can we make sure that there will be men of imagination who have the knack of inventing new hypotheses.

(Popper 1957/1991: 157)

If The Scientific Institution fails to impose mental discipline upon the individual scientist, if it instead perverts the tradition of critically discussing new ideas into a tradition of deferring to experts, if it leads scientists to employ unscrupulous methods in order to survive, and if it appeals to the power of community and communalist thinking to keep its party hierarchy in line, then the institutions of science are not well-designed. And if the members of The Scientific Institution are motivated primarily by self-interest, if they are more concerned with their own advancement than they are with discovering truth and explaining phenomena that we do not understand, then no matter how well-designed the institution might be, it has not been properly manned.

I think that this is almost the situation of The Scientific Institution today. I think that the regulative ideal of truth has almost been replaced by the regulative ideal of power. And I think that we can no longer appeal to The Scientific Institution to police its scientists – any more than we can appeal to the police to police itself – because The Scientific Institution can no longer be regarded as disinterested.

The Scientific Institution today forms a hybrid with Big Business and Big Government and Big Education – not The Scientific Institution, but The Big-Science-Big-Business-Big-Government-Big-Education Institution, in which the interests that have traditionally been regarded as scientific might actually count last in a decision regarding the acceptance of a new theory or technology (let alone in a job decision, or in a decision to publish a journal article). We can no longer assume that The Scientific Institution will impose mental discipline upon the individual scientist to preserve a tradition of critical discussion. Indeed, if Kuhn is right, then the scientist who tries to critically discuss new ideas may well find himself trying to impose an unwanted mental discipline upon a community that will respond, with Kuhnian approval, by ostracizing him.

There are many attractions of communalist thinking. But its primary vice is that it uses the power of community to punish individuals who criticize its authorities. This is the way it has always been, and while I am not an inductivist, I see no reason to think that it is any different now.

On the contrary, I see every reason to think that this kind of punitive communalist thinking has worked its way into the very fabric of the West. And it is very easy to see why. Nobody still believes that it is possible to prove that their theories are true. But this only makes it more important for authorities to protect their authority (for they would, after all, otherwise cease to be authorities). And what better way for The Scientific Institution to protect its authority than to define knowledge and truth as what its experts believe, and to exclude those who dare to question it?

But this belief that there are experts who have a special kind of knowledge that cannot be questioned – and especially not by non-experts – is the royal road to closed society. And for all the current talk about open society, it is the road upon which we are now traveling.

III

This brings me to the problem of bureaucracy. It is well known that Popper broke with the communists because he could not reconcile himself with their cavalier sacrifice of human life. But Popper remained a socialist for several more years, until his experiences in Vienna convinced him that there are dangers in socialism that are far more threatening than the problems that it is supposed to solve. Indeed, Popper told me only shortly before his death that he would still consider himself a socialist "were it not for the power problem." But what are the dangers that he saw in socialism? And what, exactly, is the "power problem"? Popper once explained it to me like this:[7]

> When I was a young man I was an ardent socialist. But I revised my views – not on the general humanitarian issues, but on the practical possibilities of socialism – when there was a socialist government in Vienna.

It was immediately after the First World War. There was terrible hunger and homelessness in Vienna. Popper, at the time, was working in a home for destitute children. And he had been assigned, as one of his duties, the job of cleaning and binding their little cuts and scratches:

> I had a certain amount of material to bind their wounds, and I had some iodine, which was then the main thing that we put on a wound to disinfect it. Well, you know that children come all the time with all sorts of things. And before long I needed a new bottle of iodine. For *this* I had to make an application to the magistrate. I first had to travel to the centre of Vienna, some fifteen miles away, where our bureaucrats met. Then I was sent from there across town to a doctor.

---

7 Popper told me this story, I think back in 1985, during one of our walks around the Kenley aerodrome. Years later, I found that he had told the same story twenty years earlier to his Introduction to Scientific Method class. I am sure he told it many times. I have, in any event, reconstructed it here, in the first person, partly from memory and partly from the transcript of Popper's 29 November 1966 class lecture that exists in the Karl Popper Archives, Box 378, file 4.

The doctor viewed me with great suspicion and questioned me for a long time, but he finally gave me a prescription. And with that I had to travel to a hospital at the other end of Vienna, where I was given a bottle of iodine like this!

Popper held up his hand with his thumb and forefinger spread about an inch apart:

It was, of course, the last time that I asked the socialists for iodine! The amount of work that went into getting that little bottle of iodine, and the amount of lost time from my real work with the children, was so absolutely out of proportion, that I actually preferred, from then on, to pay for it out of my own pocket rather than undergo that sort of thing again.

Popper told me that this one experience taught him "a lot of things," and that it eventually led him to change his mind about socialism:

I saw that we social workers who were really working with the people were like the soldiers at the front. And there on top of us were the administrators. It taught me that the administrators were in the main interested in their own advancement rather than in helping us to help the children. And it taught me that the central problem of socialism would be the problem of dealing with bureaucracy. You have a certain idea to help people, and you even get some money to do so. But how do you make sure that three-quarters of it does not disappear before it ever reaches them? So much of this administration went into red tape and into nothing at all! That, of course, was very many years ago. But I have hardly ever found a socialist of any degree of power in his party who would even admit that this was a central problem.

Lenin may or may not have admitted that bureaucracy is a central problem for Marxism. But some people regarded the bureaucrats of socialist states as a new ruling class – or community, if you will – that exploited people as much as had the old capitalists of the past. And others thought that bureaucracy eventually transformed socialist radicalism into a conservatism in which the party leaders were far more concerned with preserving their power and authority than with serving the needs of the people whom they were supposed to represent.

But bureaucracy is not a problem peculiar to socialism. Bureaucrats everywhere are often more interested in their own advancement than in helping others. And socialism, in any event, never quite cornered the market on red tape.

Bureaucracy can be found in almost every large-scale economic system, and in almost every organization that deals with people on a mass scale. It can now be found in many small-scale organizations as well. I do not think that it can any longer be defended on the grounds of efficiency. But it can be defended by arguing that large-scale organizations generally do not know the people they serve and must therefore institute rules to protect themselves against fraud. It can also be defended by arguing that some form of bureaucracy is necessary if we want to have large-scale organizations at all.

You cannot, however, argue that bureaucracy promotes open society. For you do not have to look too far in a bureaucracy to find most of the things that are characteristic of closed society. There is, first of all, the imposition of an authority structure, with rigid procedural rules and impersonal superior–inferior relationships. This, in turn, leads to the transformation of human beings into little computers, programmed to follow a set of well-defined rules and capable of performing limited tasks according to them, but unable, or at least unwilling, to think for themselves even so far as to distinguish between those rules and the ends that they are meant to achieve. It leads, almost inevitably, to what Popper called "the tyranny of the petty official" (1945/1991 vol. 1: 4). And it leads, in the end, to a consolidation of power in the hands of an oligarchic elite – or community, if you will – that is able to manipulate the rules, as well as information and communication, so as to perpetuate its own power.

It is hard to imagine how any of this could possibly set free the critical powers of man. But it is very easy to see how much of it has worked its way into The Scientific Institution.

Today we no longer believe that scientific knowledge can be rationally justified, and many have "inferred" from this that it also cannot be true. But philosophers of science continue to attribute authority to The Scientific Institution – while simultaneously acknowledging that this authority, and indeed even the membership of The Scientific Institution, is based upon nothing more than the consensus of its members. All of this, I think, is entirely in keeping with communalist bureaucratic thinking and with the "progress" that The Scientific Institution is so often said to have made. For it means that The Scientific Institution, or at least the philosophers of The Scientific Institution, have finally demonstrated – have agreed amongst themselves – that the elephants, indeed, do go all the way down.

This is the threat that Popper saw in socialism and its "power problem." We have already seen its effects in the Soviet Union. The problem that faces us now is how to facilitate science and society on a large scale without losing the individual's freedom in a labyrinth of rigid and impersonal rules. It is the problem of how to use bureaucracy in such a way that the rules exist for the sake of the human individual – for the sake of free citizens and their free social life – and not the other way round. This is a problem that we have not yet solved and do not yet know how to solve. I do not think that we will solve it by following the experts of The Scientific Institution. But I do think that we should all be thinking about how to solve it, along with the problems of authority and community, since its prevalence today poses one of the greatest threats to our freedom and open society.

IV

There is one more problem that those of us who are interested in open society should be trying to solve. It is the practical problem whether freedom and open society are worth paying money for. I am by no means being facetious in raising this problem, or in calling it "practical." Freedom, we all say, is priceless. "Give me liberty or give me death!" But matters apparently change when we are asked to pay money for it. For many people seem willing to put it in jeopardy, if not to sacrifice it entirely, if they see an opportunity to make a few dollars by doing so.

It is well known that corruption in the countries of the former (current?) socialist bloc is now reaching unprecedented levels. But the most disturbing thing about this corruption is that it is not only Mafia racketeers and professional criminals who engage in it. Tax evasion, bribery, and the black market now seem to be a normal way of life for ordinary working citizens who want simply to lead a decent bourgeois existence. I have even heard experts say that such corruption is and ought to be tolerated by the state because it facilitates a rapid transition to capitalism – and, *hence* (?!), to freedom.

Part of the fallacy here is the easy equation of freedom with the ability to acquire and manipulate material objects. This, no doubt, is a certain kind of freedom. But it is one that all too easily conflicts with the freedom to say what you think is true. This is the freedom that Popper thought was important for an open society. And it is a freedom that people seem willing to sacrifice when they step outside the law.

But could it possibly be true that this corruption is not only tolerated, but actually encouraged by the state?

Popper was wary of historical predictions. But he was willing to predict the formation of black markets in a state that did not enforce its laws against them while simultaneously pursuing policies that resulted in a shortage of commodities. It is, likewise, easy to see that there will be a good deal of tax evasion in a society in which the state raises its taxes exorbitantly, but fails to prosecute those who evade them.

But why would a state encourage criminal activities amongst its citizens? Why would it enact laws that are difficult to obey, and sometimes even contradictory, only to make little or no effort to enforce them?

One simple answer that we can never entirely rule out is stupidity. Another – and it may be difficult to decide which is the more charitable – is that the state has found an easy and effective way to control its citizens. Those who engage in criminal activity will most likely want to keep a low profile. They will, as a consequence, be less likely to criticize their government. And if they do speak out, their culpability makes it very easy for the government to silence them. In this way, a state can even perpetuate the myth that it is only the lawless amongst its citizens who are dissatisfied with it.

REFERENCES

Kuhn, Thomas S. 1962. *The Structure of Scientific Revolutions*. The International Encyclopedia of Unified Sciences, ed. Otto Neurath, Rudolf Carnap, and Charles Morris. Chicago: University of Chicago Press. Vol. 2 (2).

—— 1970. "Logic of discovery or psychology of research?" In *Criticism and the Growth of Knowledge*, ed. Imre Lakatos and Alan Musgrave. Cambridge: Cambridge University Press.

Popper, Karl R. 1945. *The Open Society and Its Enemies*. London: Routledge & Kegan Paul; repr. Routledge, 1993.

—— 1957. *The Poverty of Historicism*. London: Routledge & Kegan Paul; repr. Routledge, 1991.

—— 1963. *Conjectures and Refutations*. London: Routledge & Kegan Paul; repr. Routledge, 1991.

—— 1994. "Science: problems, aims, responsibilities." In *The Myth of the Framework*, ed. M. A. Notturno. London: Routledge.

—— Archives. "The Open Society and the democratic state." Box 6, file 6.

4

POPPER AND TARSKI

David Miller

In his tribute to Tarski on his seventieth birthday Popper wrote: "I have never learned so much from anybody else" (1972/1979: 322). Without repeating everything that Popper has ever said, this chapter attempts to summarize and to evaluate what he learnt from Tarski about truth, and to explain its value not only for logic and for the theory of knowledge but for the philosophy of the open society.

Introduction

In note 72 in Popper's *Replies to My Critics* (1974b) we read:

> Alfred Tarski recently told me that he was "slightly shocked" to find himself indexed in *O.S.* [*The Open Society and Its Enemies* (1945/ 1966)] almost as often as was Marx. While this is an exaggeration, it does emphasize my interest in his work at that time.

Note 72 is appended to a passage in his reply to Lakatos (Popper 1974b: 1001) where Popper observes that he made use of Tarski's "rehabilitation of the idea of absolute or objective truth" almost as soon as he learnt about it, lecturing on Tarski's work at Bedford College in 1935 (see also 1974a/1976: 108), and referring to it in print in the first edition of *The Open Society* in 1945. The most significant of these references is in note 23 to chapter 8 ("The Philosopher King"), which contrasts the "absolutist" theory of truth (restored to repute by Tarski) with pragmatism and relativism. In the text Plato is even given a modicum of credit because "he retained enough of the Socratic spirit to admit candidly that he was lying" (1945, vol. 1: 126 [1966, vol. 1: 144]), in contrast to "the pragmatist successors of Hegel" for whom the truth is identified with what serves our purposes or perhaps even the purposes of the state.

In Addendum I ("Facts, Standards, and Truth: A Further Criticism of Relativism") to volume 2 of *The Open Society and Its Enemies*, added in 1962 to the fourth edition, Popper described "intellectual and moral relativism" as the "main philosophical malady of our time" and prescribed Tarski's theory of truth as a part of the treatment (1966: 369). He hinted also that a full cure would be impossible without recourse to his ill-fated theory of approach to the truth, and without the adoption of his non-authoritarian, or non-justificationist, theory of knowledge, critical rationalism. (For my own version of critical rationalism see Miller 1994.) Having earlier cited (in note 23 to chapter 8 of *The Open Society*) Russell's linking of relativism and fascism (1935: 77), Popper made plain that a surrender to relativism would undermine, and perhaps even destroy, the open society in which some of us live.

That the symptoms of malignant relativism have not generally eased in the succeeding thirty-five years is obvious. Yet not everyone is frivolous, or postmodern, and there are many philosophers who are not afflicted by it and are quite happy to endorse the absolutist theory of truth (and even some workable theory, as yet undiscovered, of approach to the truth). What is striking is how opposed people are, almost unanimously, to taking the booster medicine, the final part of the cure. Indeed, the doctrine that all our knowledge must be justified (at least in part), though an intellectual scam, is still often upheld as the guardian of rationality against relativism, for example by Sokal and Bricmont (1998: ch. 4; see Miller 1999 for comments). It is not surprising that the most hard-bitten relativists are almost always disappointed justificationists who have finally seen through the pretensions of justificationism (Jarvie 1995). In these circumstances we may doubt whether critical rationalism, the complete disavowal of all demands for justification, is really a necessary part of the cure for relativism.

Part of my purpose in this chapter is to show that, independently of all questions of whether proof, or certainty, or justification (complete or incomplete) is possible, a theory of objective truth is needed to prevent us from slipping into conventionalism, and from that into outright relativism. But I stress that it may not be sufficient for this purpose. It is decidedly not sufficient to protect us from falling into an analogously dangerous type of absolutism (Popper 1966 [1945], vol. 1: Addendum I, §7), the view that, as it happens, we are in possession of the objective truth, that we have – unjustifiedly, perhaps, but unerringly – lighted on the truth. Indeed this may be true. We may indeed be in possession of what I shall call a criterion of truth. The important point is that we must not stop there.

"Truth matters" says Novak (1995: 14); "Even for those unsure whether there is a God, a truth is different from a lie." But "Truth is the light of God within us" (ibid · 15)

Truth is not manifest, and even when we are on the right track we have to decide whether or not it is the right track, and whether we shall stay on it. Is it the truth that we want, and is this the way forward? The idea that truth is absolute is never more dangerous, nor more easily confused with certain or rationally supported truth, than when we happen to be right. In this sense the critical rationalist attitude that Popper advocated (1966 [1945], vol. 2: 238) – I may be wrong and you may be right, and by an effort we may get nearer to the truth – is an indispensable ingredient of the life that an open society offers.

It makes sense only if "I may be wrong" and "you may be right" make sense whoever is right and whoever is wrong.

Popper's appreciation of Tarski's theory of truth

Popper was one of the first philosophers to take to heart Tarski's theory of truth. He has recorded in a number of places the liberating effect of the theory on him, how it made him appreciate, after years of indecision (see the brief report 1962: 6), that truth is not a shadily metaphysical concept teetering on the edge of contradiction but one that, provided some elementary precautions are observed, can be taken for granted by the most commonsense of realists. (See 1963/1989: ch. 10; 1972/1979: chs. 2, 7, and 9; and 1974a/1976: 98f. and §32.) His reaction to hearing Tarski's explanation that "Snow is white" is a true statement if and only if snow is white may be compared with Carnap's report that in similar circumstances "the scales fell from my eyes" (Coffa 1991: 304). Yet their situations were not quite identical. Carnap had himself come close to defining truth adequately for certain types of language, but had been unable to see the connection with simple factual truth. Popper was never primarily interested in formulating a definition of truth; an opponent of definitions, he saw clearly that Tarski was not attempting an analysis of truth (1945/1966 vol. 2: note 39 to ch. 11; the point is made very clear in Etchemendy 1988: 53–64). Popper's problem, he tells us (1963/1989: 223), was that

> although I accepted, as almost everybody does, the objective or absolute or correspondence theory of truth – truth as correspondence to the facts – I preferred to avoid the topic. For it appeared to me hopeless to try to understand clearly this strangely elusive idea of a correspondence between a statement and a fact.

Tarski set all this right – so much so that Popper goes on (224f.): "Thanks to Tarski's work, the idea of objective or absolute truth – that is truth as correspondence with the facts – appears to be accepted today with confidence by all who understand it."

This last remark hardly does justice to the situation. For clear and unambiguous as Tarski's contributions to the subject are (with one or two exceptions), their significance has remained controversial (Etchemendy 1988: 51). The mathematical complexity of Tarski's formal investigations is doubtless, as Popper suggests, one source of failure to understand some aspects of his work (1963/1989: 225); another, he suggests, is that Tarski's theory of truth offers no criterion of truth – though, we shall see, that is one of its major advantages. But what is missing, from both Tarski's and Popper's accounts, is a convincing description of the problem situation of the correspondence or absolutist theory. It is true that Tarski cites Aristotle's formulation, and also gives a rough formulation in contemporary philosophical language; a formulation that, he says, "[f]rom the point of view of formal correctness, clarity, and freedom from ambiguity ... obviously leaves much to be desired" (1936a: 155). He also stresses the problem posed by the semantical paradoxes (which must afflict any theory of truth, not only the correspondence theory). Popper's presentation of the correspondence theory, and its defects, is not very much more revealing; he dismisses in a few lines (1963/1989: 223) variants proposed by Wittgenstein and Schlick, yet he says little – beyond the refrain that the idea of correspondence was unclear – to explain why so many earlier and present-day thinkers have been disposed to reject it. In the face of Tarski's disclaimers, and Popper's championship, it has been commonly doubted that a viable version of the correspondence theory has been provided, or even a viable theory of truth.

In what follows I shall first give a very condensed statement of those features of Tarski's theory relevant to this discussion, and add some clarifying remarks. I shall then look more closely at two problems that Tarski's theory seems to be competent to deal with, each of them closely connected with the idea that truth is correspondence to the facts, and each significant beyond the boundaries of logic and the theory of knowledge. One of them, the problem of how objective truth is to be distinguished from objective knowledge of the truth, was most definitely in the air in Vienna, and elsewhere, in the early 1930s, and is hardly a novelty today. The second problem, the problem of selectivity, has been more rarely discussed, even though it seems to lie behind many of the standard criticisms of the correspondence theory. In conclusion I shall indicate briefly some consequences that the resolution of these problems has for the theory of the open society.

Tarski's theory of truth

Tarski stated his central task to be that of constructing "a materially adequate and formally correct definition of the term 'true sentence'" in accordance with "the intentions which are contained in the so-called classical conception of truth ('true – corresponding with reality')" (1936a: 152f.; emphases suppressed). The central difficulty was the difficulty of avoiding the semantical paradoxes, such as the paradox of the liar.

If U is the statement "U is not true" (the strengthened liar), then U can in an intuitive manner be proved to be both true and not true, and its existence precipitates the question of whether there can be any consistent theory of truth that accords with commonsense norms. Tarski's answer was that there is not. Indeed, if there is anything that can rightly be called Tarski's theory of truth (in contrast to Tarski's T-scheme, Tarski's material adequacy condition for definitions of truth, and Tarski's method for defining truth for quantificational languages) it is surely this: the claim that truth is not universal, and can be defined in a consistent way only for restricted languages. With the second part of this claim I am in agreement, but not with the first.

Following Leśniewski, Tarski repudiated the idea that the semantic paradoxes are to be traced to linguistic or grammatical irregularities – as Russell earlier (1918: 133–5, for example, but in many other places) and Ryle (1951) later maintained – and pinned the blame squarely on a false assumption – the unrestricted assumption of all instances of the T-scheme (see Tarski 1944: note 7):

X is true if and only if p,

where "X" is replaced by the structural-descriptive name of a statement, and "p" by that statement (or a translation of it). It is easily seen that if X is the statement U above then the corresponding instance of the T-scheme

"U is not true" is true if and only if U is not true

is contradictory (because U = "U is not true"). In this way Tarski showed that there is actually a contradiction between the two requirements that he imposed on any definition of truth: the condition of material adequacy, which requires that all instances of the T-scheme (the T-sentences) be derivable from the definition of truth, and the condition of formal correctness, which requires at the very least that no contradiction be derivable from the definition of truth. (A formally correct definition allows the elimination of the defined term from all contexts in which it is present; in addition, it does not allow the derivation of new conclusions from which the defined term is absent. If a contradiction were derivable when a definition was added to a consistent background theory, this second condition would fail; the definition would be creative.) Cutely put, formal correctness requires that a purported definition of truth should be a *definition* of truth, while material adequacy requires that it be a definition of *truth*. In unrestricted form these two conditions conflict.

Tarski's solution was to restrict the material adequacy condition, requiring that not *all* instances be derivable from the definition of truth, but only those for the statements of what he called the object language. This is distinguished from the metalanguage, in which the definition, and the T-sentences, are formulated. In other words, to realize a formally correct definition of truth we are compelled to sacrifice its material adequacy. A good definition will be materially adequate for the statements of the object language, and for these statements instances of the T-scheme will be consequences of the definition. T-sentences may be derivable even for a few statements in the metalanguage that contain the word "true" (for example, a T-sentence may be derivable for the truth-teller paradox, the statement W = "W is true"), but others will not be. This is frequently misunderstood. It is mistaken of Simmons (1993: 13), for example, to suggest that it is because the application of the predicate "true" is limited to statements of the object language that "there are restrictions on what we may substitute for 'X' and for 'p'" in the T-scheme. The predicate "true" may be applied (not always correctly, of course) to any statement. Any T-sentence whatever may be formulated by substitution in the T-scheme: replace "X" by the structural-descriptive name of a statement from either the object language or the metalanguage, and replace "p" by the statement itself (or by a translation). But not every T-sentence is derivable from the definition of truth (or, to use Tarski's unfortunate expression in 1944: §6 and §8 (pp.52a, 53b), "can be asserted in the language").

It is important to appreciate that Tarski does not say that the strengthened liar U is ungrammatical or ill-formed or meaningless, a position attributed to him by Quine (1962: 8), Engel (1989: 115), Grim (1992: 31–3), and many others. As Popper demonstrated so effectively (1963/1989: ch. 14), the attempt to deny meaning to paradoxical statements does not really get to grips with their intransigence. How indeed could Tarski condemn the liar to meaninglessness if he intends the term "true" to be correctly defined and hence eliminable from all contexts? Full eliminability would imply that there exist meaningless or ill-formed sentences from which the word "true" is absent. Nor does the sentence U turn out to be "simply true" (as *The Cambridge Dictionary of Philosophy* puts it (1995: 726)). That U is true is not ruled out, to be sure (though it could happen that a formally correct definition of truth would classify it as false). But U would not be *simply* true; it would be *demonstrably* true within set theory, given the definition of truth.

It is somewhat astonishing that so many commentators on Tarski's theory of truth misjudge or even ignore his prime concern: his concern to show – by providing a correct definition of truth – that the correspondence theory of truth can be formulated in a way that is free from contradiction. Mackie, for example, endorses the formula (1973: 53; emphasis suppressed) "To say that a statement is true is to say that things are as, in it, they are stated to be" (which, except for telling us only what it is to say that a statement is true, not what it is for it to be true, sounds reasonably like an informal statement of the correspondence theory of truth); and asks: "But apart from the avoidance of the paradoxes, what is the merit of Tarski's very complex procedure as opposed to our rather trivial one?" (p. 34). Anyone who understands what Tarski was trying to do would realize that a definition of truth that employs semantical primitives (such as "as things are stated to be") can hardly escape the suspicion of being inconsistent. Even more alarming is the apparent dismissal of the paradoxes as peripheral. (Later, Mackie (1973: ch. 6), has a great deal to say about the paradoxes; but what he says there on pp. 250–3 about Tarski's solution is mostly mistaken.) Field (1972: 91), to take another example, wonders out loud why Tarski should have sought a definition of truth in which there are no semantic primitives; and, without even mentioning the paradoxes, goes on to endorse the view that the main point was to bring semantics into the fold of physicalism. McDowell (1978: 116) agrees. I disagree. A glance at the paragraph from Tarski (1936b: 405f.) to which Field alludes reveals that the main aim always was to show that a consistent version of the correspondence theory of truth can be developed; and not even physicalists, I suppose, think that every concept that cannot be defined in physical terms is inconsistent. (See also Etchemendy 1988: 53f., and Kirkham 1992: 202–5, who claims that Field has attributed to Tarski a version of physicalism that he would not have acknowledged.) That is why Tarski emphasized that the solution to the problem of the establishment of scientific semantics is "closely connected to the theory of logical types" (1936b/1956: 406). It explains in addition why he saw his task as one of providing, where possible, an explicit definition of truth, rather than an axiomatic theory, an aspect of his work that Mackie (1973) admits that he is unable to explain.

It should be mentioned in conclusion that for a certain rather wide class of languages Tarski did show how a materially adequate and formally correct explicit definition of truth can be constructed (though, as far as I know, he gave no detailed proof of material adequacy). He proved also that there is no singular formula of elementary arithmetic that is true of just the Gödel numbers of true statements of elementary arithmetic; in brief, arithmetical truth is not arithmetically definable (Tarski's theorem), though it is definable in second-order arithmetic (see Boolos and Jeffrey 1974/1989: ch. 19).

Truth and criteria of truth

We hardly need any deep result from mathematical logic to show that it is impossible to provide proof or justification of all true statements. That much should be clear from traditional skeptical arguments. But there is a closely related possibility: that of a criterion of truth, which is not so easily extinguished, though often confounded with it. Skepticism has encouraged many writers quietly to abandon the search for certainty, in practice if not in principle, and even for (partial) justification, and to turn their minds to the task of searching for, or constructing, a criterion of truth; a method or procedure for identifying which statements are true and which false. A criterion of truth, as I understand it, need not provide a proof or justification of all true statements, or even an intuitively compelling definition of truth; what it must do is to provide a workable procedure for classifying statements as true and false. Popper stressed on a number of occasions (1963/1989: 225; 1972/1979: 46, 317f., 321f.) that one of Tarski's contributions was to show that there exists no general criterion of truth.

It is quite possible that a criterion of truth for some class of sentences might exist, and it might even fall within its own scope. Papal infallibility ("Every statement made by the Pope *ex cathedra* is free from error in all matters pertaining to faith and morals") could be such a criterion (though I do not suppose that it is) if it counted as an article of faith. We may even, in toy cases, construct a correct criterion of truth. Take, for example, the tiny language (adapted from Miller 1985/1996: §4) whose sentences are defined by

"Snow is green" is a sentence.
"The moon is square" is a sentence.
Appending any sentence to the words "It is not true that" yields another sentence.
These comprise all the sentences.

The two sentences

A sentence is true if it contains an even number of letters.
A sentence is false if it contains an odd number of letters.

provide a criterion of truth for this language (given the availability of methods of counting), and may themselves be added to the language. Tarski's theorem states that for elementary arithmetic no such criterion is possible, even if in its application we are allowed to make appeal to the full resources of arithmetic. (We may be able to prove all the true statements of arithmetic, and disprove all the others; but we cannot prove the true ones to be true or the false ones not to be true.) Yet Gödel's first incompleteness theorem is really all that is needed to rule out the possibility of an applicable criterion of truth for arithmetic; the complete theory of the natural numbers is not even recursively axiomatizable, so there exists no effective procedure that will eventually classify statements correctly amongst its theorems or its non-theorems, let alone a procedure that will classify the theorems as true and the non-theorems as false. Note that Tarski's and Gödel's results do not show that there are not other classes of arithmetical statements (not to mention other theories) that can be endowed with criteria of truth; the impossibility of a general criterion of truth does not imply the general impossibility of a criterion of truth. What these negative results together do indicate is that a definition of truth is possible even if an accompanying criterion is not possible.

Popper sometimes emphasized this aspect of Tarski's work (for example, 1966 [1945], vol. 2: Addendum I, §§2f.; 1972/1979: 320). Sometimes he mixed in also the question of certainty; for example when he wrote (ibid.: 321f.) that Tarski's theorem is "of the greatest interest if we remember the classical conflicts between the Stoics (and later the Cartesians) on the one side, and the Sceptics on the other" and claimed that Tarski's work resolved the conflicts; and when he wrote (ibid.: 46) that truth, as Tarski defines it, "is an objectivist or absolutist notion of truth ... [but] not absolutist in the sense of allowing us to speak with 'absolute certainty or assurance'. For it does not provide us with a criterion of truth."

I do not deny that a common expectation of a criterion of truth is that it bring proof or certainty, or at least some degree of justification, in its wake. But as noted above, we can at least imagine a criterion of truth (for a limited range of statements) that is not itself justified (completely or incompletely), and is therefore not able to justify (completely or incompletely) the statements that it identifies as true. The impact of Tarski's and Gödel's work is not so much to silence the demand for certainty – that it did not do so in Gödel's case is obvious (1961?/1995) – as to make plain (to all who want to see) that we may understand (and even, granted enough logical apparatus, define) what it is for a statement to be true without having access to any procedure that, properly followed, says whether or not the statement is true.

Why this is so important in the development not only of Popper's ideas, but also of Carnap's, is that by the time Tarski's work had become known it was obvious that, even if adequate criteria of truth exist for empirical statements, or any others, they can provide no proper understanding of truth. Procedures that allow us to classify statements as true and false are valuable as far as they go, and no one denies that some procedures are needed at the empirical level, but they are criteria of truth only if they perform the classification correctly; that is, truly. It is therefore imperative that we have an understanding of truth that is independent of any means we adopt for classifying statements as true. Without such an independent understanding we are doomed to fall into the trap of defining truth in terms of the procedures we use to classify it. The eventual outcome is inevitable: truth becomes a matter of decision, of convention, and ultimately of political might. (Musgrave 1997 suggests that it may lead also to idealism.)

For Popper the situation had been a difficult one. His emphasis on the testing of previously conjectured hypotheses required the adoption of some empirical procedure (or procedures) for classifying as true or false those statements he called basic statements (singular statements describing observable states of affairs). He recognized that no basic statement could be justified (in any objective sense) by any subjective experience; but experience could not be ignored if the method were not to cease to be an empirical one. This was the fate of Neurath's proposal, according to which, in effect, a basic statement can be deleted if it is inconvenient. Popper accordingly recommended a procedure that consisted in the taking of an unfounded (or conjectural) decision to accept a basic statement in the light of (that is, as a result of) an appropriate experience (1934/1959: §29). To some extent what counts as an appropriate experience – in particular, at what stage we decide to stop testing further – is unquestionably a matter of agreement that is motivated by extraneous and even arbitrary factors such as time, cost, and interest (as stressed in his 1974b: 1114); it is "a free decision" (1934/1959: 109). What Popper never said was that the truth value of an accepted basic statement is also a matter of free decision.

What he did do, rather unfortunately, was to describe his procedure as a form of conventionalism restricted to singular statements (1934/1959: 108f.). Many have therefore concluded that he "put forth a position essentially indistinguishable from Neurath's" (Coffa 1991: 367; see also pp. 365f.). But this interpretation is pretty well refuted by Popper's comparison between this aspect of the empirical method and the verdict of a jury (Popper 1934/1959: 109f.; my emphasis):

By its decision, the jury accepts, by agreement, a statement about a factual occurrence – a basic statement, as it were … the verdict plays the part of "a true statement of fact." But *it is clear that the statement need not be true merely because the jury has accepted it*. This fact is acknowledged in the rule allowing a verdict to be quashed or revised.

He rather spoils his own case when he says three paragraphs later that the jury's decision can be challenged only on procedural grounds, but the point is already made: the truth of a basic statement is not constituted by the decision to accept it as true.

Yet how much easier this would all have been had Tarski's definition of truth been available. With his clear distinction between truth and the procedures by which we may in some cases identify truth, there is no difficulty in acknowledging that our procedures, though often satisfactory, are fallible; there is more to being true than being identified to be true. Again, conjectures can be characterized not negatively as statements that have not been identified to be true, but positively as statements that may be true whether we identify them or not. Best of all, we can understand in what way true statements correspond to the facts. This correspondence is not something that can be shown – we cannot put a true statement such as "Snow is white" against a fact, and compare one with the other. But this does not matter, since what is primary is not what can be shown, but what can be said. And the instances of the T-scheme say what can be said: "Snow is white" is true if and only if snow is white.

Imperfect correspondence

For critical rationalists, one of the most irritatingly inconvenient of linguistic conventions is the presumption (in all natural languages I know anything about) that when a speaker utters a declarative sentence in ordinary discourse he does more than use it to say what it says. My uttering "Snow is white" involves me, it is said, not only in saying that snow is white, but also in saying, or implicating, that I am certain, or know, or have good grounds for believing, that snow is white; or at least that I have applied some criterion of truth (in the sense already outlined) that has inspired me to the utterance. Yet the art of conjecture, so central to the critical rationalist mode of existence, is hardly even a method, let alone a criterion of truth. If I wish to conjecture that snow is white I am therefore obliged to say something on the lines of "I conjecture that snow is white" (even though this in its turn apparently involves me in saying more than I wish to say).

Tarski's work shows clearly that this convention (which may be less forceful in writing than in speech) is an unfortunate one. It provides an excellent example, to set beside Popper's example of the semantic paradoxes, of how "natural languages, which were among Hayek's prize examples [of institutions that had grown organically] ... may be in urgent need of critical improvement" (Shearmur 1996: 35, reporting a real intellectual difference between Hayek and Popper). A second example from the pragmatics of language is the convention, less peremptory but quite as seditious, that takes a speaker to be speaking truly only if he is not selective but gives a report "omitting no detail, however slight" (in the often used words of P. G. Wodehouse). The problems that this convention poses for the correspondence theory of truth are not as widely discussed as they deserve to be. It hardly needs to be said that Tarski's theory solves these problems without remainder.

One aspect of the problem appears with the thought that, if there is ever a correspondence between a statement and a fact, it must be a correspondence between the statement and some linguistically untouched (or "unconceptualized") part of the world (usually the physical world); and therefore no statement will ever count as true, for no statement can never say enough. This doctrine that the only truth is the whole truth is a familiar component of the idealist tradition: "all judgements are partly true and partly false" (Ewing 1934: 208). It is worth mentioning also at this point an older criticism of the theory that truth consists of an "identity of structure" between a judgment and a fact (one version of correspondence theory of truth, later revived by Schlick 1925: §10); namely that "[such] wholes cannot be analysed into materials subsumed under an external form – i.e. a form which can be what it is, unaffected by the differences of the material which it unifies" (Joachim 1906: 26). Joachim based this conclusion on a rejection of the possibility of "purely external relations" but this feature is not central. What is valid in his criticism is that reality does not have, independently of what is said about it, a structure that judgments or statements are attempting to capture (compare Popper 1946: 213f.). What is not valid in Joachim's criticism is the conclusion that statements about the world cannot be perfectly true.

A related problem is provoked by the phenomenon of vagueness. Language, we may admit, is usually vague, whilst the world is not vague. How then can there be a strict correspondence between true statements and the world? The conviction that such a correspondence is impossible has led to numerous attempts over the years to go beyond the correspondence theory of truth. (For some useful critical remarks see Quine 1960: §26.) The most famous of these attempts is fuzzy logic, which – far from taking vagueness seriously, as its official ideology suggests – is at heart a project to reduce vagueness to precision. (The motivation is computational.) I agree with Black (1963: 6) and Dummett (1975: 312) that vagueness is in this sense not eliminable. Tarski's T-scheme shows that for normal purposes it need not be eliminated. The statement "Snow is white" is doubtless vague, but according to Tarski it is true if and only if snow is white. That does not postulate a vague aspect to the world, but states – vaguely, of course – a condition on the world that has to be satisfied if the statement "Snow is white" is to be true.

The problem of selectivity arises also in the philosophy of history, where it is associated with the view that all writing of history is falsification of history, in the bad sense of distortion of history. (For a discussion of related issues see Popper 1945/1966: ch. 25, §3 and Popper 1957: §31.) Joachim (1906: 16), writes characteristically:

> though a chronicle may, from one point of view, "correspond" detail for detail with the historical events, yet for its reader, even if not its writer, it may be radically false. For it may entirely miss the "significance" of the piece of history, and so convey a thoroughly false impression.

Indeed, we can find something like the same view even in Popper's writings in this area. Writing of situational models (1994: 172), he says: "Can any model be true? I do not think so. Any model, whether in physics or the social sciences, must be an oversimplification. It must omit much, and it must overemphasize much." But oversimplification alone need not imply falsehood. Granted, if a model is understood not as a linguistic item but as a physical or mathematical object, such as an orrery (a model of the solar system) or an urn model of the spread of infectious diseases, or a picture, then it will omit much, and overemphasize much, and it is trite that it is not true. Where such a concrete model, or picture, fails is in not saying which of its (positive or negative) features we are to pay attention to, and which we are to ignore: such information can be conveyed only by language. To be sure, some of these provisions are conventionally understood – a picture is one-sided, two-dimensional, perhaps framed – and normally we know – without being told – that these features are to be disregarded. But the model or picture does not tell us this. Figurative language, as its name suggests, is in a similar boat. What this illustrates is the inadequacy of the doctrine that scientific theories should be represented by models, indeed the inadequacy in general of the picture theory of truth. We may well wonder what makes the descriptive use of language possible, but we should not underestimate its achievements.

I do not deny that the selective use of true statements can indeed mislead, or "convey a thoroughly false impression" (Joachim). It can mislead because there is often, though not in courts of law, an unspoken presumption (to some extent formalized in the logic programming system PROLOG; see Gillies (1996: §4.2)) that the speaker tells the whole truth, or at least the whole relevant truth. There are also problems arising from the contextual variation of what a statement says, problems that I cannot discuss here. But the presentation of too many true statements can be just as misleading, as statisticians know. All we should conclude from this is that some facts may, in some situations, be more salient than others; we should not conclude that true statements do not correspond to the facts.

Concluding remarks

If there is one thing that an objectivist theory of truth, such as Tarski's, makes plain, it is that there is an ineradicable dualism of facts and decisions, a dualism, we might say, that patrols the boundary of the realm of facts itself. The decision to accept a true factual statement X as true is not identical with the statement X, nor is it identical with the state of affairs that X describes. Tarski showed that, by employing a metalanguage for which truth is undefined, we may define, and effectively make redundant, the idea of truth for statements of an object language. But the truth of a statement, far from being brought down to the level of a fact, as correspondence theorists have often put the matter, is in this way raised to the level of a statement for which truth is not yet defined. A decision to accept a statement as true therefore always goes beyond the statement itself, and even beyond its truth.

This conclusion, I suggest, has nothing to do with the failures of justificationism (which I do not for a moment want to diminish), and everything to do with the unbridled power of the descriptive use of language. We are always falling short of what we can achieve. But – to use another phrase often employed by P. G. Wodehouse – we can, as the first canto of *In Memoriam* says, rise on the stepping stones of our dead selves to higher things.

REFERENCES

Black, M. 1963. "Reasoning with loose concepts," *Dialogue* 2: 1–12; references are to the reprint in Black, *Margins of Precision*. Ithaca: Cornell University Press, 1970.

Boolos, G. S. and Jeffrey, R. C. 1974. *Computability and Logic*. Cambridge: Cambridge University Press; 3rd edition, 1989.

The Cambridge Dictionary of Philosophy. 1995. Ed. R. Audi, Cambridge: Cambridge University Press.

Coffa, J. A. 1991. *The Semantic Tradition from Kant to Carnap. To the Vienna Station*. Cambridge: Cambridge University Press.

Dummett, M. A. E. 1975. "Wang's paradox," *Synthese* 30: 301–24.

Engel, P. 1989. *La norme du vrai*. Paris: Gallimard; references are to the English translation, *The Norm of Truth*, Toronto and Buffalo: University of Toronto Press, 1991.

Etchemendy, J. 1988. "Tarski on truth and logical consequence," *Journal of Symbolic Logic* 53: 51–79.

Ewing, A. C. 1934. *Idealism: A Critical Survey*. London: Methuen.

Field, H. 1972. "Tarski's theory of truth," *Journal of Philosophy* 49: 347–75; references are to the reprint in Platts 1980: 83–110.

Gillies, D. A. 1996. *Artificial Intelligence and Scientific Method*. Oxford: Oxford University Press.

Gödel, K. 1961?/1995. "The modern development of the foundations of mathematics in the light of philosophy," in S. Feferman *et al.* (eds) *Kurt Gödel. Collected Works*, vol. 3: *Unpublished Essays and Lectures*. New York and Oxford: Oxford University Press, 1995, pp. 374–87.

Grim, P. 1992. *The Incomplete Universe*. Cambridge, Mass.: MIT Press.

Jarvie, I. C. 1995. "The justificationist roots of relativism," in C. M. Lewis (ed.), *Relativism and Religion*. London: Macmillan, pp. 52–70, 125–8.

Joachim, H. H. 1906. *The Nature of Truth*. Oxford: Clarendon Press.

Kirkham, R. L. 1992. *Theories of Truth. A Critical Introduction*. Cambridge, Mass.: MIT Press.

Mackie, J. L. 1973. *Truth, Probability and Paradox*. Oxford: Clarendon Press.

McDowell, J. 1978. "Physicalism and primitive denotation: Field on Tarski," *Erkenntnis* 13: 131–52; references are to the reprint in Platts 1980: 111–30.

Miller, D. W. 1985. *Russell, Tarski, Gödel: An Internal Study Aid*, Coventry: University of Warwick; Portuguese translation, "Russell, Tarski, Gödel: um guia de estudos," *Ciência e Filosofia* (São Paulo), 5, (1996), 67–105.

—— 1994. *Critical Rationalism. A Restatement and Defence*. Chicago and La Salle: Open Court Publishing Co.

—— 1999. "Sokal and Bricmont: Into the Frying Pan," http://www.warwick.ac.uk/ philosophy/miller/sokal.html

Musgrave, A. E. 1997. "The T-scheme plus epistemic truth equals idealism," *Australasian Journal of Philosophy* 75: 490–6.

Novak, M. 1995. *Awakening from Nihilism: Why Truth Matters*. London: Institute of Economic Affairs.

Platts, M. de B. (ed.) 1980. *Reference, Truth and Reality*. London: Routledge & Kegan Paul.

Popper, K. R. 1934. *Logik der Forschung*. Vienna: Julius Springer; references are to the English translation, Popper 1959.

—— 1945. *The Open Society and Its Enemies*. London: George Routledge and Sons; 5th edition, London: Routledge & Kegan Paul, 1966; one-volume Golden Jubilee edition, London: Routledge, 1995.

—— 1946. "Why are the calculuses of logic and arithmetic applicable to reality?," *Aristotelian Society, Supplementary Volume* 20: *Logic and Reality*: 40–60; references are to the reprint in Popper 1963/1989: pp. 201–14.

—— 1957. *The Poverty of Historicism*. London: Routledge & Kegan Paul.

—— 1959. *The Logic of Scientific Discovery*. London: Hutchinson; expanded English translation of Popper 1934.

—— 1962. "Julius Kraft 1898–1960," *Ratio* 4: 2–12.

—— 1963. *Conjectures and Refutations*. London: Routledge & Kegan Paul; 5th edition 1989.

—— 1972. *Objective Knowledge*. Oxford: Clarendon Press; 2nd edition 1979.

—— 1974a. "Intellectual autobiography," in Schilpp 1974: 3–181; reprinted as *Unended Quest*. London: Fontana, 1976.

—— 1974b. "Replies to my critics," in Schilpp 1974: 961–1197.

—— 1994. *The Myth of the Framework*. London: Routledge.

Quine, W. V. O. 1960. *Word and Object*. Cambridge, Mass.: MIT Press.

—— 1962. "Paradox," *Scientific American* 206; references are to the reprint "The ways of paradox" in Quine, *The Ways of Paradox*. Cambridge, Mass.: Harvard University Press, 1966: 1–18.

Russell, B. A. W. 1918. "The philosophy of logical atomism," in *The Philosophy of Logical Atomism*. La Salle: Open Court.

—— 1935. "The ancestry of fascism," in *In Praise of Idleness*. London: George Allen & Unwin; references are to the reprint in Russell, *Let the People Think*. London: Watts & Co., 1941, pp. 61–79.

Ryle, G. 1951. "Heterologicality," *Analysis* 11: 61–9; reprinted in Ryle, *Collected Papers*, vol. 2. London: Hutchinson, 1971: 250–7.

Schilpp, P. A. (ed.) 1974. *The Philosophy of Karl Popper*. La Salle: Open Court.

Schlick, M. 1925. *Allgemeine Erkenntnislehre*, 2nd edn. Berlin: Julius Springer; English translation, *General Theory of Knowledge*. La Salle: Open Court, 1985.

Shearmur, J. F. G. 1996. *The Political Thought of Karl Popper*. London: Routledge.

Simmons, K. 1993. *Universality and the Liar. An Essay on Truth and the Diagonal Argument*. Cambridge: Cambridge University Press.

Sokal, A. and Bricmont, J. 1998. *Intellectual Impostures*. London: Profile Books.

Tarski, A. 1936a. "Der Wahrheitsbegriff in den formalisierten Sprachen," *Studia Philosophica* 1: 261–405; references are to the English translation in Tarski 1956: 152–278.

—— 1936b. "O ugruntowaniu naukowej semantyki," *Przegląd Filozoficzny* 39: 50–7; references are to the English translation in Tarski 1956: 401–8.

—— 1944. "The semantic conception of truth and the foundations of semantics," *Philosophy and Phenomenological Research* 4: 341–75; references are to the reprint in A. P. Martinich (ed.), *The Philosophy of Language*, 2nd edn, New York: Oxford University Press, 1990: 48–71.

—— 1956. *Logic, Semantics, Metamathematics. Papers from 1923 to 1938*, translations by J. H. Woodger. Oxford: Clarendon Press.

5

POPPER'S IDEAL TYPES: OPEN AND CLOSED, ABSTRACT AND CONCRETE SOCIETIES[1]

Ian Jarvie

Popper presents his central notions of closed and open societies as tools for historical interpretation: history is the struggle to navigate the transition from an earlier and less desirable form of society to a later and more desirable form. Various criticisms can be made of his historical claims.[2] Since *The Open Society* is philosophical, not historical, in its aims, these criticisms can easily be shown to be beside the point (provided philosophy can be distinguished from history). Discarding these historical claims, however, would also lose their suggestiveness. How can they be reintroduced? Weberian ideal types can do the philosophical work without the historical claims, so I propose we treat closed and open in that way. Popper also holds up science as a model for the open(-minded) society. If we treat this view of science as also an ideal type, his lack of concern with the deviation of his model from the real history and sociology of science need not damage the philosophical points being advanced.

An ideal type, according to Weber, is an analytical construct built out of empirical materials but, since it is an idealization, it corresponds to no concrete reality. The ideal type is created for purposes of thought and exists nowhere; it is in this sense utopian, but it is rooted in reality, so that it is criticizable, though not for its idealizations as such. The power of the philosophical notions of open society and of science as an open society in miniature is that, read as ideal types, they not only help us to criticize and to reform our social and political institutions, but also help expose the grave deficiencies in the social organization and politics of real, existing science and point to the need for reform.

Historical criticisms of *The Open Society*

Popper's great book is organized around a contrast between open and closed societies. *The Open Society and Its Enemies* presents this contrast in the form

1 Appropriately enough, I hope, the idea of treating Popper's master social concepts as ideal types is something I first came across in Gellner 1964: 84n.
2 John Hall and John Watkins find sociological, historical, and even historicist deficiencies in *The Open Society and Its Enemies*. See their papers in this volume.

of an interpretation of the history of the philosophy of politics and of history, viewed as an arena for debate between partisans of these two contrasted modes of social organization. Such historical interpretations are, Popper holds, to be judged by their fruitfulness not by their truth or falsity. No one can doubt the fruitfulness of the open and closed interpretation considering the extra-ordinary monograph Popper was able to build; a work which shifted the locus of debate in political philosophy from democracy to openness.

Popper's initial presentation of the book's master notions is historical. In the Introduction to *The Open Society and Its Enemies* he contrasts life in earlier tribal or "closed" society with modern life in an open society. Tribal society is uncritically submissive to magical forces, as contrasted with a society which is open and sets the critical powers free. Popper admits that the work of building open societies that aim at humaneness and reasonableness, at equality and freedom, "is still in its infancy" (1945, vol. 1: 1). Humanity has not yet fully recovered from the shock of the birth of openness.[3] Tribalism is seen as the ancestral form of human society. He writes of it as emphasizing "the supreme importance of the tribe without which the individual is nothing at all" (ibid.: 9), i.e. a kind of collectivism.[4]

In chapter 10 of the book, eponymously entitled "The Open Society and Its Enemies," a theoretical chapter he was tempted to place at the beginning (ibid: 5), Popper elaborates. The first step from tribalism toward openness and individualist humanitarianism was made, he says, in Ancient Greece. The early Greek tribes were not unlike, he hypothesizes, Polynesian peoples, such as the Maoris (we recall that Popper was writing this in New Zealand). He does not deny that there are significant differences between Greeks and Maoris:

> There is no standardised "tribal way of life." It seems to me, however, that there is one distinguishing feature which is common to most, if not all, of these tribal societies. I mean their magical or irrational attitude towards the customs of social life, and the corresponding rigidity of these customs.
>
> (Ibid.: 172)

Whilst also allowing that tribal customs, though rigid, do change, he goes on to say that the comparatively infrequent changes

> have the character of religious conversions, or of the introduction of new magical taboos. They are not based upon a fully rational attempt to improve social conditions. Apart from such rare change, taboos

---

3 It still surprises me that Popper incorporates the Freudian idea of birth trauma into his work.

4 This is historical speculation. Anthropologically and biologically we might expect small-scale band organization to be the form of early human society. Tribalism can arise only with greater population density than we envisage in the earliest times.

rigidly regulate and dominate all aspects of life ... institutions leave
no room for personal responsibility.

(Ibid.: 172)

Popper finds evidence in Ancient Greek texts of the unevenness of change
from tribalism toward openness. The Greek philosopher Heraclitus, he observes, did not distinguish clearly between the institutional laws of tribal life
and the laws of nature, "Both are taken to be of the same magical character."
So Heraclitus does not yet have the key idea of openness. We must take care
not to suppose that the changes under discussion are abrupt, sharply differ-
entiating before and after; rather, change is gradual, uneven, *and reversible*.
Popper readily admits that magical and tabooistic thinking survive down into
our own (supposedly utterly modern) society. In brief, there are no real societies at either of the poles open and closed: Popper's own qualifications
deconstruct the initially historical presentation. Instead, openness is an ideal;
its achievement a matter of degree. The relative openness of the modern West
resides in that we have made social space for choice and decision between the
unchanging laws of social life and man-made taboos. This space, which we
try to expand, is the arena of personal responsibility, a social space where we
are permitted, even encouraged, to assess choices rationally by estimating
their consequences, to decide, and to take responsibility for the outcome.
Sometimes we may expand space by altering the social framework.

Openness permits a critical attitude to choices, and even to the social
framework that constrains choices. A critical attitude is identified with rationality. Is Popper identifying magical and tabooistic thinking with irrationality?
An affirmative answer to this question is widespread and it is a serious
misunderstanding.[5] Popper does not say that magic and taboo are irrational
per se. What he says is much more subtle: what is judged irrational is a magical
or tabooistic *attitude* to human custom and to human law. This attitude is
not a mere matter of psychology: it is institutional, not a state of mind.
Attitude as state of mind is one meaning of the term, as when we confess to
having an attitude of hostility to someone, we may mean no more than that
we have inner feelings of hostility. But the word has another and better-
established meaning. An attitude is also a stance, or posture, or, even, a
policy. A statue can be described as being that of a person striking an heroic
attitude. When we ask, "what is to be our attitude toward something or
other?," we are asking a question about stance. Shall we treat it with respect,
with disdain? shall we ignore it? shall we investigate it? and so on. Feelings
may background our choices, but they are not necessarily embodied in the
attitude. Our attitude manifests itself in action, it is not found in some
elusive (introspected) mental state. Quite possibly, stance and subjective

---

5 Main credit for this misunderstanding should probably go to Imre Lakatos, who, however, merely
stated crudely a prejudiced misunderstanding that was in the air.

feeling could be in conflict. A scientist could have a subjective attitude of conviction, of being correct. Yet the same scientist could, as part of an institution, foster and implement an attitude of skepticism and the demand for testing, even to their own work. The same goes for superstitions: we could believe them, fear them, yet still adopt a critical attitude. We could take a critical attitude to a magical belief, such as that this spell will turn you into a frog, or to a taboo, such as that people in certain states are unclean and it is forbidden to approach them. Such an attitude would be manifest in our proposing to test the spell and, if the result was negative, condemn the practice of terrorizing people with threats of spells. The taboo could be assessed as to whether it causes those under it to suffer and those believing in it to mistreat them. Such a rational approach is no mere thought experiment: magical and tabooistic thinking in our own society is sometimes subjected to this kind of rational assessment. The crimes of witchcraft and sorcery, for one, have long been removed from our law books and serious accusations are now almost unknown. Many taboos and superstitions have simply faded away because we do not take them seriously enough to oppose them. Witchcraft, sorcery, taboo, and superstition have not been, cannot be, refuted. Proving a negative, such and such *does not exist*, is impossible. A rational attitude has rather led to the conclusion that they are unnecessary and harmful. That attitude, that policy, explains their atrophy. A socially instituted attitude has re-conditioned subjective attitudes, rather than vice versa.

The point is of the greatest importance. Popper holds that the difference between science and magic does not lie in the content of their *claims* but in the *attitude* adopted to these claims, the way they are approached by their adherents. In the case of magic and taboo the attitude is uncritical; its contrast is critical. The critical attitude is what Popper attempts to capture and institutionalize in his methodological rules for science. Thus he has no difficulty with the fact that there may be ideas in science – the alchemical search for the philosopher's stone; Newton's theory of action at a distance – that resemble those behind magical practice and were even perhaps inspired by them in historical fact. What marks science and its rationality is an attitude to, a way we treat, ideas. The beginnings of science, on this account, lie in the adoption and institutionalization of the rational attitude, not in a new and superior kind of idea. Within scientific institutions ideas get massaged into testable form, and, if they fail the tests, they become candidates for replacement. In the absence of suitable replacements their status is ambiguous.

In *Logik der Forschung* (*LdF*) Popper had presented science as an invisible college governed by rationally debated and adopted rules of procedure. The attitudes embedded in the rule of this college are strongly to be contrasted with the attitudes of magic and taboo. Rules of the college are strictly secular and, indeed, since one need not enter it, optional. People are free not to join, members are free to try to alter this or that rule. The rules are not surrounded with a magical aura, or sanctioned by the dread of taboo. In *LdF* science was explicitly compared to the disinterested search for truth in a jury trial. In Popper's discussion, science, magic and taboo, and jury trial are all typified, simplified, idealized. They function as ideal types. It cannot be denied that in our society, magical and tabooistic attitudes toward science and jury trial linger on. Similarly, disinterested and critical inquiry can and does occur in predominantly magical and tabooistic societies. The ideal types assist our thinking: they alert us to alternatives, and allow us to be critical of our attitudes and their institutional embodiment and so to be able to contemplate alteration. Under Popper's hand this ideal type of science as an institutionalization of the attitude of open-mindedness and rationality is given a central place in his social thinking.

Popper in *The Open Society* ambitiously generalizes his *LdF* ideas about the social character of science. He takes the rationality of scientific institution(s) as a model for an attitude that he recommends be institutionalized throughout society. From government downwards there should be institutions that embody an attitude of independent-minded, coolly critical, assessment – of rules, laws, institutions, policies, and so on, by means of an estimate of their likely consequences. Institutions should be built to foster such ways of choosing as well as, reflexively, to encourage a critical attitude towards the institutions themselves. A society with such an attitude toward itself and its components is an open society, and a paradigm for the open society is the open institution of science. Indeed, Popper thinks that the connection is stronger, possibly even approximating a sociological law:

> There can be sociological laws, and even sociological laws pertaining to the problem of progress; for example, the hypothesis that, wherever the freedom of thought, and of the communication of thought, is effectively protected by legal institutions and institutions ensuring the publicity of the discussion, there will be scientific progress.
>
> (1945/1962, vol. 2: 322, note 13)

Seeking a metaphor to characterize the alternative, the closed-minded society, Popper proposes the ancient one of the organism. In an organism each part plays its role and no other: the legs cannot become the brain, nor other parts the belly. If conceived of as an organism, the way society and each part of it functions, is a natural given. Popper contrasts this to the situation in an even partially open society, where we can observe competition between parts to assume other roles, members trying to displace others, for example in the class struggle, where the ruled endeavour to become the rulers. The very existence of such struggle constitutes a rejection of a natural order of parts and, to the degree that it is open, makes nonsense of the comparison of society to an organism (1945, vol. 1: 173–4).

Although I present Popper as deconstructing his own historical presentation, it is vulnerable to still further criticism. What Popper offers is an historical myth about openness: it is a story about origin. It does not offer sufficient conditions for openness, as he always maintained that these were not present, hence his story is not quite an explanation of the origin of openness. His story offers, rather, a description of factors conducive to openness. It is a materialist, not an idealist theory. It goes thus. How did the transition from the closed to the open society begin in Ancient Greece? Popper argues that population pressure created tension within the ruling class, presumably in a struggle for the spoils, which was meliorated by the creation of daughter cities or colonies. But cultural contact and commerce on the periphery created even more stress, as non-traditional classes, including foreigners, emerged to disrupt the prior social order. By the sixth century BC there were revolutions and reactions, the birth of free thought, and clear evidence of the strain of civilization. The strain comes from the demands which the breakdown of the closed society makes on the citizen: to be rational, to think for oneself, to be autonomous, and, above all, to take responsibility for the way things are in one's society. Popper concludes of the strain of civilization: "It is the price we have to pay for being human." This astonishing remark might seem to equate "being human" with being "civilized" and, perhaps, *fighting the tribal in our breasts*. It warrants a digression to deal with it.

Any equation of being human with not being tribal would create an unsustainably inconsistent position for one of Popper's humane and enlightened stance. It is not hard to see that it is a misreading. It occurs in a passage where Popper is contrasting the open and the closed societies. As we have seen, these concepts are far from being fully and satisfactorily discussed, especially when they are related to concrete historical events, such as those that occurred in Ancient Greece. Popper is explicit, however, that the process of transition from the one form of society to the other is only partial. He draws attention to the continued existence of magic and tabooistic thinking in our present society. There is a sub-text of allusion to Nazism as the tribalism of modern Germany and Austria. What perhaps he fails sufficiently to emphasize is that tribal society is only partially present *amongst tribes*. Tribes are treated differently at different places in the book: first they are concrete, then they are historical, then not quite historical, and lastly they are metaphor. Popper uses tribe as a metaphor to condemn contemporary barbarism with his expression the *return* to the tribe, where the return is a step back from openness rather than a step back in time. Furthermore, intentionally or not, the return advocates going *all the way* – though it is doubtful whether it would be successful. "Tribal" or "closed" and "open" or "rational" are here being deployed as metaphors, or rather, as "ideal types," decidedly not as concrete descriptions. Thus we can interpret the strain of civilization as falling on tribesmen also, *to the extent that they are civilized*, that is, to the extent that their society compels individuals to be rational, to look after themselves and to take responsibility – to increase their rationality. In this respect I think it is a fact that *all known societies are to a greater or a lesser degree open (civilized); none is completely closed (uncivilized)*. Civilization is a matter of degree. This concludes the digression.[6]

Possibly this interpretation is too charitable, as Popper does write this sort of thing:

> Thus when we say that our western civilisation comes from the Greeks, we ought to be clear what that means. It means that the Greek[s] began that greatest of all revolutions, a revolution which started just yesterday, as it were, for we are still in its initial stage – the transition from the closed to the open society.
>
> (1945/1946 edn, vol. 1: 153)[7]

Popper here gives the distinct impression that genuine closed societies exist historically, as all of them, up to the time of the Ancient Greeks, were closed; that as a matter of fact most societies are closed, namely akin to herds, societies to which the organic metaphor can properly be applied, not only because of the magical or tabooistic attitude to social custom, but also because there are no phenomena like class struggle or upward social mobility.

We have seen how Popper's qualifications to his initial historical presentation can fend off the criticism that open and closed represent pseudo-anthropology. What would his answer be to the charge that they are false history, that they in no way correspond to what actually happened? Popper presents historical interpretations as neither true nor false, but rather, like methodologies, fruitful or barren (Jarvie 1960). So they can be criticized for being fruitless, but not as severely as hypotheses for being false. For example, his own attention to discussions of openness led him to ask whether some of the arguments to be found in Greek writings were directed at opponents whose very existence is missing from the historical record. The most controversial case was his suggestion that some surviving arguments suggest that there may have been a forgotten movement for the abolition of slavery. Still, this does not deal with all criticism, which I doubt can be stemmed.

Let me turn, instead, to the value of his interpretation. How do we show that the contrast of open and closed can be fruitful? My suggestion is that first we treat them as Weberian ideal types. What more can I say in favor of treating "open" and "closed" as ideal types? There is a decisive argument, I think, and it comes from Popper himself; we could call it "Popper's hermeneutic rule" (see chapter 11 of Jarvie 1987):

> *Popper's Hermeneutic Rule*   Always try to reformulate the position under discussion in its logically strongest form.

---

6 Awareness of this is signalled in footnote 8 to chapter 10 of the first edition of *The Open Society*, where Popper notes that the strain of civilization is clearly expressed in Heraclitus, with traces in Hesiod, long before the time Hellenic society begins to disintegrate. This note is preserved in later editions.

7 This passage, only slightly rewritten, is preserved in the 1962 edition at the foot of vol. 1: 175.

This rule is the opposite of any apologetic rule; that is, it does not recommend that you defend pet ideas by any means to hand. Rather, it enjoins us that where an author has formulated a promising position in a way that as vulnerable to some obvious objection, the commentator should first try to improve upon it before subjecting it to criticism – not for the author's sake but for the sake of the inquiry. Weak positions easily knocked down do not advance inquiry. We learn more from criticizing strong positions, whether they in the end succumb to criticism or not.

To interpret Popper as treating the transition from the open to the closed society as a series of real historical events sits uneasily with certain remarks he makes at various places in the text. Furthermore, such a claim is easily refuted by the evidence of anthropology.[8] Allowing that neither tribes nor totalitarian societies are ever completely closed, Popper suggests that the nearest to being closed are petrified societies, of which Ancient Egypt is the best example. Examples of complete closedness are to be found not in history but in some of the dystopias of fiction. None of these objections shows the notions of "open" and "closed" to be without analytical interest, unable to assist our inquiries. They remain immensely illuminating. Therefore, it better accords with Popper's Hermeneutic Rule to ignore his failure to posit open and closed as ideal types and proceed to treat them as such.

One argument for the fruitfulness of open and closed as ideal types is that they led Popper to devise a second contrasted pair, concrete society and abstract society, better to analyze historical trends in social organization. In the American edition of 1950, and subsequently, Popper added this second pair of ideal types to his conceptual armoury. Their significance has been little commented on. The passages from chapter 10 that we have been discussing were extensively re-worked for the new American edition, although the line of argument was not altered in any way.

The ideal types Popper introduced in 1950 are those of the "abstract society" as contrasted with "concrete" society.

> As a consequence of its loss of organic character, an open society may become, by degrees, what I would like to call an "abstract society." It may, to a considerable extent, lose the character of a concrete or real group of men, or of a system of such real groups.
>
> (1945/1950 and subsequent edition, vol. 1: 174)

Popper offers as an illustration a thought-experiment society in which people never meet face-to-face. Individuals go about in closed motor cars and commu-

---

8 These issues were first broached by Ernest Gellner, in a generous Foreword he contributed to my *Revolution in Anthropology* (1964). Somewhat ungraciously, I tried to answer him in an appendix (III) added to the proofs of the book. For the second edition, thinking better of my ungraciousness and my defensiveness, I deleted the appendix. They are reiterated by him in his 1964: 84–5n, and p. 159n.

nicate by typed letters or by telegrams, with artificial insemination for repro-
duction. This is a "completely abstract or depersonalized society." Yet, Popper
notes, elements of this abstraction do permeate our modern society.

> There are many people living in a modern society who have no, or
> extremely few, intimate personal contacts, who live in anonymity
> and isolation, and consequently unhappiness. For although society
> has become abstract, the biological make-up of man has not changed
> much; men have social needs which they cannot satisfy in an abstract
> society.
>
> (Ibid.: 174–5)

This whole passage is interpolated before the passage about the Greek
origins of the transition from closed to open (from p. 153 of the first edition)
quoted above. It is problematic. Our bodies prevent direct contact soul-to-
soul the way advocates of the concrete society see as ideal. This condition is
universal, so in the transition passage from the new material discussing the
abstract society back to the older text discussing the open society Popper
stresses that there is some element of exaggeration in his discussion of the
trend toward abstraction in the open society. "There never will be or can be
a completely abstract or even a predominantly abstract society – no more
than a completely rational or even a predominantly rational society" (ibid.:
175). We still form real groups, his concession continues, although it is
doubtful if they provide for a common life, that is, for our social needs.
There are, however, gains as well as losses from the growing abstractness.
Personal relations are no longer determined by accidents of birth; spiritual
bonds can play a role when biological bonds are less prominent. Modern
open societies function largely by way of abstract relations such as exchange
or co-operation. The picture painted is inherently bleak, contributing to
what he calls the strain of civilization.

The notions of concrete and abstract yield further fruit, leading Popper to
formulate a very important methodological point. It is, he says, with the
analysis of these abstract social relations that modern social theory is mainly
concerned. What he could have added, but did not, is that *precisely because* so
many social relations are abstract and none of them is fully concrete it is hard
for their actors to think out consequences of action, intended and unintended,
whereas in a face-to-face society (the preferred term in sociology for what
Popper terms "concrete"), actions and their consequences are readily seen,
and when expectations are dashed magical thinking explains this away. When
we think of the actions of modern government, with which our relations are
entirely abstract, it is obvious how the problems are compounded. Governments take actions like writing laws or creating new institutions which have
consequences intended and unintended on such an enormous scale that con-
tinuous effort is required to try to track down whether they have succeeded in

their aim, whether they have thwarted their own aim, whether the intricacies of implementation have resulted in little or no effect, or perhaps in monstrous unwanted effects. Much social and political discussion turns on these questions, upon which most of the conventional social sciences have surprisingly little to say, partly because they shy away from viewing social reform as tests of their ideas.

A clear example is the imposition of taxes. Sociologists and economists play down the fact that the imposition of a new tax is always a shot in the dark. Despite the existence of extensive statistics on modern economies, they are by no means fully understood. Thus, whenever taxes are introduced, or even just reformed, either to close loopholes, rectify injustices, or seek new sources of revenue, much discussion of outcomes is guesswork. Outcomes concern not just tax yield *versus* collection cost: there are also questions of effect on different economic activities, on overall economic activity, as well as political effects (costs). Even an effective and responsibly crafted tax reform can produce political backlash, as in the attempt to replace ratable value property taxes with a "community charge" system in the United Kingdom in the late 1980s and the early 1990s. This contributed to the fall of the Prime Minister herself. Electors, having little say on individual tax measures, tend to punish the government as a whole.

Here we see also the fruitfulness of Popper's basic sociological idea: the social organization of science, we remember, was Popper's model for the organization of the open society. Science is both concrete (laboratories, annual meetings, and the like) and abstract (in many senses). One could point to the Internet, that evolving wonder, as a realization of abstract social relations in the fields of science and of scholarship. The seventeenth-century metaphor of an invisible college is at last a reality. Scientific work and scientific groups can be realized by persons who never meet one another and who communicate by electronic means. Many see in all this a portent of a wider aspect of our future, as such advanced communication gets set to replace face-to-face communications in the workplace, in the market, in education. My guess is that such predictions are similar to predicting the demise of walking, the demise of the book, the demise of the movie. The social logic of the technology is different; instead of replacement, new technology characteristically adds layers that enhance and supplement older forms; replacement is unusual. Civil society does not become purely electronic but, because of the electronic pressure groups, for example, its agencies can recruit more widely, be better informed, and mobilize more quickly than before.

So much for science as abstract society. What of science as concrete or face-to-face society as a model for the open society? At first this looks promising. The Socratic seminar is an attractively egalitarian ideal. All serious questioners are welcome. The rules are the minimal ones of civility, clarity, and rationality. The group engages in an effort of cooperative problem solving. We see this projected forward into the Royal Society of the seventeenth century and the

Town Meeting of the New England colonies.[9] At this point the fruitfulness of the ideal types of open and closed, abstract and concrete, show in their pointing us toward a critique of Popper's ideas on openness. It is hard to see the Socratic seminar exemplified in today's Big Science and Big Government.

Popper's contemporary, Michael Polanyi, did not accept the Socratic seminar as a model for science or for society. His ideal free society, he said, is not the open society. His social philosophy drew different conclusions for science and for society from Big Science. Real scientific progress, in his view, required a considerable amount of intellectual and of social discipline. The ignorant and the incompetent needed to be weeded out, and knowledge and traditions of inquiry passed on directly by those in whom they were embodied, the leaders of the profession. Hierarchy and expertise were thus unavoidable. Polanyi was a democrat who argued that scientific values were a special case that needed the protection of elitist enclaves inside an open society, especially protection of freedom of thought and communication as well as protection from political interference: his concern for the autonomy of science led him to acknowledge as unavoidable limits to the autonomy of scientists, limitations similar to those in force in any protected guild.

Thomas Kuhn varied Polanyi's picture a little by distinguishing the social organization of science during periods of stability from those during periods of revolutionary upheaval. The stable normal science was Polanyite, the revolutionary periods were ones of disorganization and breakdown so severe that it was doubtful if there was science going on at all. These were modifications of detail: Kuhn took for granted the privileged position of science as a closed social organization within a free and open society. The Manhattan Project in which he had played a minor role had shown at first hand that an open society could close off an area of science and technology from public scrutiny and yet make progress. Within the project the scientific work was sub-divided into compartments which were sealed off from one another. Yet a Socratic seminar was permitted or tolerated, but only inside compartments, and only amongst the top echelon.

When Popper was confronted with the Polanyi/Kuhn position he recoiled, admitting its accuracy and deploring the fact that this was the state of affairs at the same time.[10] This is the only occasion I know of when he faced the fact that science as it has actually developed, as opposed to its Socratic ideal type, has social (as well as intellectual) features opposed to Popper's own social and political ideals. The encounter was inconclusive.

What has happened is a beautiful example of a boot-strap operation and so it is an illustration of the power of ideas, in this case Popper's. Popper's Socratic ideal type of science led him to his bold interpretation of the whole of human

9 See Jarvie and Agassi 1979.
10 See Popper in Lakatos and Musgrave 1970.

history as a struggle to generalize from that model of inquiry into nature to the conduct of all our affairs. Jury trial, Parliamentary democracy, the Royal Society of London, all of these were argued to be embodiments of the same idea. But, it turns out not to be the case that science permanently embodies the Socratic ideal type. The advent of Big Science in the twentieth century can be seen as the case of technology, money, politics, careerism, and many other factors altering the institutions. We can now judge this development not just by the standard of the Socratic seminar but by the derivative notions of open and closed, abstract and concrete. Having now achieved a high degree of openness in society at large, we can look critically at the changing social embodiment of science, once the source of our ideal type, and declare its present degree of openness deficient. These ideal-typical notions have more than demonstrated their fruitfulness.

REFERENCES

Gellner, E. A. 1964. *Thought and Change*. London: Weidenfeld.

Jarvie, I. C. 1960. "Professor Passmore on the objectivity of history," *Philosophy* 35: 355–6.

—— 1964. *The Revolution in Anthropology*. London: Routledge.

—— 1987. *Philosophy of Film*. London: Routledge.

Jarvie, I. C. and Joseph Agassi. 1979. "The rationality of dogmatism." In Th. Geraets (ed.), *Rationality Today*. Ottawa: University of Ottawa Press, pp. 353–62.

Lakatos, Imre and Alan Musgrave. 1970. *Criticism and the Growth of Knowledge*. Cambridge: Cambridge University Press.

Polanyi, Michael. 1958. *Personal Knowledge*. London: Routledge.

Popper, K. R. 1945 (and later editions). *The Open Society and Its Enemies*. London: Routledge.

6

THE SOCIOLOGICAL DEFICIT OF
THE OPEN SOCIETY, ANALYZED
AND REMEDIED

John A. Hall

The Open Society and Its Enemies can usefully be seen as a paean of praise to
bravery. For one thing, we should open our theories to refutation, not least by
writing as clearly as possible. More generally, we should embrace *Gesellschaft*
and so reject the cosy womb-like certainties of *Gemeinschaft*. In this view,
history is seen as an endless oscillation between systems dominated by the
cowardice of the weak and those marked by the fearlessness of the strong.
This essay concentrates on the historical sociology that lies at the heart of this
position. I argue that this view is defective, both as an interpretation of the
historical record and as a foundation for an open society – as is particularly
clear when attention is drawn to some basic elements of a more veridical
general account. All this can be formulated differently: despite the inspiration to be derived from the normative call to bravery, an open society in fact
depends on more solid social foundations.[1]

So as to be as clear as possible, three points characterizing and delimiting
the nature of this essay should be made. First, a background presupposition to
everything that follows is enthusiastic approbation of Popper's rewriting of
liberalism in terms of openness. The insistence on basing society on Socratic
dialogue seems to me exemplary, perhaps especially because it makes clear that
objectivity results, as Popper famously stressed, from a process of social criticism (Popper 1945/1962, vol. 2: ch. 23). As it happens I have nothing especially
original to offer by way of positive critique, but make my generalized admiration apparent so that the import of the negative critique that I do offer is not
misunderstood. In other words, my contribution is to offer a realistic sociological complement to a philosophically brilliant normative demand. Secondly,
concentration is exclusively on the historical sociology within *The Open Society and Its Enemies*. No discussion is offered of Popper's related claim that
social and natural sciences share a unified method (see Stokes 1997); nor is his

---

1 My argument echoes that of Gellner 1985: ch. 1. Where Gellner's interest was in Popper's attitude
 toward positivism, mine is in his historical sociology.

social philosophy compared to his epistemology more generally (see Bunge 1996). Further, I do not engage in the debate begun so effectively by Jeremy Shearmur as to the political orientation that should logically derive from Popper's *Weltanschauung* (Shearmur 1996). Thirdly, I do not seek to place Popper within the context of his time, not least since this task is now being performed at such a high level by Malachi Hacohen.[2]

The best way to turn to substantive matters is to suggest that Popper's great treatise contains three assertions: that there is a perennial revolt against freedom, that this is much encouraged by the activities of intellectuals, and that periods of rapid social change create instabilities which do much to undermine open societies. As each of these points is considered in turn, it is worth emphasizing that it is the *combination* of the three that makes the most powerful version of Popper's argument. Nonetheless, even this version does not give us a proper historical sociology of the open society, as will be made particularly clear by presenting key elements of that necessary account.

Beyond psychologism

Everything remains to be said for Popper's arguments against psychologism, made as a defence of Marx against Mill (Popper 1945/1962, vol. 2: ch. 14). It is indeed the case that what we take to be basic human instincts are very often the product of societal influence. This point continues to have real bite when applied to modern social science. Most obviously, it undermines what might be termed the hard programme of rational choice theory, that is, the onto-logical view which sees human beings as calculators of material interest. The trouble with this position is not that people do not calculate, for of course they do, but that what they value – that is, what counts to them as "interest" – varies enormously; in technical terms, preference formation needs to be understood in sociological terms rather than in those of rationalist deductivism (Hall 1993).

My first critical point against Popper concerns his own psychologism – which is to say that I wish to "hoist him by his own petard," to damn him in terms of his own argument. Strictly speaking this is not fair. For Popper's defence of the autonomy of sociology contains an explicit reservation that social science can benefit from the careful and limited use of psychological variables (1945/1962, vol. 2: 97–8). I entirely agree with this, as will be-come apparent later when making my own generalization about the radicalizing effect of political exclusion. Nonetheless, Popper's interpretation of break-

---

2 Hacohen 1996. Cf. Eidlin 1997. I differ from both authors given that their accounts of the abstractness of Popper's universalism lead to considerable sympathy for communitarianism of some sort. The contrast between society and community should not be accepted uncritically; its either/or quality has done much to mislead modern social theory.

downs of democratic systems in terms of a universal human tendency, that of "the perennial revolt against freedom," is very far from being limited and careful.[3] For one thing, the contrast in values is simply too stark, there being a great deal to be said for distinguishing a comprehensible, even desirable demand for security from out-and-out tribalism. More fundamentally, the variety of the historical record just cannot be seen in terms of this polar opposition. Even a short perusal of Juan Linz and Alfred Stepan's classic collection on *The Breakdown of Democratic Regimes* (1978) makes utterly obvious that a whole set of material social forces – from demographic pressures to threatened militaries and from defeats in war to economic collapse – have to be taken quite as much into account as does the "cowardly" ideological demand for moral unity.

But it is possible and desirable to save brilliant Popperian insights, to reconstruct them so that they gain plausibility, and to do so in such a way that the argument as a whole can be advanced. The claim that I wish to make is that the desire for moral unity, for an end to the splitting between social reality and the self, is distinctively Western. Perhaps there is something to the notion that a tribal past leaves an intellectual legacy: certainly Islam encodes egalitarian demands, and thereby has little sympathy for the mundane workings of political power (Crone 1980). Nonetheless, the unleashing of what Freud termed "oceanic feelings" is still best seen as Western. As a civilization, Islam brims, so to speak, with confidence, being utterly bereft of any self-doubt about its worth (Cook and Crone 1977). Occidental civilization seems entirely different. Greek comedies, histories and travel writings, both before and after Plato, show considerable nostalgia for primitive life, and contain anthropologies – doubtless more projection than reality, but revealing on that very account – of simple peoples who share property and/or women.[4] The conclusion to be drawn is thus that what Popper takes to be a universal human psychological trait is in fact the product of a particular culture.

There is a great deal to be said in favor of Popper's analysis of one of the sources of this cultural tradition. Such admirers of Sparta as Plato were indeed threatened aristocrats, attracted to a world in which their own social position had been assured.[5] The production of communist ideas at a later period can equally be seen as the result of threats to the position of intellectuals. The outpouring of utopian thought at the time of the Reformation exemplified by the works of More and Campanella owed a very great deal to the ending of

---

3 This psychological drive received its fullest and clearest statement in Popper 1945/1962: ch. 10.

4 I draw here and in the next paragraphs on knowledge gained at a conference on "Pre-Modern Communism" that I organized with Patricia Crone in 1992. I learnt a great deal from her comments, and from P. Cartledge's "Utopias in Ancient Greece: Fact or Fantasy?".

5 Popper's views about the Laconists have been powerfully supported by Wood and Wood 1978. Dawson 1992: ch. 2 offers some cautionary words on this interpretation.

monasticism, that is, of a specialized communist world which had guaranteed intellectuals high status.

Nonetheless, Popper misses an additional early source of utopian thought in the West. Religious communities convinced that the millennium was at hand were able to translate ideas of sharing into actual practice. The most obvious and important example of such sharing (which does not really deserve to be considered in Freudian terms as mere craven desire to return to the past) is that between the disciples of Jesus Christ in the period immediately after his death – if, that is, we are to believe the testimony of Acts of the Apostles. But the inhabitants of Leyden in 1535 were equally prepared to sink individual difference within a common cause (Cohn 1961). It is worth noting that such sharing was by no means always voluntary. Just as the admirers of Sparta favored hierarchical regimentation, so too did such reformation sects as the Hutterites (Scribner 1992). This proved to be a continuing tension. Thus in Rousseau, whose importance is seriously underplayed by Popper, there is at once an admiration for authority and the desire for Spartan simplicity (Shklar 1969; Blum 1986). Whilst Rousseau's work was most immediately used by the creators of a bourgeois republic of virtue, the admiration for authority could be split from egalitarianism altogether, as in fascism, with the two forces remaining most tightly allied in actually-existing socialism (Kolakowski 1974).

As the dream of moral unity is written into the heart of our civilization, both in the polis envy of the civic virtue tradition and in Christianity, it is extremely important to stress that only very particular conditions have led to the success of social movements seeking to suppress social diversity. We will see later that this holds true within the modern industrial era, but it is worth stressing immediately that it applies equally to pre-modern circumstances. Sparta stands as the exemplar of war communism: a small minority of the military fit were forced into a totalitarian way of life in order to survive in an extremely hostile environment. Expectations of the millennium break the pattern of normal routines quite as much – although it is important to note that consequential utopian practices have tended to be very short-lived. One reflection that follows from this is the strangeness of the fact that both fascist and communist intellectual traditions have been based on highly unusual circumstances. Differently put, the abnormal has been theorized excessively. A second reflection – that will gain ever greater force as we proceed – can be put negatively: social change *per se*, that is, changes in the rythms of social and economic life, does not correlate closely with the triumph of utopian "total" politics.

The dangers of idealism

Let me turn to the second criticism. Popper's viewpoint adds idealism to psychologism in stressing that open societies are threatened by the betrayal of the intellectuals, traitors within the gates of the open society who play upon the fear of freedom.[6] It is in this spirit that he places at the front of his treatise a passage from Samuel Butler's *Erewhon*:

> It will be seen … that the Erewhonians are a meek and long-suffering people, easily led by the nose, and quick to offer up common sense at the shrine of logic, when a philosopher arises among them who carries them away … by convincing them that their existing institutions are not based on the strictest principles of morality.
>
> (Popper 1945/1962, vol. 1: v)

Idealism itself can usefully be seen as comprising two theses. The strongest thesis is that language or culture provides us with a single, monolithic and coherent set of concepts which dictates the way in which we can live. The analysis of human action, by this account, becomes far less important than appreciation of the ideological codes which determine action. It can be said immediately that this general view, massively present in modern philosophy and social science, is often mistaken, largely because most ideological systems contain options of belief within them. But it is not completely mistaken. For one thing, "the closing of the gates of interpretation" in Islam seems to have produced an ideological system far less flexible than its Christian rival, and one whose austerity may well account for the limitation of certain social options within it. For another, my argument against Popper's psychologism has been to reinterpret it in terms of this sort of idealism, as a strain within Western thought that surfaces again and again, particularly amongst intellectuals.[7]

This brings us to a second, more sociological version of idealism, namely the one which claims that intellectuals determine the pace of socio-historical change. Popper very largely endorses this view. Again, there is some, occasional truth to this. World history is partly patterned by the emergence of world religions, one element in all of which is a claim to power by intellectuals based on a monopoly of literacy. Further, the Jacobins and the Bolsheviks, as well as the lumpen-intelligentsia so prominent within fascism, most certainly affected the historical record. But Popper's idealism is excessive because it fails to recognize the many occasions on which there have been intellectuals with more or less repulsive ideas who have failed to have any impact on social development. If the notion of betrayal by intellectuals makes any sense, it can certainly be applied to the political theory of Jean-Paul Sartre. But this modern Jacobin mercifully had no impact on the historical record. Equally, there have been many totalitarian theorists, characteristically mixing together egalitarian and hierarchical ideals, but most have been ignored.

---

6 It is worth recalling that Popper later admitted – in his *Unended Quest* (1976: 113) – that he had initially intended to call his great treatise "False Prophets: Plato–Hegel–Marx".

7 A particularly striking account of the endless love for the polis is that of Rawson 1991.

It is worth emphasizing here that all this should be a source of comfort for liberal democrats. *Pace* Popper and Butler, people are not normally easily led by the nose – meaning that they, rather than any enlightened elite, can be relied upon to calculate their own best interests.

Patterns of history

I can move to my third and final point, on which most time will be spent, by again making a reservation about what has just been said. On occasion, Popper qualifies the psychologism plus idealism that marks his account by noting that social disruptions were necessary for people to become prone to the messages of the intelligentsia. He describes the failures of social democrats in Weimar, for example, as a prelude to his characterization of fascism (1945/1962, vol. 2: 60–1). This is sensible, and it usefully helps us distinguish, for example, between the myriad forces causing a state breakdown from the revolutionary groups who sometimes seize the opportunity that this provides (Goldstone 1991). Nonetheless, my third criticism is that the implicit general historical account that Popper offers is deeply flawed, in large part because it omits far too much. To substantiate these views, let me first recall Popper's general account before suggesting an alternative.

Popper's dialectic of development

Popper's best-known claim is that Western civilization begins with the Greeks, in the Great Generation that pioneered rational criticism. If the first volume of his book describes in detail the way in which this view was attacked by Plato, considered at once as a real humanitarian aware of the sufferings brought about by the transition to openness and as a disaffected and threatened aristocrat, the twelfth chapter of the book describes repetitions of the pattern, that is, of outbursts of openness followed by renewed revolts against freedom. We are offered a view of history as an endless dialectic of development.

The first renewed progressive moment is identified by Popper unhesitatingly as that of early Christianity, whose universalism is contrasted unfavorably with mere Jewish tribalism, for all that it then became linked to a pattern of authority that ensured the coming of the Dark Ages. Those Dark Ages are seen very conventionally by Popper as ending only in 1789, the ideals of which year are uncritically endorsed as universalist and meritorious. The reaction against these views is effectively then seen as twofold, with Hegel playing the key role in both.

On the one hand, Hegel becomes the paid court philosopher of the Prussian state producing all sorts of mystical nonsense in order to keep the *ancien régime* in being. Real and higher freedoms were invented together with a philosophy of history glorifying the Prussian state, both of which were designed to undermine the universalism of the revolution. On the other hand, Hegel proved to be absolutely vital in defeating the spirit of the earliest German nationalism. Although Popper has much to say about Herder and Fichte, both of whom he regards as nothing but apostles of tribalism, with the latter's ideas resulting from the basest material motives, his account of the earliest German nationalism is ambivalent, if not actually positive:

> At the time when Fichte became the apostle of nationalism, an in-stinctive and revolutionary nationalism was rising in Germany as a reaction to the Napoleonic invasion. (It was one of those typical tribal reactions against the expansion of a super-national empire.) The people demanded democratic reforms which they understood in the sense of Rousseau and of the French Revolution, but which they wanted without their French conquerors. They turned against their own princes and against the emperor at the same time. This early nationalism arose with the force of a new religion, as a kind of cloak in which a humanitarian desire for freedom and equality was clad.
>
> (Popper 1945/1962, vol. 2: 55)

These ideas were a threat to the King of Prussia. Hegel is held to have been employed to counter this, to argue that the notion of popular sovereignty, that is, of some sort of Rousseauean superpersonality of the people, was meaningless given that the people was a mere formless multitude without leadership. In this manner, nationalism became illiberal, for all that it retained traces of liberalism within it. But it is worth highlighting the fact that Popper's deepest view is that nationalism *is* tribal, and a historical mistake. A footnote stresses that the Dan-ube area needed an international federation, and that the failure to create one had been a disaster; Popper is further particularly critical of Wilson's adherence to historicism, though curiously enough not to Masaryk's, on the grounds that anyone with a sense of history could see that the intermingling of peoples in this area was so great that any attempt to create homogeneous societies was doomed to be vicious (1945/1962, vol. 2: 51, 312, 318).

Finally, Popper notes the failure of social democracy, suggesting that it was no accident that it failed to oppose the war, and that it anyway had few ideas to deal with the depression and a poor record of opposition to fascism (ibid.: 60–1, 162–5). This leads into his magnificent pages on the nature of fascism (ibid.: 60–78). No equivalent pages on the nature of communism are offered, but Popper's distaste for its historicism is clearly apparent when citing the catastrophic decision of German communists to co-operate with fascism on the grounds that the sooner the last apotheosis of capitalism is over, the sooner can the new order be expected (ibid.: 162–5).

A sociological alternative, or, the importance of exclusion

In lieu of a complete alternative account, I offer four points that at least suggest what such an alternative account would look like.

The first point is negative. Skepticism should be shown to the claim that civilization begins with the Greeks. Popper sensibly distinguishes the ideas of the critical rationalists from those of the Laconists, and one could add to and so reinforce his positive case an institutional awareness of the way in which hoplite warfare empowered a peasantry against the upper classes (Bryant 1990). It was this latter factor that led to the creation of a society in which power was dispersed rather than being concentrated in any single set of hands. Still, the social struggles that then took place between tyrants and people were *within* a world that rested on slavery. This is not a world that adherents of the open society should admire, let alone mythologize. Surely, Hume and Smith, who made this point, were right to seek an entirely different exemplar for our civilization (Hont and Ignatieff 1983: especially introduction)?

My second point is positive. A more accurate and appropriate historical moment for the underwriting of the notion of the open society is, as Montesquieu and many of the Scottish Moralists realized, that of early modern Europe. Here was an acephalous society in which power was very distinctively in several sets of hands – in which, to put the point in different words, negative resisting powers were enhanced and generalized.[8] Kings were balanced by at least three estates of the realm, nobles, churchmen and burgers, with the additional restraint in some places of a fourth estate of peasants. If this was the consequence of the Fall of Rome, the legacy proved to be enduring. Gibbon realized this when stressing the benefits of multipolarity rather than empire:

> The division of Europe into a number of independent states, connected, however, with each other, by the general resemblance of religion, language, and manners, is productive of the most beneficial consequences to the liberty of mankind. A modern tyrant, who should find no resistance either in his own breast or in his people, would soon experience a gentle restraint from the example of his equals, the dread of present censure, the advice of his allies, and the apprehension of his enemies. The object of his displeasure, escaping from the narrow limits of his dominions, would easily obtain, in a happier climate, a secure refuge, a new fortune adequate to his merit, the freedom of complaint, and perhaps the means of revenge. But the empire of the Romans filled the world, and, when that empire fell into the hands of a single person, the world became a safe and dreary prison for his enemies ... To resist was fatal, and it was impossible to fly.
>
> (Gibbon 1903: 93)

In a multipolar system too much brutality to one's own population could lead to gain for an opposing state – as Montesquieu so clearly stressed when

---

8 There is a large literature on this point. See *inter alia* McNeill 1964, 1985, and Mann 1986.

reflecting on the skills and wealth that the Huguenots brought to Holland and East Anglia after their expulsion from France in 1685 (Montesquieu 1969: ch. 6). In consequence, states learned, albeit slowly and imperfectly, to restrain themselves, even to make their countries attractive to merchants and artisans. If this relative self-control helps explain the emergence of capitalism, its eventual triumph has quite as much to do with multipolarity. Capitalism had states rather than a state, meaning both that no single centre could discipline or control economic life and that every effort had to be made to imitate the leading edge of economic and military power.

This is the social portfolio appropriate as a foundational base for the open society. To begin with, the rise of the West, for all the viciousness with which it then treated the rest of the world, was miraculous in combining affluence with relatively soft political rule. Adam Smith was right to stress that commerce and liberty went together, at least in their first instantiation (Winch 1978, 1996). A further feature is less well understood, but it is quite as important. The stress of many eighteenth-century thinkers on sociability, polish, and refinement has often been seen as engaging oddity, as with Samuel Johnson's insistence on lowering the shades of his carriage when out of town on the ground that nature was too unruly. But something serious is being said here, and it involves the notion of civility.

Civility is best seen as arising, both in the past and in the present, out of stalemate consequent on different sources of power being unable to defeat each other, that is, as a decision to live together whilst tolerating differences of belief which are then consigned to private life (Gellner 1994; Hall 1995; Karl 1990; Colas 1997). The nature of this attack on enthusiasm, on those holders of absolute truth prepared to enforce it, become particularly apparent in the work of Benjamin Constant. His famous lecture contrasting the liberty of the ancients with that of the moderns insisted that the morally unified world of the polis was antithetical to a complex division of labor – and that ignorance of this point had led to the Terror (Constant 1988; Holmes 1984). In general, universalisms which seem meritorious – the Christian doctrine of Grace, the civic nationalism of the French Revolution – can be very vicious, as the "heretics" of the Later Roman Empire and of Medieval Europe as well as the inhabitants of the Vendée would attest. I believe such ideologies to result from periods when the socially sophisticated suffer political exclusion: they universalize against particular tyranny, but populate their views with vivid pictures of the villains responsible for their fate. All in all, an open society is a very complex affair: it accepts difference, either with resignation or enthusiasm, insisting only on a limited measure of agreement. This is quite as important an achievement as democracy and affluence given that the former can lead to tyranny and the latter to the denial of fundamental freedoms.

My third point concerns the period between 1789 and 1945 that is at the centre of *The Open Society*. My prior abstract judgment was that Popper's account makes far too much of the role of intellectuals. Analysis can now demonstrate that understanding of the key social forces of the age is missing from Popper's account, leading him to identify the wrong guilty party of modernity.

The most important accounts of modernity have stressed the impact of industrialization. A new social world gave rise to – and created conditions for self-awareness of – both nations and classes, the salience of both causing horrendous difficulties for *anciens régimes*. To my mind, the two most striking explanatory schemas of nineteenth- and twentieth-century history stress the simultaneous, layered interaction of both forces. Karl Polanyi's *The Great Transformation* – a great social science treatise that arose from inter-war Vienna, in many ways superior in quality to those offered by Hayek, Schumpeter and Popper – bases its case on the division of capitalism by states (Polanyi 1944). The endless change demanded by the market will, Polanyi insisted, sooner or later be resisted by some national society, preferring to keep its way of life rather than to endlessly adapt to the impersonal logic of the international market. Ernest Gellner's account of nationalism rather differently notes that fundamental conflict comes when social inequality and national difference are superimposed on each other: classes can be integrated but nations – whatever exactly they are! – will mobilize when the new industrial structure of opportunity, that is, a more homogenous world based on a single language, puts them systematically at a disadvantage.[9]

These are brilliant accounts, and my main point is that something of this order is needed in order to go beyond Popper's slim mapping of our social destiny. As it happens, my own views do not quite accord with Polanyi's and Gellner's; spelling out the difference is relevant since it allows proper identification of the guilty party of modernity.

In the abstract, a strong case can be made, in the spirit of Max Weber, for a more political interpretation of the mobilization of classes and nations.[10] In the years to 1914, the American working class was not socialist, the British was laborist, with only the German and still more the Russian working classes having genuine political consciousness. This fact seems to be best explained by the nature of the regime with which workers had to interact: political exclusion bred mobilization and ideological strength, whilst the granting of early citizenship in liberal states seems to have diffused conflict, in particular making class demands industrial rather than political.[11] Differently put, when workers have the chance to reform, they will not

9 Gellner 1983 – which makes much of the difficulty of defining "the nation." On Gellner's theory as a whole see the essays in Hall 1998.

10 Weber's comments about the German working class of his own time can be found in his wartime reflections on the historical sociology of Wilhelmine Germany (1978: 1391). I am generally influenced here by Mann 1993.

11 There is a substantial literature on this point. See *inter alia* Waisman 1982, Geary 1984, McDaniel 1987, Katznelson and Zolberg 1986, McKibbin 1990, and Mann 1986, vol. 2: chs. 15 and 17–19.

become revolutionary. As it happens, I believe that the spirit behind this interpretation of classes holds as true for nations (Hall 1994: especially ch. 6). Most of the peoples in Austro-Hungary sought their historic rights, and would not have sought to secede from a more liberal entity wedded to federalism and to consociationalism. Supranationalism can work, in other words, as long as it is not linked to authoritarian imperialism. In a nutshell, the possibility of voice tends to undermine the attractions of exit. The ambivalence at the heart of Popper's account of early German nationalism derives from his nearly recognizing this.

The general implication of this analysis is that the guilty party of modernity has been the established elite whose refusal to allow for political modernization led to radicalization of social forces. More generally, the social changes brought by capitalism and industrialization did not by themselves cause strains that doomed open societies. Mobilization depends far more upon political arbitrariness than upon mere social change.

In more concrete and particular form, this analysis applies to the political elite of Wilhelmine Germany – it being important to remember that it was actions in Berlin and not in Vienna that were responsible for the First World War. Why did Germany undertake the disastrous policy, and in 1939 one might add as much as in 1914, of starting a war likely to be lost since it had to be waged on two fronts? (Snyder 1991: ch. 3 and passim; Mann 1993: ch. 12; Hall 1996: ch. 3 and passim.) The best answer seems to be found in the fact that the German state was but half-modernized, at once a curious combination of court and of late development. It excluded both workers and middle-class nationalists, but felt ever more threatened and constrained by their ideologically intensifying demands. In order to deal with this situation the regime gave something to everyone – that is, a *Weltpolitik* appealing to the Social Democrats and to some industrialists, and an Eastern policy beloved by the army – rather than weighing up priorities. Such diplomatic licentiousness made enemies everywhere, so creating that encirclement from which in 1912 it was decided to break out. None of this was necessary. On the one hand, it was within the realm of possibility to have created settled institutions for German society, and these would have diminished and diffused the tensions of modernization. On the other hand, no economic necessity dictated the view that the health of the nation depended upon territorial expansion. The political elite felt threatened by domestic and then by international pressures that it had itself created, but the fact that it had no capacity – no single center after Bismarck where priorities could be given to overall strategy – by means of which it could have done better meant that the guilt to be assigned has more of the nature of causal responsibility than moral failure (Aron 1979).

My fourth and final point concerns war. It was defeat in war – rather than rapid social change *per se* – which unleashed the revolutionary forces of the twentieth century with which Popper was concerned. He was of course quite right to stress that the First World War ended badly. The putative link between nationalism and self-sufficiency remained, with the nationalizing practices of new states being at once particularly repulsive and a certain source of instability given the presence of large neighboring "homelands" (Brubaker 1995). Further, the allies made a harsh treaty which they were then not prepared to enforce. In contrast, the Second World War ended in such a way as to ensure stability (Maier 1981; Ruggie 1982). Nationalism was ignored, and both Japan and West Germany were reconstructed from the outside. Of course, the creation of a prosperous and liberal world in the West, a world in which nation-states lose their bite because of the creation or re-assertion of a larger, American dominated international political and economic society, stands in stark contrast to the deprivations endured under actually existing socialism. Still, to note that the way wars end matters is important: open societies are fragile, and no wave of social evolution guarantees their emergence and maintenance. If we can hope that lessons from inter-war Central and Eastern Europe have been learnt, it is still far too early to say that the openness of every country in the region is assured – not least since many regimes resemble Wilhelmine Germany in being politically only half-modernized and thereby potentially prone to praetorian politics (Snyder 1990).

Conclusion

It makes sense to conclude with an admission that leads to a summation. Popper's view of the open society and of the dangers that it faces is not, as noted, neatly split into the three elements distinguished here. Whilst I do not think that my division, made only for heuristic purposes, has distorted the account given of Popper's theory, recognizing it as a unity brings attention back to historicism, the fundamental devil that *The Open Society and Its Enemies* seeks to exorcise. It is here, it seems to me, that Popper must be convicted of gross and dangerous exaggeration. His magnificent demonstration of the dangers of what might be termed "totalizing history-worship" lead to a naive blindness to the impact of such social and historical forces as geopolitical conflict and political exclusion. Open societies rest upon decent institutions quite as much as upon bravely adopting critically rational attitudes, and their creation depends very much upon assessing social and historical forces such as war and political exclusion so that they can be manipulated and mastered. History is neither utterly determined nor a simple site upon which we can act: discovering the options that are genuinely available requires sustained analysis. In this matter we cannot do without those sociologies which attempt to map patterns of history. Such moderate historicisms are both necessary and desirable. Having no map at all can be as disastrous as having a misleading one.

REFERENCES

Aron, R. 1979. "On liberalisation." *Government and Opposition* 14.

Blum, C. 1986. *Rousseau and the Republic of Virtue*. Ithaca: Cornell University Press.

Brubaker, R. 1995. "National minorities, nationalising states, and the external national home-lands in the New Europe." *Daedalus* 124.

Bryant, J. 1990. "Military technology and socio-cultural change in the ancient Greek city." *Sociological Review* 38.

Bunge, M. 1996. "The seven pillars of Popper's social philosophy." *Philosophy of the Social Sciences* 26.

Cohn, N. 1961. *The Pursuit of the Millennium*. 2nd edition. New York: Harper.

Colas, D. 1997. *Civil Society and Fanaticism*. Stanford: Stanford University Press.

Constant, B. 1988. *Benjamin Constant: Political Writings*, ed. B. Fontana. Cambridge: Cambridge University Press.

Cook, M. and P. Crone. 1977. *Hagarism*. Cambridge: Cambridge University Press.

Crone, P. 1980. *Slaves on Horses*. Cambridge: Cambridge University Press.

Dawson, D. 1992. *Cities of the Gods*. Oxford: Oxford University Press.

Eidlin, F. 1997. "Blindspot of a liberal: Popper and the problem of community." *Philosophy of the Social Sciences* 27.

Geary, D. 1984. *European Labour Protest, 1848–1945*. London: Methuen.

Gellner, E. 1983. *Nations and Nationalism*. Oxford: Blackwell.

—— 1985. *Relativism and the Social Sciences*. Cambridge: Cambridge University Press.

—— 1994. *Conditions of Liberty*. London: Hamish Hamilton.

Gibbon, E. 1903. *The Decline and Fall of the Roman Empire* vol. 1. London: Everyman.

Goldstone, J. 1991. *Revolution and Rebellion in the Early Modern World*. Berkeley: University of California Press.

Hall, J. A. 1985. *Powers and Liberties*. Oxford: Blackwell.

—— 1993. "Ideas and the social sciences." In J. Goldstein and R. Keohane (eds), *Ideas and Foreign Policy*. Ithaca: Cornell University Press.

—— 1994. *Coercion and Consent*. Oxford: Polity Press.

—— 1995. "In search of civil society." In J. A. Hall (ed.), *Civil Society*. Oxford: Polity Press.

—— 1996. *International Orders*. Oxford: Polity Press.

—— 1998. *The State of the Nation: Ernest Gellner and the Theory of Nationalism*. Cambridge: Cambridge University Press.

Hacohen, M. H. 1996. "Karl Popper in exile: the Viennese progressive imagination and the making of *The Open Society*." *Philosophy of the Social Sciences* 26.

Holmes, S. 1984. *Benjamin Constant and the Making of Modern Liberalism*. New Haven: Yale University Press.

Hont, I. and M. Ignatieff (eds) 1983. *Wealth and Virtue*. Cambridge: Cambridge University Press.

Karl, T. 1990. "Dilemmas of democratisation in Latin America." *Comparative Politics* 22.

Kolakowski, L. 1974. "The myth of human self-identity." In L. Kolakowski and S. Hampshire (eds), *The Socialist Idea: a Reappraisal*. London: Weidenfeld and Nicolson.

Katznelson, I. and A. Zolberg (eds) 1986. *Working Class Formation*. Princeton: Princeton University Press.

Linz, J. and A. Stepan (eds) 1978. *The Breakdown of Democratic Regimes*. Baltimore: Johns Hopkins University Press.

Maier, C. 1981. "The two postwar eras and the conditions for stability in twentieth-century Europe." *American Historical Review* 85.

Mann, M. 1986. *Sources of Social Power* vol. 1: *A History of Power from the Beginning to AD 1760*. Cambridge: Cambridge University Press.

—— 1993. *Sources of Social Power* vol. 2: *The Rise of Classes and Nation-States, 1760–1914*. Cambridge: Cambridge University Press.

McDaniel, T. 1987. *Autocracy, Capitalism and Revolution in Russia*. Berkeley: University of California Press.

McKibbin, R. 1990. *Ideologies of Class*. Oxford: Oxford University Press.

McNeill, W. H. 1964. *The Rise of the West*. Chicago: Chicago University Press.

Montesquieu. 1969. *The Spirit of the Laws*. Cambridge: Cambridge University Press.

Polanyi, K. 1944. *The Grand Transformation*. Boston: Beacon Press.

Popper, K. R. 1945. *The Open Society and Its Enemies*. London: Routledge & Kegan Paul; 4th revised edition 1962.

—— 1976. *Unended Quest*. London: Fontana.

Rawson, E. 1991. *The Spartan Tradition in European Thought*. Oxford: Oxford University Press.

Ruggie, J. G. 1982. "International regimes, transactions and change." *International Organization* 36.

Scribner, R. 1992. "Practical utopias: pre-modern communism and the reformation." Paper prepared for the Pre-Modern Communism conference 1992.

Shearmur, J. 1996. *Popper's Politics*. London: Routledge.

Shklar, J. 1969. *Men and Citizens*. Cambridge: Cambridge University Press.

Snyder, J. 1990. "Averting anarchy in the New Europe." *International Security* 14

—— 1991. *Myths of Empire*. Ithaca: Cornell University Press.

Stokes, G. 1997. "Karl Popper's political philosophy of social science." *Philosophy of the Social Sciences* 27.

Waisman, C. 1982. *Modernisation and the Working Class*. Austin: University of Texas Press.

Weber, M. 1978. "Parliament and government in reconstructed Germany." In *Economy and Society*. Berkeley: University of California Press.

Winch, D. 1978. *Adam Smith's Politics*. Cambridge: Cambridge University Press.

—— 1996. *Riches and Poverty*. Cambridge: Cambridge University Press.

Wood, E. M. and N. Wood. 1978. *Class Ideology and Ancient Political Theory*. Oxford: Oxford University Press.

7

A WHIFF OF HEGEL IN
THE OPEN SOCIETY?

John Watkins

Ernest Gellner's letter of invitation to participants in the conference in Prague on the fiftieth anniversary of *The Open Society and Its Enemies* indicated various areas in which contributions would be welcome. I chose the parallel between the principles of the open society and of the scientific community as understood by Popper; this would be a welcome opportunity to make good an omission from my contribution, "The Unity of Popper's Thought," to the Schilpp volume on Popper. I had intended this to cover his moral, social and political thought; but that got squeezed out by the lengthening discussion of the relation between his conjecturalist epistemology and his indeterminist metaphysics. In Prague I would have an opportunity to discuss affinities between his negative, falsificationist methodology and his negative utilitarianism, and between his conjecturalist-cum-critical rationalism and his Periclean view of democracy ("Although only a few may originate a policy, we are all able to judge it"), and between his conception of scientific method and his rejection of utopian in favor of piecemeal social engineering. More generally, I would be investigating the parallel proclaimed by Gellner when he wrote that Popper's "social ethic consists essentially of the commendation of the virtue of *openness*, which is the social equivalent of *falsifiability* – the holding of social principles without rigidity, in a spirit which is willing to learn, innovate, experiment, and change. Social and cognitive health are analogous, and the wider society is but the scientific community writ large" (Gellner 1974: 172).

I had devoured *The Open Society* as a student at LSE in 1947. It seemed urgently relevant to the then state of the Western world. On the home front, neither dreams of utopian engineering nor historicist beliefs were altogether extinguished; speaking of the immediate post-war era, Lord Boyle remarked that there were those who believed that one could run a peacetime economy like a wartime one and who believed in the inevitability of socialism (Boyle 1974: 844). On the foreign front, one great enemy of the Open Society had been crushingly defeated with the help of another, and the latter was now systematically taking over Eastern European countries one after another. Moreover, a good many Western intellectuals welcomed these developments. (There were others who viewed communism with a certain distaste but wearily regarded its eventual triumph in the West as inevitable.) Some Western commentators fell in with the Soviet title of "People's Democracies" for the newly subjugated countries, and a highly vocal minority claimed that these exemplified *true* democracy. When I first went to LSE people of that persuasion seemed to be dominating the student body. (They especially hated Ernest Bevin, then Foreign Secretary. At one Student Union meeting a speaker defiantly declared that he was in favor of Bevin's anti-Soviet foreign policy having experienced communist terror during a year behind the Iron Curtain. There were cries of "No" and "Lie"; an angry girl in front of me turned to her companion and said, "What's the chairman doing? Why doesn't he stop him?") Against that background *The Open Society* had for me, and many others, a shining quality.

But as the years passed the ideas of that book seemed, for those of us fortunate enough to be on the Western side of the Iron Curtain, to lose their urgency just because they had largely won out over here. None of us, it seemed, any longer believed in historical inevitability, let alone in the inevitability of communism; nor were politicians any longer dreaming of Utopian reform. And although, as we now know, Open-Society ideas were quietly infiltrating some dissident circles inside the communist bloc, the sullen truce of the Cold War seemed to rule out all thought of an intellectual-cum-political liberation over there. So far as I know, Western friends of the Open Society were completely surprised by the serial collapses of communist systems in 1989–90. Prior to that astonishing debacle it had generally seemed to us that over large areas of the earth Open-Society ideas either had won out or else had no hope of doing so.

I say this by way of apology for the fact that while I would take down *The Open Society* to consult some passage, or to look at changes to a new edition, or to browse among its footnotes, I never re-read it straight through until I was preparing for the Prague conference. And when I did I got a shock. In my recollection of it, *The Open Society* had demolished certain speculative philosophies of history without putting another one in their place; surely its concepts of a closed society and an open society were not given any sort of historicist underpinning, but depicted ideal types analogous to economists' models for pure monopoly and perfect competition? Methodological individualists may exhibit in their models some dynamical tendencies, for instance an economy going through a cycle of boom and slump, generated by the interactions and feedbacks among the hypothetical agents; but they do not postulate one-way historical developments in real societies. Or consider Social Contract theorists. With the possible exception of Rousseau they were methodological individualists, and in depicting a progression from a state of nature to a political state they generally claimed to be offering only an idealized, hypothetical, *as-if* "history." Hobbes, for example, showed how rational agents would act if they found themselves in a state of nature; and although he was inclined to believe that savage people in America approximate to this condition, he agreed that it may very well be that there never was a time when a pure state of nature existed. And although a sovereign should not allow it to happen, a nation state may slip back towards a state of nature. Indeed in ancient Persia, according to Sextus Empiricus, upon the death of their king the people were left lawless for five days "in order to learn by experience how great an evil lawlessness is."[1] Off the cuff, I would have said Popper's *The Open Society* is consistent with there never having been a fully closed society, and with fluctuations in either direction between closedness and openness.

I should have learnt better from Gellner. Back in his 1964 book he had a remark, admittedly tucked away in a footnote, to the effect that while Popper's stereotype of tribal life may be useful as an ideal type, "it is most questionable whether tribal society is indeed generally 'closed'" (Gellner 1964: 84–5n). Some months before the Prague conference there had been a conference on Popper in Warsaw. In the course of a characteristically fluent and impressive talk given without notes, and since published, Gellner remarked that Popper "is desperately attracted precisely by those things that he also rejects," instancing historicism as an example (Gellner 1996: 78). I did not attend closely to that at the time; but I now think that Gellner was on target. When I got round to re-reading *The Open Society* straight through I detected in it what seemed to me an unmistakable trace of Hegelian historicism. I was so startled that I scrapped my previous plans and decided to concentrate on this. Most of what I will say relates to volume 1 of *The Open Society*.

In its application to World-History the Hegelian Dialectic, as I understand it, has the following components:

1   As World History progresses there occurs, from time to time, a decisive, dialectical turning point. The dominant Idea or "thesis" of the previous epoch engenders a countervailing Idea or "antithesis" and a new epoch commences.
2   A dialectical turning point has a once-and-for-all character; it cannot be reversed and will not be repeated. It is unique.
3   The new epoch is ushered in by certain Historic Individuals who embody the new thesis or Idea. These may be individual people, a Charlemagne or Frederick the Great, for example; or they may be collectives, a nation, for example, or a city-state.
4   The transition period is a time of trauma usually involving war.

Hegel of course had something steering these historical developments, namely the World Spirit. I did not include this in the above sketch since it has no counterpart in Popper. I do not claim that a full-blooded Hegelianism is stalking *The Open Society*, only that there is in it a significant whiff of Hegelian historicism, the grin of the Cheshire Cat without the cat. I will now try to

---

1 For references see Watkins 1973: 48.

establish this claim by drawing attention to counterparts in *The Open Society* to each of the above components.

(1) In Popper's case the turning point is, of course, the move from a Closed to an Open Society. What makes a society *closed*? Popper offered two kinds of answer. The first was in terms of size and togetherness. Closed societies tend to be small, primitive, and face-to-face, held together by semi-biological ties; they tend to be socially and politically arrested, and lacking upward mobility (Popper 1945/1966: vol. 1: 173–4). They are the opposite of what he called an "abstract" society in which, in the limit, no one would actually *meet* anyone, transactions being done by typewritten letters, telegrams, etc. This sociobiological characterization led him to equate being closed with being tribal. But size and togetherness are not constitutive of a closed society. An open society may be small; Popper declined to use Graham Wallas's term "The Great Society" partly because Periclean Athens was small (ibid.: 202–3); and in a small open society there may well be a lot of face-to-face togetherness. For Popper, the essential characteristic of a closed society was a certain cast of mind, namely a magical attitude. Popper wrote: "It is one of the characteristics of the magical attitude of a primitive tribal or 'closed' society that it lives in a charmed circle of unchanging taboos, of laws and customs which are felt to be as inevitable as the rising of the sun, or the cycle of the seasons" (ibid.: 57). Conversely, what chiefly makes a society *open* is the shift to an opposite mental attitude, that of critical rationalism.

(2) So far there is nothing inconsistent with my previous, naively methodological individualist, understanding of *The Open Society*. But now a significant trace of Hegelianism enters. As I said, for Hegel a dialectical turning point in World History cannot be reversed (though it may, of course, be taken up and transformed by a later dialectical development), and nor will it be repeated. How did Popper view the historical transition from a closed to an open society? Were there many of them and could the transition go in either direction, as I once supposed, from open to closed as well as from closed to open? Popper's answer to this last question is clear. Many people, finding the "strain of civilization" too much, have *wanted* to return to a closed society. But this is like a longing to return to the womb: it cannot be fulfilled. Sparta's dominant aim, according to Popper, was to arrest all change and return to tribalism; but that was impossible (ibid.: 182). "We can never return to the alleged innocence and beauty of the closed society"; attempts to do so will instead result in the Inquisition, the secret police, and a romanticized gangsterism (ibid.: 200).

So any transition can only be one-way, from closed to open. Was there a time when all mankind lived in closed societies? Popper came very close to answering *yes*. He assumed, and we may go along with this, that there was a time when they all lived in tribes; and he added that, although there is no standardized "tribal way of life," there seem to be some characteristics that can be found in most, if not all, of these tribal societies, namely their magical or irrational attitude towards the customs of social life (ibid.: 172). If we drop all cautious qualifications from the above, we get: *There was a time when all mankind lived in tribal societies, and all tribal societies share a magical or irrational attitude.* Conjoining this with (1) above we get: *There was a time when all mankind lived in closed societies.* Indeed, at one point Popper appeared to equate *tribal* with *closed* by verbal fiat: "In what follows, the magical or tribal or collectivist society will also be called the *closed society*" (ibid.: 173, his italics).

By the time Popper was writing *The Open Society* quite a few more or less open societies were in existence (even if some of them had recently been over-run by romanticized gangsterism), rather as quite a few political states were in existence when Hobbes was writing *Leviathan* (even if one of them had recently been torn by civil war). And had Hobbes asserted that there had been a time when all mankind was in a state of nature, he would presumably have agreed that this means that there have been *several* transitions to nationhood in the course of human history. Does an analogous proposition hold for transitions to open societyhood? Well, quite a few of those existing in Popper's day, including the one in New Zealand in which he wrote *The Open Society*, may be seen as daughter societies of pre-existing open societies. But could *all* of them properly be seen as descendants of *one* original prototype? Has this epoch-making transformation occurred only once in the long course of human history? It was when, during my re-reading of *The Open Society*, I began to suspect that Popper's answer was *yes* that I scrapped my previous plan and decided to concentrate on the trace of Hegelian historicism that was becoming apparent.

At one point Popper said that the Greeks were the *first* to break out of tribalism and the closed society (ibid.: 171), which is consistent with lots of subsequent break-outs occurring independently elsewhere. However he invariably spoke of *the* transition to the open society. Was this like speaking of *the* whale? Was he referring to a type rather than to its tokens? I can't make out whether Popper merged type and token here or held that this type has only one token. In either case his view seems to have been that there has been *one* transition, that this was inaugurated by the Greeks, and that it is still going on. After describing "the transition from the closed to the open society" as "one of the deepest revolutions through which mankind has passed," he went on: "Thus when we say that our Western civilization derives from the Greeks, we ought to realize what it means. It means that the Greeks started for us that great revolution which, it seems, is still in its beginning, the transition from the closed to the open society" (ibid.: 175). (So far as I can see, "still in its beginning" means only that no society is *perfectly* open; see ibid.: 294, note 6.) It is as if any (more or less) open society that came into existence later had an umbilical cord stretching back to the primal one.

Indeed, he sometimes seemed to suppose that memories of ancestral traumas are somehow transmitted to descendent societies. A longing to *return* to a closed society could not yet have existed while all mankind lived in closed societies. If the Greeks were the first to break out, it could only have been among those of them who remembered the old days that the longing to return first arose. A methodological individualist can allow that cultural "memories," nostalgic or otherwise, of *x* can be kept alive, by folklore, in later generations with no direct experience of *x*. Suppose that Freud's hypothesis in *Totem and Taboo* that a band of brothers in the primal horde killed and ate their father had been true; one can imagine that awesome event becoming legendary among their descendants. But unless one is a Lamarckian one cannot agree that memories and feelings originally associated with a singular historical event should become hereditary. Now Popper held that nostalgia for the warmth and security of a closed society became endemic in Western societies. How did this happen? He detected in the anti-scientific and pro-medieval ideas of a twentieth-century author a "romantic hysteria ... produced by the dissolution of the tribe and by the strain of civilisation" (ibid.: 242); yet this man could have had no personal recollections of "the dissolution of the tribe"; did he perhaps inherit a group-memory of it? However that may be, the point remains that for Popper the transition to an open society is not something that has happened at various times in various parts of the world. What happened in Greece was like a Hegelian dialectical shift in being a crucial and *unique* turning point in World History.

(3) The third point was that according to Hegel the new epoch is ushered in by certain Historic Individuals who embody the new thesis or Idea. This brings me to what Popper called the "Great Generation," which he introduced by saying that it "marks a turning-point in the history of mankind" (ibid.: 185). As Paul Feyerabend might have asked, what's so great about the Great Generation? Well, it certainly included some great *individuals*, among them Democritus, Pericles, and Socrates. But in what sense did these individuals constitute a *generation*? There is a certain ambiguity about this term. Let me turn for a moment to a rather similar ambiguity exhibited more obviously by the term "cohort." This originally meant an organized body of soldiers within a Roman legion. Let us use "cohort$_{rom}$" for that sense. Nowadays "cohort" often means a group of individuals selected according to some common demographic feature(s), such as being a member to the post-war "baby boom." Let us use "cohort$_{dem}$" for that sense. A cohort$_{dem}$ is obviously very different from a cohort$_{rom}$. The answer to "Could one belong to it without being aware of doing so?" is *yes* for the first and *no* for the second, whereas to "Can it act in a unified way?" it is *no* for the first and *yes* for the second.

To which of them is Popper's idea of the Great Generation more analogous? Popper said that its members were all living "in Athens just before, and during, the Peloponnesian war" (ibid.: 185). By itself, that tells in favor of a cohort$_{dem}$ analogy. But he also described the Great Generation as a "great humanitarian *movement*" (ibid.: 70, my italics), which seems to tell in the other direction. Yet he obviously did not mean that this Generation's members literally ganged up to form a movement, which would in any case have been impossible because, as Levinson pointed out, they were scattered over more than a century (Levinson 1953: 285). Is there any way of transcending these conflicts? If Hegel had extended the concept of an Historic Individual to social bodies intermediate between human persons and nation-states, this would have accommodated the Great Generation rather well. They could constitute a kind of dialectical "movement" without being a movement in any crude sense, and the different facets of the open-society philosophy which they respectively contributed could be seen as being amalgamated by this Historic Individual, which would embody the Idea of the new epoch.

(4) The final point was that a dialectical shift is far from being what Bradley, in a memorable phrase, called "a ballet dance of bloodless categories"; the shift from thesis to antithesis typically involves political and military as well as conceptual conflict. Popper wrote: "the political and spiritual revolution which had begun with the breakdown of Greek tribalism reached its climax in the fifth century, with the outbreak of the Peloponnesian War" (Popper 1945/1966, vol. 1: 183). From his narration, which drew heavily on Thucydides, of events in that drawn-out struggle I will pick on one significant detail. When I read *The Open Society* as a student I soon forgot about the Long Walls linking Athens to Piraeus. Of what philosophical interest were they? At one time Popper was thinking of calling the book "A Social Philosophy for Everyman"; why did Everyman need to know about these walls? Well, Athens had embarked on *the* epoch-making transition from the closed to the open society, and in that transition *sea-communications* were of great importance: "Perhaps the most powerful cause of the breakdown of the closed society was the development of sea-communications and commerce" (ibid.: 177). Popper saw this as leading naturally to an *empire*: "tribalist exclusiveness and self-sufficiency could be superseded only by some form of imperialism." (ibid.: 181).[2] Seafaring and commerce "became the main characteristics of Athenian imperialism" (Popper 1945/1966, vol. 1: 177); and the Athenian empire needed a *navy* to protect it. It became clear to contemporary enemies of the open society that if they were to defeat this new democracy they would need to destroy Athens's empire, which would involve destroying Athens's navy. Which brings us to the walls: "But the naval policy of Athens was based upon its harbours, especially the Piraeus, the centre of commerce and the stronghold of the democratic party; and strategically, upon the walls which fortified Athens, and later upon the Long Walls which linked it to the harbours of the Piraeus and Phalerum" (ibid.: 177–8). When the Long Walls were completed, "the democracy could enjoy security so long as it upheld its naval supremacy" (ibid.: 179).

If Hegelian World History has the features attributed to it above, and if each of those features re-appears in Popper's account of the progression from a closed to an open society, then there is indeed a whiff of Hegel in *The Open*

2 Why did Popper defend Athenian imperialism? According to Hacohen, "Popper seems to have read Viennese progressives' dashed hopes for the Habsburg Empire and their grand designs for a cosmopolitan Central Europe into classical Athens" (Hacohen 1996: 475).

Society. What significance, if any, does this have? Well, it surely heightened the interest of what he wrote about Athens to see Athens as the locus for that critical turning point. If our Western civilization somehow depends on what happened there, then any significant detail is of vital interest. I suspect that this is one reason why volume 1 was generally found more exciting than volume 2. There might seem to be a whiff of historicism in the latter's use of tidal metaphors: the tide of rationalism, which had been rising during the previous three centuries, "has now turned" (Popper 1945/1966, vol. 2: 229) and we are now at "The High Tide of Prophecy"; but these expressions seem to denote intellectual fashions with no historicist underpinning.

But there were dangers. The thesis that mankind was imprisoned in closed-societyhood before the Athenian break-out is vulnerable to counter-examples which would not have hit the thesis that Athens achieved a remarkably good approximation to the ideal type of an open society. Indeed, a counter-example is actually mentioned in *The Open Society* itself. Tucked away in the footnote 9 to chapter 10 is the following sentence: "It is hardly an accident that the oldest known civilization, that of Sumer, was, as far as we know, a commercial civilization with strong democratic features; and that the arts of writing and arithmetic, and the beginnings of science, were closely connected with [Sumer's] commercial life" (Popper 1945/1966, vol. 1: 295). So something like what happened in Greece had happened two millennia earlier in city-states in Mesopotamia. And who can be sure that there were not comparable anticipations in early Egyptian, Hittite, or Chinese civilizations? Or consider the peopling of that part of the world in which Popper wrote *The Open Society*. In that book the Maoris get only this brief mention: "The early Greek tribal society resembles in many respects that of peoples like the Polynesians, the Maoris for instance. Small bands of warriors living in fortified settlements, ruled by tribal chiefs or kings ... waging war against one another" (ibid.: 171–2). This misses out on the Polynesians' striking feats of navigation. According to my encyclopedia, Polynesia started being opened up as a result of ocean voyages made in large sailing canoes; the explorations appear to have begun between 3,000 and 4,000 years ago and to have gone on until the Maoris settled New Zealand about 1,000 years ago. Was that done by men in thrall to the unchanging taboos of a closed society?

But exposure to counter-examples is perhaps the least of the dangers. More serious is the downgrading of mankind's mental capacities in the pre-Athens era implied by Popper's view of the transition from closed to open societyhood. We are going along with his assumption that there was a time when all mankind lived in societies that were "tribal" as opposed to "abstract": small, face-to-face groups, held together by semi-biological ties. This is plausible; Hobbes himself allowed that our forebears lived in groups or bands rather than as isolated individuals in a Hobbesian state of nature; and there could be no moves toward abstract societies before the advent of postal and telegraphic services. But as we saw, to those sociobiological characteristics of a tribal society Popper added a certain cast of mind, namely a magico-irrational attitude. (It is really the supposed shift from this attitude to its antithesis, namely a critical-cum-scientific attitude, that renders the transition from a closed to an open society *dialectical* in something like Hegel's sense.) We cannot know it, but assume for argument's sake that all tribal societies have engaged in what we today would regard as magical practices. Is this to impute irrationalism to them? Well, magic can be looked upon as a kind of primitive technology: instead of just planting you plant-and-chant, and it works rather well.[3] But perhaps that rationalizes magical practices a shade too easily. Again, magic can be looked upon as a comforting accompaniment to practices with a pragmatic rationality of their own. You plant as you would anyway, and make some music. Mythologies may envelop tribal hunting but the latter has its own inner discipline; as Roger Sandall put it, you can trust a Palaeolithic hunter, but not a professor, if you want to know whether there's a bear in the cave or a croc in the creek (Sandall 1997: 250). But perhaps that line underplays the dark side of magical thinking. Someone who recognized this side was Charles Darwin, and I will conclude this paper by contrasting his views in *The Descent of Man* with Popper's views on the thinking abilities of people in primitive societies.

I begin with a criticism which Darwin made of Wallace. Wallace had briefly flirted with a theological argument which depended on his claim that the brains of primitive men 35,000 years ago were too big for them: "Natural selection could only have endowed the savage with a brain a little superior to that of an ape, whereas he actually possesses one but very little inferior to that of the average members of our learned societies" (Wallace 1869: 392); savages were swollen-headed. Darwin retorted: "He [man in the rudest state] has invented and is able to use various weapons, tools, traps, etc. ... He has made rafts or canoes for fishing or crossing over to neighbouring fertile islands. He has discovered the art of making fire"; it was by these inventions that "man in his rudest state has become so pre-eminent ... I cannot, therefore, understand how it is that Mr. Wallace maintains, that 'natural selection could only have endowed the savage with a brain a little superior to that of an ape'" (Darwin 1874: 72–3). It was clear to Darwin that "man mainly owes to [his mental faculties] his predominant position in the world" (ibid.: 196). Although Darwin mentions "strange superstitions and customs," such as the sacrifice of human beings to blood-thirsty gods, only in passing, he seems to have accepted that they were widespread. That he regarded them as deeply irrational is indicated by his remarking that "it is well occasionally to reflect on these superstitions, for they show us what an infinite debt of gratitude we owe to the improvement of our reason, to science, and to our accumulated knowledge" (ibid.: 146–7). If we had asked him how such irrationality fits in with his views about the evolution of our species, he

---

3 See Jarvie and Agassi 1967 and 1973.

could have answered that mental faculties capable of inventing traps and canoes are also capable of inventing myths and superstitions.

Darwinism is conspicuous by its absence from *The Open Society* (there are some references to social "Darwinism").[4] There are lots of references to Darwin and Darwinism in *Objective Knowledge*. However, there is no sign that Popper read *The Descent of Man*. Indeed, where he got his low view of primitive people's mentality is something of a puzzle. One begins to wonder whether he may not have adjusted human pre-history to make it a suitable backdrop for the Athenian revolution. The Lascaux Cave's galleries of glorious animal pictures, dating from around the fourteenth century BC, were famous by the time he was writing most of the pieces in *Objective Knowledge*. But he seems not to have revised his estimate of tribal mentality upwards. In his latter-day Darwinian phase, when he retraced our evolutionary pre-history he usually went back, not to *Homo erectus*, say, or *Homo habilis*, but much further, to the amoeba. The praises he heaped on this small creature – variations on "From the amoeba to Einstein is but a step" occur no less than six times in the book – mirror his dispraise of "primitive man." Gellner has been called "the Big Daddy of Big Ditch thinking,"[5] the Big Ditch being, roughly, the discontinuity between the cognitive superiority of modern, industrially successful societies and the cognitive backwardness of pre-modern societies. Was Popper a founder of Big Ditch thinking? Gellner said not. True, he gave us "the fundamental opposition of Closed and Open Societies, the latter linked to freedom and science, the former excluding both"; but then he (Popper) appears to think that the scientific attitude "has been with us ever since the amoeba" (Gellner 1992: 51). Elsewhere Gellner spoke of Popper's "doctrine that the amoeba was a good Popperite" (Gellner 1979: 251n).

But Gellner did not get this quite right: the amoeba is not yet a *good* Popperian. If Einstein scores alpha-plus in that respect the amoeba scores only beta-minus. For there is a step the amoeba has failed to take. Like Einstein, it attacks problems with conjectures; and like Einstein's, its conjectures are liable to refutation. But unlike Einstein, the amoeba does not consciously seek out error-elimination (Popper 1972: 24–5; Popper 1963/1972: 52). The amoeba is pre-critical and not fully scientific. On a scale with the amoeba at one end and Einstein at the other, where does tribal or primitive man belong? Popper's answer was that, lacking a critical attitude he *belongs with the amoeba!*[6] That seems to me a *reductio ad absurdum* of Popper's idea that before the transition to an open society which began in Athens in the fifth century BC, mankind was uniformly sunk in closed-society, pre-critical irrationality.

---

4 I go a little into Popper's relation to Darwin in Watkins 1995.
5 By Roger Sandall 1997: 247.
6 "It is different with primitive man, and with the amoeba. Here there is no critical attitude" (Popper 1972: 247–8).

REFERENCES

Boyle, Edward. 1974."Karl Popper's *Open Society*: a personal appreciation," in P. A. Schilpp, (ed.), *The Philosophy of Karl Popper* (The Library of Living Philosophers). 2 vols. La Salle: Open Court, pp. 843–58.

Darwin, Charles. 1874. *The Descent of Man and Selection in Relation to Sex*. 2nd edn. London: Murray.

Gellner, Ernest. 1964. *Thought and Change*. London: Weidenfeld & Nicolson.

—— 1974. *Legitimation of Belief*. Cambridge: Cambridge University Press.

—— 1979. *Spectacles and Predicaments*. Cambridge: Cambridge University Press.

—— 1992. *Postmodernism, Reason and Religion*. London: Routledge.

—— 1996. "Karl Popper – the thinker and the man," in Stefan Amsterdamski, (ed.), *The Significance of Popper's Thought. Proceedings of the Conference on Karl Popper: 1902–1994*. Amsterdam: Rodopi, pp. 75–83.

Hacohen, Malachi. 1996. "Karl Popper in exile: The Viennese progressive imagination and the making of *The Open Society*." *Philosophy of the Social Sciences* 26: 452–92.

Jarvie, I. C. and Agassi, Joseph. 1996. "The problem of the rationality of magic." *The British Journal of Sociology* 18: 55–74.

—— 1973. "Magic and rationality again." *The British Journal of Sociology* 24: 236–45.

Levinson, Ronald B. 1953. *In Defense of Plato*. Cambridge: Harvard University Press.

Popper, Karl R. 1945. *The Open Society and Its Enemies*, 2 vols. London: Routledge & Kegan Paul; 5th edn. 1966.

—— 1963. *Conjectures and Refutations*. London: Routledge & Kegan Paul; 4th edn. 1972.

—— 1972. *Objective Knowledge: An Evolutionary Approach*. Oxford: Clarendon Press.

Sandall, Roger. 1997. "An Australian dilemma: reconciling the irreconcilable." In *Upholding the Australian Constitution*, vol. 8 (Proceedings of the eighth conference of The Samuel Griffith Society) Melbourne: Samuel Griffith Society, pp. 239–59.

Wallace, Alfred Russel. 1869. Review-article (unsigned) of Lyell's *Principles of Geology and Elements of Geology, The Quarterly Review* 126: 359–94.

Watkins, John. 1973. *Hobbes's System of Ideas*. 2nd edn. London: Hutchinson; repr. Gower Publishing Co, 1989.

—— 1995. "Popper and Darwinism." In Anthony O'Hear (ed.), *Karl Popper: Philosophy and Problems*. Cambridge: Cambridge University Press, pp. 191–206.

Part III

APPLYING THE TEXT

8

THE PROBLEM OF OBJECTIVITY
IN LAW AND ETHICS

Christoph von Mettenheim

Ethics is not a science. But although there is no "rational scientific
basis" of ethics, there is an ethical basis of science, and of rationalism.
Popper 1945/1966, vol. 2: 238

The problem of the objectivity of norms has interested me almost since the
beginning of my legal education. My first opportunity to discuss it with
Karl Popper came in 1970. He seemed to consider it as having been solved
in his *Open Society*. Although fascinated by that book, I was then still un-
convinced and remained so after our discussion. In 1980 I stumbled upon
what I believed, and still believe, to be the theoretical solution of this problem. Due to professional strain it took me some time to get it written down,
and the publication of my small book on legal theory which, of course, I
sent to Karl Popper after publication (1984), very unfortunately came at the
time of the last illness of his wife, of which I was not aware, and therefore
escaped his notice. I received no answer and did not dare to inquire, and we
only met again in May 1994. He very kindly took the time to read the
book, predicting in advance, however, that he would probably disagree with
my view of the relations between facts and norms which I had tried to
explain in our conversation. He considered the issue fundamental while I
thought, and still think, it has a bearing only on questions of methodology.
We then had a wonderful discussion by correspondence and during another visit in August 1994, but could not reach a final agreement. The
summer seminar of the University of Madrid in Santander, to which I was
invited at his kind recommendation, and for which this paper was originally prepared, should have been an attempt at "intersubjective criticism"
of our diverging views; but then came, sadly, his last illness, and his death
on 17 September 1994. The seminar, of course, was cancelled. So I am still
waiting for a discussion of my dissenting opinion. Since this was influenced by *The Open Society* more than by any other book, the fiftieth anniversary
of this unparalleled work is an occasion to present it.

I

Karl Popper's writings do not fall into the standard field of interest of a law student. I came across them almost by accident in 1966 when I was about to finish my legal studies, and was *captivated*. There is no need to explain here what I read;[1] it may be sufficient to say that I read all I could get hold of, and was convinced by every word I read. One of the views which entirely convinced me was the theory of *methodological nominalism*, as opposed to essentialism, in particular the explanation of the role which definitions should play in science, which Popper explains in chapters 3 and 11 of *The Open Society* (1945/1966, vol. 1: 31ff.; vol. 2: 9ff.). I will just briefly recall it by the example he uses, i.e. by the definition: "A puppy is a young dog." According to Popper this kind of definition does not occur in science, but in science we only use definitions which are to be read the other way round, that is, as it were, from right to left. The word "puppy" would then be not the question, but an *answer* to the question: "What shall we call a young dog?"

I am not going to expound on this theory here because there are many examples ready at hand to demonstrate its truth, such as, for instance, physical effects of the influence of velocity on frequencies, which we no longer explain, but simply recall, by using the name of "Doppler-Effect"; or names for new elements, or nuclear particles, and many others. Popper has explained methodological nominalism so thoroughly in *The Open Society* that there is no need to explain it here. But I would like to quote the devastating summary of his criticism of the opposite view, the view of methodological essentialism, which he has put at the beginning of his discussion of the two views, where he says:

> The development of thought since Aristotle could, I think, be summed up by saying that every discipline, as long as it used the Aristotelean method of definition, has remained arrested in a state of empty verbiage and barren scholasticism and that the degree to which the various sciences have been able to make any progress depended on the degree to which they have been able to get rid of this essentialist method.

These are very strong words, and Popper even adds: "This is why so much of our 'Social Science' still belongs to the Middle Ages."

This struck me very deeply. On the one hand I could not find – and still have not found – any fault in Karl Popper's theory of methodological nominalism or, vice versa, in his refutation of essentialism. His theory of definition,

---

1 I first read "What is dialectic?" because this concerned something I had always wanted to know, and had never been able to understand. The paper had been included in the anthology *Logik der Sozialwissenschaften*, ed. Ernst Topitsch (Popper 1965).

supported as it is by Tarski (1965), seems to me a just evaluation of the role which definitions should play in science.

On the other hand I was, when I first read this in 1966, a young lawyer thoroughly trained to base my legal opinions on *clear concepts* which I had to take from the statutes I was expected to expound and to apply. It may be known that, other than in the Common Law countries which rely on the rule of *stare decisis*, the German legal system depends very strongly on written statutes, and most of the problems which a lawyer is expected to solve arise, or at least *seem* to arise, from the concepts used in these statutes, i.e. concepts like "property," "negligence," "fraud," "damages," "copyright," etc. Continental lawyers, especially when they are young, even incline to the belief that, at least in private law, the solution to *any* conflict arising between two parties can, and must, be derived by a logical inference from the existing statutes.[2] In a legal system based on written statutes there simply seemed to be no other way than to read a definition from left to right, i.e. to *start* from the concept and *then* find out the meaning of this concept – which was precisely the method Karl Popper had rejected to strongly.

There not only seemed to be no other way, but I was even convinced that this kind of legal system, which is by no means a German invention, and which is presently spreading all over Europe by the increasing importance of statutes in the European Community, was highly beneficial to society. Moreover, it appeared to me to be the only possible way of putting into practice Karl Popper's idea of piecemeal social engineering, as proposed in the *Poverty of Historicism* (1957: ch. 21) and *The Open Society* (1945/1966, vol. 1: 158f.), since piecemeal social technology would require some kind of *instrument* for bringing about the desired limited changes And this instrument, I thought, could only be legislation, implying the enactment of statutes which would then have to be expounded, starting from the concepts they used.

So there seemed to be a major clash between methodological nominalism – which I believed to be right – on the one side, and the practice of law and the theory of piecemeal social engineering – which I believed also to be right – on the other side. For a long time I saw no way of reconciling these two views, and this was the problem from which I started my own endeavors. Putting it more generally, one might say that my problem was how to fit legal theory into Karl Popper's epistemology. This was the problem he and I started to discuss in 1970.

II

In order to make this problem more transparent for the non-lawyer I will give an example of a typical legal problem as it may pose itself in the everyday life

---

2 In my opinion, which I have explained in *Recht und Rationalität*, this view is mistaken; but this does not prevent it from being taught in universities and thus being widely spread.

of legal profession. It has deliberately *not* been chosen from among the big problems of life and death because, I believe, in questions of methodology these grand issues will usually not contribute to our understanding, but may impair our judgment. Methodology, I think, has to do with rationality, and for a critical rationalist therefore must have to do with exploring the *limits* of rationality. But questions of life and death tend to boil down to problems of morality which, I believe (and have tried to show in von Mettenheim 1984: 80ff.), will go beyond the limits of rationality and which everyone must decide on his or her own responsibility. The same holds for the problem whether positive law can be unjust, or illegal, or illegitimate, and whether there can be a right, or even a duty, to resist this law for instance in cases of the violation of human rights.[3] In view of the history of my country I have not the slightest doubt that the answer to this question must be affirmative. But I also think it is not a problem of rationality. It could be better compared with the situation in which someone is trying to smash my head with a cudgel: what I need most urgently then is not a good argument against killing people, but a good weapon to defend myself.

The situation of what I call a *legal problem* is entirely different. Looking at it with the eyes of a practicing lawyer the situation might be this:

> X is a promising young attorney recently settled down, and good fortune prompts one of the important retail corporations of the country to seek X's advice. They intend to print, at enormous expense, a new catalogue of their assortment in beautiful many-coloured print and in an edition of many thousand copies. And since they have a new marketing director who wants to demonstrate her abilities, their advertising slogans go to the very edge of unfair competition, and sometimes beyond it. They ask our young lawyer for a legal opinion. X now has the choice: to stay on the safe side and reject most of the slogans on the grounds of unfair competition. X will then risk losing the client and the income. Or, X can try to leave the advertising as aggressive as possible and then risk that some competitor of the client may obtain an injunction preventing the further use of the catalogue. X will be lucky if the client only presents a bill for printing expenses, and not also for lost profit in Christmas turnover, which might mean the end of X's economic existence.

---

3 For this problem see the famous controversy between H. L. A. Hart, "Positivism and the Separation of Law and Morality" (my retranslation from the German translation), and Gustav Radbruch, "Gesetzliches Unrecht und übergesetzliches Recht" ("Legal Injustice and Supralegal Justice" – my translation), *Süddeutsche Juristenzeitung*, Tübingen 1946, p. 105, in which Hart took the side of positivism while Radbruch blamed this attitude for having been responsible for national socialistic legislation.

The example shows two features which are characteristic of legal problems. One of them is that the lawyer *wants* to do the right thing by some other will than his own, and his problem is to find out what exactly he is expected to do. This, I think, is what turns his problem into a legal problem. It is only the fact that he wants to obey the law; without this it might have been a problem of power, or of morality. But the will to conform to pre-existing binding rules raises the specific problem of law, the problem of finding out what exactly these rules expect him to do. The other feature, which is not characteristic of all but of many legal problems, is that the task of the lawyer consists in approaching as close as possible to the borderline between legality and illegality. Philosophers concerned with ethics tend to overlook that law not only has to do with crime, or with traffic accidents, where violations are mostly accidental, or at least uncontrolled; it also includes fields like company law, anti-trust law, or tax law etc., where people will deliberately go to the very edge of legality, because if they do not others will, and will thereby gain an advantage over them. And even if the borderline between legality and illegality has not been approached deliberately, the problem will remain the same in cases where chance has placed the facts close to this line, which happens surprisingly often. So it might be said as a generalization that the legal problem is the problem of defining this borderline between legality and illegality as precisely as possible, thereby making legal decisions predictable, or at least improving their predictability[4]. That is what raises the methodological problem of objectivity in law, or in legal decisions.

III

I will now first try to explain what I believe to be the solution of this problem, and then, in a last and final section of this chapter, I will come to the question on which Popper and I disagreed.

III.1

It is possible that some would consider my recipe for a solution of the problem a weird concoction of Kant and Popper, consisting, basically, of three ingredients, namely (1) Kant's Principle of the Autonomy of the Will, and (2) an instrumental use of Kant's Categorical Imperative, and (3) an application of the Rationality Principle. They might say that these three ingredients have been thrown together in a pot, then have been left to ferment for some years, and finally were thoroughly stirred by someone who did not know what was in the pot.

---

4 In von Mettenheim (1984: 62ff.) I have tried to show that one of the important *empirical* reasons underlying the claim for justice, and for equal rights, can be found in the need for predictability.

III.1.a

Those who think I have done just that, may be right. But if they are, if indeed I did not understand what Kant, or Popper, *really* meant, then this would only demonstrate the principle of the autonomy of the will as *I* understand it; for it would show that I have "made my Kant myself."

In his *Religion within the Limits of Pure Reason* Kant says that, in a certain sense, everyone must "make his God himself";[5] and in his *Metaphysik der Sitten* he explains that "even the Saint of the Gospel must first be compared with our ideal of moral perfection before we can recognize him as a Saint,"[6] In this same sense I think it is right, and very important from a *methodological* point of view, to say that we must "make our legislator ourselves." We must realize that, exactly like moral decisions, legal decisions and legal opinions are our own decisions and opinions for which we ourselves must bear responsibility. We bear this responsibility not only once when we decide to become lawyers, and not only every morning when we decide to do our duty and go to the office and not to the races, but for each and every decision we make;[7] and we bear it even if we only try to abide by the law, because it depends on our thoroughness, our diligence, and last but not least on our abilities, whether or not we have properly understood the law. If we omit to read the complete text of a statute then, in this sense, we have "made" the wrong legislator. In the same way we have "made" the case which we may be about to decide. I have read dozens of judgments which had to be reversed simply because the judge omitted important elements of the statute to be applied; and even more judgments where he or she took a wrong view of the case because she or he omitted to read important parts of the file. That is the main reason why we need Courts of Appeal.

III.1.b

But if we "make" our own legislator, does this not leave too much room for the individual will? Does it not lead to subjectivism, to relativism, and to arbitrariness of legal decisions? I think not.

---

5 Immanuel Kant, *Die Religion innerhalb der Grenzen der blossen Vernunft* (Königsberg 1773), footnote to 4th Piece, Part 2, section 1; Popper quotes this passage in section 6 of "Kant's critique and cosmology" (Popper 1989).

6 My translation from Immanuel Kant, *Grundlegung zur Metaphysik der Sitten* (Riga 1785), section 2; see also the beginning of the Conclusion of *Kritik der praktischen Vernunft* (Riga 1788).

7 The short discussion of the abridged version of this paper in Prague has shown me that I should be even more explicit on this point. I think it is doing injustice to Kant to impute to him the view that the autonomy of the will only goes as far as *recognizing* the saint, while, after that, we can rely on his authority. Whoever argues like that is (in words used by Popper in a different context) only an unconscious witness to Kant's originality because he fails to grasp, even after more than 200 years, the most important point of Kant's message of the autonomy of the will. This message (as I understand it), is that there is *no* authority, neither in law nor in ethics, not even if we try to obey, and that therefore the responsibility for *all* our decisions, every day and every second, rests only with us (see also the quotation from Popper's *Open Society* at the end of this chapter).

In my view the situation in law – and the same would apply to ethics – is not very different from that in the natural sciences. In the natural sciences we have learned from Karl Popper's *Logic of Scientific Discovery* (1959)[8] that the laws of nature are of our own making. They are not given to us by some authority from outside, but we ourselves invent them; and then, in a second step, we criticize them by experiment in order to find out whether they conform with reality. The idea that we "make" our own legislator is, after all, very similar to this idea that the laws of nature are our own invention. In fact, both these ideas are implications of what Kant proudly called his "Copernican Revolution" of philosophy; for like Copernicus, who had turned the physical universe upside down by placing the sun instead of the earth into its centre, Kant turned the universe of thought upside down by placing *man* instead of God, or nature, or some other authority, into its centre.

So I think the idea that we "make" our own legislator should not worry us too much. Instead we should look whether it is not possible to establish the *objectivity* of legal decisions by objective *criticism*, as it is done in the natural sciences. This is where the true problem lies, and where we seem to run into trouble because, clearly, other than the laws of nature, legal statutes or the laws of morality cannot be *refuted* by experiment but only *violated* by offence. Popper's criterion of falsification by experiment obviously does not apply to these laws.

III.2

This is the point where the second ingredient of my concoction comes in, i.e. the *instrumental* use of the Categorical Imperative.[9] Once more, I wish to emphasize that it does not worry me too much whether I properly understood what Kant *really* meant by *his* Categorical Imperative,[10] as long as the way *I* understand it gets us where we want to go. But I would not like to take the credit for a discovery which, I believe, was Kant's.

I contend that we can criticize legal decisions in two different ways, both of which are based upon on the assumption (which I have explained in more detail in *Recht und Rationalität* [1984: 52ff.], but cannot discuss here) that, in the future, similar decisions must be made in similar cases, i.e. on a generalization of the principle underlying the decision. If we make this assumption, then we can try to look for contradictions by finding, or even inventing, examples in which the application of the rule would *conflict* with some other

---

8 This was Popper's own translation of his *Logik der Forschung* (Vienna: Springer, 1934).

9 I have put the word "instrumental" in italics because I wish to emphasize that, contra Hayek in his late work *Law, Legislation and Liberty* (1973, 1976), I do *not* consider the Categorical Imperative, or any related principle of the universality of legal or ethical norms, as an ethical law *in itself*, but only as an instrument for the criticism of (real or proposed) decisions. For my criticism of Hayek's views see von Mettenheim 1984: p. 70f., notes 4, 5. About Popper's view on this point I am not sure; this was one of the questions we would have wanted to discuss.

10 I have been criticized for pretending to be the only one who properly understood Kant.

rule which we also assume to be valid. For instance, we may argue that it is contrary to the rule of equal rights of men and women to let the husband have the last word if parents do not reach agreement over the education of their children. That is, I think, one way of *objective* criticism.

The other way is to discuss the *empirical* effects which would result from the generalization of a decision. If, for example, we assume a supreme court decision according to which it is illegal, and therefore inoperative, to pledge the future wages of a person as a security for a loan, then this may help the borrower in the individual case; but the effect of generalizing this decision might well be that, in future, bank loans can only be obtained by the rich who can offer better securities than only wages.[11] There may be further ways of objective criticism, as for instance the historical approach of trying to reconstruct the problem situation as it had been seen by the legislator when he was passing the law, but I think the two methods mentioned in the text are by far the most important.

It is easy to see that this kind of criticism will never reach the degree of certainty (or corroboration) which can be reached in the natural sciences. It must always be based on the assumption of what *would* happen, and how human beings *would* react, if we *did* decide this way or the other, and on the assumption that future cases *would* be decided in the same way. It thus has to rely on a reality which does not yet exist, but is only hypothetical. But I would not admit that, for this reason, this criticism is subjective or relative. It may be less certain than criticism by experiment. But certainty and objectivity should be distinguished. The objectivity of this criticism is based on the fact that the assumptions it has to rely on will normally be fairly simple and based on common experience, and, at any rate, can be discussed in terms of probability.[12] That makes them uncertain; but it does not affect their objectivity; just as the objectivity of quantum theory is not impaired by the fact that most of its problems are problems of probability.

III.3

The third ingredient of my recipe is even more technical, and I will try to be very brief about it. If we make *moral* decisions then it seems clear to me that the responsibility for these decisions rests with ourselves (1945/1966, vol. 1: 61; see quotation at end of this chapter). This becomes most obvious if we decide to disobey the law. But with legal decisions the situation is slightly

---

11 This is, I believe, a fair example for the "unavoidable unwanted consequences" (Popper) which may be caused by legal decisions as by social reforms, and it is, therefore, the point where Popper's theory of piecemeal social technology gains *methodological* importance for legal theory. Cf., for instance, Popper 1957: 64ff.

12 In his "propensity interpretation" of the probability calculus Popper has shown that this is possible although we are dealing with singular events. See Popper 1983: 286ff.

different, because what makes our decision a *legal* decision is the fact that we *want* to obey the law. And our problem is to find out what exactly the law expects us to do. We may find that the statutes which we wish to apply are not sufficiently clear, or are even contradictory, and that they do not yield the information we need in order to make our decision. Since all legal arguments based exclusively on the wording of a text normally come to an end fairly soon, we can only hope to solve our problem by the introduction of *new information* which will have to come from outside the text.[13] But from where do we take this new information? Do we pretend to act as we think the historic lawgiver would have acted? Even if the statute is more than 100 years old and we may be dealing with a problem of our time, resulting from developments he could never have thought of? Or do we just rely on our own individual experience? It seems that, at this point, the sluices have been opened to the floods of subjectivism and of relativism.

But I think this fear is unfounded. I suggest that, at this point, we make use of a *fiction* which, as an empirical theory, we all know, would be untenable. We know that some of our statutes are centuries old while others have only recently been passed. And we know that in democratically governed countries the passing of a law may be influenced by very strange circumstances, bordering on chance more often than not. We further know that the majority of parliament which passed the law may no longer exist, and that the official who drafted the text, and who, we hope, knew what it was about, may also long be dead. Therefore we know for certain that such a person as "the legislator," or such a thing as the "will of the legislator," does not exist.

But in spite of all this I suggest that we *pretend* the legislator to be a rational being, existing here and now, and having at his disposal all the *true* knowledge available in our time[14]. If we adopt this fiction, which is nothing else than an application of the *rationality principle*,[15] to an object of Popper's "World 3",[16] then we may assume that all existing laws[17] conform with the will of this fictitious legislator; and we may, in expounding these laws, and eliminating the contradictions we are bound to find, use all the true knowledge available

---

13 At this point further inquiry into the *meaning* of the text would not get us anywhere, but would, by suggesting an inquiry into the "real" meaning of terms, or concepts, used in the text, clearly lead into the erroneous methodological approach of essentialism and thereby into the "empty verbiage and barren scholasticism" criticized by Popper.

14 This may include the knowledge about the historic lawgiver and the problem situation from which he started, which may have been based on misconceptions.

15 For this see Popper, "Rationality and the status of the rationality principle," in *Les Fondements Philosophiques des Systèmes Économiques, Textes de Jacques Rueff et en son Honneur* (1967); now also included in Popper 1994b: 177ff; Watkins 1978.

16 I will explain this in section IV. 3.

17 This also applies to laws which have been valid for a long time, because the legislator could decide to abolish them. If he decides not to do this they are carried by his will. Cf. Popper 1966, vol. 1: 61(see the quotation at the end of this chapter).

in our time; and our decision may be criticized on the basis of this knowledge. The objectivity of this knowledge would, I contend, establish the objectivity of that criticism; and the objectivity of the criticism would, in turn, establish the objectivity of the decision. We cannot be certain to have found the right decision, because it will have to be based on uncertain knowledge. But I contend that this would not affect its objectivity. And by striving for objective criticism we would be serving law, and justice, by helping to increase its predictability.

IV

This gives me the clue for the third and final section of this chapter. It may have been noticed that I have put some emphasis on the fact that, as I think, my theory of law (if I may call it so after this very sketchy outline) is an *objectivist* theory. My reason for emphasizing this is that this was the point where Karl Popper and I disagreed. He thought that I attribute too much importance to the role of the will of the individual, and that this makes my theory subjectivist, and relativistic, leading, as he claimed, to Nietzsche and Hitler. And I think that all I did was to transpose his epistemology into legal theory, consistently using no other elements than those I have found in his works.

IV.1

At the bottom of this lies the fact that I do not entirely agree with Karl Popper's theory of *critical dualism*, i.e. of the "dualism" of facts and norms, or decisions. I disagree with only one aspect of it which I believe to be inconsistent with his other views, and which, I think, is important only from a methodological point of view, and mainly for legal reasoning, but which Popper considered as fundamental in our correspondence. It is his view that, because it is impossible to reduce decisions or norms to facts or descriptions, we must accept a *dualism* of norms and facts. And connected with this is his view that the concept of "validity" or "rightness" of a norm may be used in exactly the same sense as the concept of "truth" with respect to facts or descriptions. He explains these views in chapter 5 of the *Open Society*. Let me therefore quote Popper himself (1945/1966, vol. 1: 63f.):

> Critical dualism thus emphasizes the impossibility of reducing decisions or norms to facts; it can therefore be described as a dualism of facts and decisions. But this dualism seems to be open to attack. Decisions are facts, it may be said. If we decide to adopt a certain norm, then the making of this decision is itself a psychological or sociological fact, and it would be absurd to say that there is nothing in common between such facts and other facts. Since it cannot be doubted that our decisions about norms, i.e. the norms we adopt,

clearly depend upon certain psychological facts, such as the influence of our upbringing, it seems to be absurd to postulate a dualism
of facts and decisions, or to say that decisions cannot be derived
from facts. This objection can be answered by pointing out that we
can speak of a certain decision which has been submitted, or considered, or reached, or been decided upon; or alternatively, we may speak
of an act of deciding and call this "decision." The situation is analogous with a number of other expressions. In one sense, we may speak
of a certain resolution, which has been submitted to some council,
and in the other sense, the council's act of taking it may be spoken of
as the council's resolution. Similarly, we may speak of a proposal or a
suggestion before us, and on the other hand of the act of proposing
or suggesting something, which may also be called "proposal" or "suggestion." An analogous ambiguity is well known in the field of descriptive
statements. Let us consider the statement: "Napoleon died on St.
Helena." It will be useful to distinguish this statement from the fact
which it describes, and which we may call the primary fact, viz. the
fact that Napoleon died at St. Helena. Now a historian, say Mr. A,
when writing the biography of Napoleon, may make the statement
mentioned. In doing so, he is describing what we called the primary
fact. But there is also a secondary fact, which is altogether different
from the primary one, namely the fact that he made this statement;
and another historian, Mr. B, when writing the biography of Mr. A,
may describe this second fact by saying: "Mr. A stated that Napoleon
died on St. Helena." The secondary fact described in this way happens to be itself a description. But it is a description in a sense of the
word that must be distinguished from the sense in which we called
the statement "Napoleon died on St. Helena" a description. The making
of a description, or of a statement, is a sociological or psychological
fact. But the description made is to be distinguished from the fact
that it has been made. It cannot even be derived from this fact; for
that would mean that we can validly deduce "Napoleon died on St.
Helena," which obviously we cannot.

IV.2

This does not convince me. I do not doubt, of course, that we must distinguish between the laws of nature and ethical or legal norms. Ethical or legal
norms can be violated; the laws of nature cannot. Only the statement of such
laws can be refuted. So there is an obvious difference. And I do not doubt
either that we can, and must, distinguish between a norm, or decision, and
the fact that it has been adopted, or reached. But I doubt very strongly that
these distinctions will justify the assumption of a "dualism" of facts and norms
(or decisions); for if the nebulous term "dualism" is to be given any meaning

at all, then this must at least be different from the meaning of the term "identity," and would therefore imply that norms (or decisions) are *not* facts, i.e. that they are *excluded* by definition from the concept of "facts." But Popper's examples, or analogies, which I have just quoted, are *all* derived from *statements of facts*. Both "Napoleon died on St. Helena" and "Mr. A stated that Napoleon died on St. Helena" are statements of facts; and they therefore show that, *within* the class of facts, we can distinguish between one fact, or statement of fact, and another fact, or statement of fact. They therefore show that the class of facts can be *subdivided*, which is trivial. But does it follow from this that we must also distinguish between facts and norms, or decisions, in the sense that norms, or decisions, are *excluded* from the concept of "facts"? I think not, because there exists no valid rule of inference yielding this result.

IV.2.a

At this point it appears to me that Popper's approach is essentialistic. He is starting from the wrong question, namely from the question of what a "norm" or "decision" *really is*. Even if his answer is only negative, because he says that norms or decisions are *not* facts, he is, in saying this, still discussing what they "are," and therefore discussing the *concept* of "norms" or "decisions." But as a methodological nominalist he ought not to discuss concepts; he ought to start at the other end, and tell us *first* what he is speaking about, and *then* suggest: let us call it a "norm," or let us call it a "decision."

But what is he speaking about? As to decisions, I propose to leave this question aside for the moment since we all know quite well what we are doing when we make decisions. Something is going on inside of us, or of others, and to this something we have given the name "decision".[18] But how about norms? What is a "norm" and what makes it "valid"? Or how do we avoid these "what is" questions which are already badly put because they are again starting from concepts and looking for their "real" meaning?[19]

In order to take a truly nominalistic approach I think we must begin by agreeing about what we wish to talk about, and I suggest that we speak about the question whether or not it would improve life if everybody did just as they pleased, absolutely uninhibited by any legal or moral restrictions, or whether it would not be better to establish some kind of patterns of behavior that we think would make life easier if they were observed by everybody. These patterns of behavior I would then propose, for the purpose of this discussion, to call "norms," and then proceed to the far more

18 An attempt at a nominalistic definition of the term "decision" might consist in assigning this term to a process in which a situation containing more than one possibility is being consciously reduced to only one reality. But in my opinion the term "decision" is an excellent example for Popper's statement that, in science, "all the terms that are really needed must be undefined terms" (1945/1966, vol. 2: 18).
19 Cf. Popper 1966, vol. 2: 14; 1977: ch. P1, sect. 4.

interesting question: *what might make other people observe them?* That seems to be the really crucial question.

It is important to see that, as I have formulated the question, it is an *empirical* question. If we ask what might make other people observe norms, then the answer must relate to the motives which, *in fact*, other people have for observing norms. This answer must then, if it is not to be beside the point, itself be a statement of facts, which may be right or may be wrong, and which can be criticized on the grounds of experience.

And because only an empirical answer would meet the question it seems clear to me that it cannot be a simple answer. Different persons may have different motives for observing norms of conduct. For some the motives may originate from the Bible, or the Talmud, or the Koran, or from other religious traditions, while others may simply think that rules of behavior will make life easier for all of us. There may even be people who think, indeed, in terms of the Categorical Imperative, and therefore believe that norms should be observed because the maxims underlying our actions should always be apt to serve as a general principle of legislation. And there may not only be different motives in different people, but in fact, I think, the motives for observing a norm may even *vary* within one individual person, depending on the kind of norm in question. Mine at least do. There are norms which I obey because I would be ashamed of myself if I didn't. Others I obey because I know that only obedience will get me what I want, as is the case, for instance, with some tax laws, or laws of civil procedure. Still others I obey because I fear punishment if I don't, as, for instance, stopping at red traffic lights when there is absolutely no other traffic in sight which I might endanger. I even admit that there are numbers of laws or norms which I have knowingly transgressed, as for instance speed limits or "no parking" signs.

These examples may seem to be unfair, or even beside the point, because traffic lights, or speed limits, or "no parking" signs, are so trivial, and to some extent even arbitrary, whereas there are other norms as, for instance, the last five of the Ten Commandments, or Hayek's "Rules of Just Conduct" (1973, vol. 2: 35ff.), where no argument is possible: it seems that at least such important norms as the commandment "Thou shalt not kill" are valid beyond question. They appear to be bearing the reason for their validity in themselves. And would not the same be true of other norms, at least in the sense that it is possible to establish objectively whether or not they are good for humankind? It is possible that Popper's proposal to use the words "validity" or "rightness" of a norm in exactly the same sense as we use the concept of "truth" with respect to facts and descriptions was intended by him to be understood in this sense, i.e. in the sense that a norm is "valid" if it works for the good of mankind, and that the question whether it does in fact work for the good of mankind allows of only one answer which, as in the natural sciences, we may hope, but never be certain, to have found.

I wish to make it quite clear that I am not at all sure whether it is fair to attribute this view to Karl Popper. I am speaking of an idea mentioned in a footnote to chapter 5 of the *Open Society* (1945/1966, vol. 1: 234 n. 5) which points in this direction. If Popper did mean this, then, I think, he would have been contradicting other thoughts of his which I am going to mention in a moment, and which I find far more important. But at any rate he himself would have been the first to say that is not really important whether he was contradicting himself or whether I misunderstood him, as long as, by a common effort, we get nearer to the truth.[20]

IV.2.d

The truth is, I believe, that the proposal to connect the concept of "validity" of norms with the concept of "truth" of facts, or descriptions, is not only wrong, but even dangerous.

It is dangerous because it implies that, as in the natural sciences, *only one* answer can be true, and that a norm which does not give the right answer is, therefore, *not valid*. It thereby implies that there can be *only one* "right" or "valid" social order, and that, as long as we have not found this, we do not have to obey the law. So it seems to me, if subjectivism leads to Nietzsche and Hitler, as Sir Karl wrote to me in one of his last letters, and with which I fully agree, this kind of objectivism leads to utopia, and therefore to Marx, which, though possibly better, is still not the way to an "Open Society."

And this view of a parallelism of truth and validity is wrong, in my opinion, because it presupposes a uniformity of mankind which has never existed, and, I hope, never will exist. Popper himself mentions in *The Open Society* and in the *Poverty of Historicism* the enormous complexity of our social order and, in particular, the fact that every attempt to influence or change it may lead to unforeseen repercussions because it entails the reactions of free human beings (cf. 1957: ch. 21; 1945/1966, vol. 2: ch. 14). If this is true, and I believe it to be, then I can see no reason why there should be *only one* "right" social order, or even *only one* "right" solution for the smaller problems which we wish to attack with the modest means of piecemeal social technology. And I think that in social engineering, other than with statements of natural laws, it does not impair objectivism, or lead to relativism, if we accept the possibility of more

---

20 This is a hint at his words in chapter 24 of *The Open Society* (1945/1966, vol. 2: 225) to which he attributed highest importance, as can be seen from his quotation in the introduction to *The Myth of the Framework* (1994b: xii).

than one solution to a social problem. If, for example, we wish to tackle the problem of drugs in our country, then there may be various ways of doing this. We may try to approach it from the angle of improving import controls. Or we may try to get hold of the money made in the sale by penetrating the banker's discretion. We may also try to do both at once, or one step after the other. And we may try to deter the dealers by publicly announcing our measures, or to take them by surprise through secrecy. Most of these measures would involve the enactment of new laws as well as the making of decisions, and it may be that one line of action is better than another because it leads to quicker results, or causes lower costs, or has fewer repercussions on the monetary market. It may also be that, depending on the initial conditions, the best line of action to be taken *varies* from country to country, or from century to century. All these questions may be discussed on the basis of objective criteria, but they will have to be criteria of probability. And where probabilty is involved there must be more than one possibility.

IV.3

If this view is right then, I believe, it takes only one further step to put norms or laws into the proper place which they should take in Karl Popper's epistemology. If norms, or laws, may be considered as instruments designed to solve problems of social engineering in a piecemeal sort of way, then, I think, we must consider them as parts of what Popper calls his "World 3," i.e. the world of the products of the human mind. Popper puts great emphasis on the reality of this world (see 1994a: chs 2 and 3; 1977: ch. P2), and he defines the concept of "reality" by proposing to call "real" anything that can create – either directly, or by mediation of "World 2," the world of mental or psychic states – changes in "World 1," the world of physical states, or bodies (1977: ch. P1, sect. 4).

In my opinion, there can hardly be any doubt that norms – and I mean the norms themselves and not the fact that we have adopted them – are "real" in this sense, because the great majority of mankind is guided by sets of norms which may differ in their contents, but which all operate through the mind of those who adopt them, and thus, by influencing their behavior, cause changes in "World 1," the world of physical states. So, according to Popper's definition of "reality," these norms are real and cannot, therefore, be excluded from the class of facts, unless we define the concept of "fact" in a way that it does not include everything that is real. In my opinion we will gain nothing, but only create a muddle, if we try to define the concept of "facts" in such a way that it no longer coincides with the concept of "reality," but will exclude from "facts" one particular class of concepts which is nevertheless considered to be describing something "real." Norms belong to "World 3," and not to a new "World 4" which we would have to invent in order to save critical dualism.

IV.4

So I think, *as a methodological concept* critical dualism should be given up. From a *purely* methodological point of view monism, that is to say a "methodological monism," is the right answer, and for legal theory, as for ethics, it is important to see this because only methodological monism will fit in with the principle of the autonomy of the will, and will thus permit to improve the objectivity of legal and moral decisions by allowing objective criticism. But I wish to emphasize once more that this by no means implies giving up the distinction between descriptive sentences and normative sentences, or the distinction between norms and facts as it is often understood in everyday language, where the members of "World 3" are mostly not included in the concept of "facts." This "ordinary language" distinction between "is" and "ought," or norms and facts, is, I think, almost as important as the distinction between black and white (which is also a distinction between facts and other facts), but it nevertheless rests on an ambiguity of language, because the concept of "facts" is once used so as to include *everything* that is real, and otherwise so as to *exclude* norms *in spite of* their reality. That is why it is *methodologically* unsound.

But this difference of opinion in questions of methodology between Sir Karl Popper and myself does not, I think, indicate an important, or even fundamental, difference of opinion in questions of philosophy. I wish to conclude this paper with his own words from *The Open Society*. They express my view better than I could have expressed it myself – which can hardly come as a surprise since I have learned it from him – and I fully subscribe to them after changing only one single word, the word "critical *dualism*," to "critical *monism*." I think these words contain the best explanation of the principle of the autonomy of the will in ethics that was ever written (1945/1966, vol. 1: 61):

> Critical *dualism* merely asserts that norms and normative laws can be made and changed by man, more especially by a decision or convention to observe them or to alter them, and that it is therefore man who is morally responsible for them; not perhaps for the norms which he finds to exist in society when he first begins to reflect upon them, but for the norms which he is prepared to tolerate once he has found out that he can do something to alter them. Norms are man-made in the sense that we must blame nobody but ourselves for them; neither nature, nor God. It is our business to improve them as much as we can, if we find that they are objectionable. This last remark implies that by describing norms as conventional, I do not mean that they must be arbitrary, or that one set of normative laws will do just as well as another. By saying that some systems of laws can be improved, that some laws may be better than others, I rather imply that we can compare the existing normative laws (or social institutions) with some

126

standard norms which we have decided are worthy of being realized. But even these standards are of our making in the sense that our decision in favour of them is our own decision, and that we alone carry the responsibility for adopting them. The standards are not to be found in nature. Nature consists of facts and of regularities, and is in itself neither moral nor immoral. It is we who impose our standards upon nature, and who in this way introduce morals into the natural world, in spite of the fact that we are part of this world. We are products of nature, but nature has made us together with our power of altering the world, of foreseeing and of planning for the future, and of making far-reaching decisions for which we are morally responsible. Yet responsibility, decisions, enter the world of nature only with us.

This, I believe, makes my point.

REFERENCES

Hayek, F. A. 1973. *Law, Legislation and Liberty*. London: Routledge & Kegan Paul; reprinted 1976.

Mettenheim, Christoph von. 1984. *Recht und Rationalitat*. Tübingen: Mohr Siebeck.

Popper, Karl R. 1945. *The Open Society and Its Enemies*. London: Routledge & Kegan Paul; 5th edn, Routledge 1966.

—— 1957. *The Poverty of Historicism*. London: Routledge & Kegan Paul.

—— 1959. *The Logic of Scientific Discovery*. London: Hutchinson.

—— 1965. "What is dialectic?" In *Logik der Sozialwissenschaften*, ed. Ernst Topitsch. Cologne and Berlin: Kiepenhener & Witsch.

—— 1977. *The Self and Its Brain*. Heidelberg, Berlin, London and New York: Springer.

—— 1983. *Realism and the Aim of Science*. London: Routledge.

—— 1989. *Conjectures and Refutations*. 5th edn. London: Routledge.

—— 1994a. *Knowledge and the Body–Mind Problem*. London: Routledge.

—— 1994b. *The Myth of the Framework*, ed. M. A. Notturno. London: Routledge.

Tarski, A. 1965. *Introduction to Logic*. New York: Oxford University Press.

Watkins, J. W. N. 1978. "Unvollkommene Rationalität." In *Freiheit und Entscheidung*. Tübingen: Mohr Siebeck.

9

MINIMA MORALIA[1]

Is there an ethics of the open society?

Sandra Pralong

In 1989, as the Berlin Wall came tumbling down and the political establishment, along with the rest of the world, needed to make sense of events, Karl Popper's *The Open Society and Its Enemies* (Popper 1945/1966) enjoyed a second birth. Its new relevance, due primarily to Popper's typology of "closed" and "open" political systems, was especially obvious in Eastern and Central Europe: the book was perhaps the only theoretical framework available in which the daunting challenge behind the unfolding events was put into proper perspective.

The collapse of communism – a closed system *par excellence* – is generally seen to entail the transformation of a centrally planned economy and of a repressive political apparatus into a market system and a democratic regime. From Popper's framework, however, it is obvious that the transition between closed and open societies represents much more than structural overhaul and institutional redesign. More profoundly, it requires a change in attitude: in individuals' perception of their universe and of their place in it.

And herein lay, in my opinion, one of the key issues related to the post-communist transitions. To the question "What do people need to change in order to build open societies?," the usual answer is: their institutions. Popper's more sophisticated approach however is to say: their way of thinking! They need to change their epistemological framework and their moral outlook (Popper 1945/1966, vol. 2: 232f.). Popper fully accounts for the ethical differences between what he calls Plato's "totalitarian ethics," in which the interests of the individual are subjected to the interests of the group (1945/1966, vol. 1: 108), and for Marx's "historicist moral theory," in which the ends justify the means (1945/1966, vol. 2: 208), both of which he contrasts with Socrates' "humanitarian" project of defense of individualism (1945/1966, vol. 1: 104f.). But, surprisingly, Popper fails to detail the different ethical standards embedded in each moral framework.

1 I have borrowed the title from Theodor Adorno's *Minima Moralia* (Verso, London, 1974), and from Andrei Pleşu's similarly titled *Minima Moralia* (Bucharest: Editura Cartea Romanească, 1988).

In this essay I will focus on identifying the criteria associated with each ethical project. Specifically, I will attempt to find, in Popper's writings, the most appropriate criterion for making moral decisions in the open society. Even though Popper doesn't make it explicit, I believe there is a particular ethical rule in the *Open Society*; it has the beauty of simplicity, it is compatible with Popper's other values, and it dovetails with Socrates' humanist project of inviting individuals to apply critical thinking to all domains, including morality and ethics.

Choosing between the two competing ethical projects – the "totalitarian" and the "humanitarian" – is, in my opinion, one of the keys to the transition from closed to open society: from ethics stem politics, and politics determines institutional design and socioeconomic organization. Yet Popper seems to underrate a key problem related to the existence of two different ethical paradigms. Not only does he fail to specify the different criteria for moral choice that are associated with each approach, but he also under-emphasizes the difficulty of *transition* from one ethical paradigm to another.

Even though I will not address here the problems involved in changing ethical standards, I will briefly outline the issue as follows: the idea of transition from closed to open society requires that we clarify the circumstances in which change is to occur, and the time-lag allowed for change to be completed. Both these elements, however, pose difficulties partly ignored by Popper, perhaps because: (a) they are somewhat implicit in his idea that change requires a moral decision between dogma and reason (1945/1966, vol. 2: 232f), and (b) because he considered change from closed to open systems to be gradual and to take generations (see especially 1945/1966: ch. 10). However, the post-communist experience points to a different expectation, namely that of *rapid* change – a transformation to be completed, if possible, within the span of a single lifetime.

This means that, in order to switch from one ethical system to the other, the *same people* ought to change their moral outlook. And what does *that* entail? If we extrapolate from what Popper calls the "logic of the situation" (1945/1966, vol. 2: 97), what is required is a change in circumstances such that it alters moral reasoning. Yet I will argue that the new circumstances of post-communism are far from providing an environment apt to induce change in moral thinking. Quite the contrary, I believe that, paradoxically, liberalism is more likely to entrench the old, discredited moral criteria, than to provide an incentive to change.

Changing moral perspectives away from "totalitarian ethics" requires that individuals abandon an instrumental ethic in which the ends justify the means, and adopt a Kantian ethic of legitimate rule obedience, along with what Popper calls "moral egalitarianism" (1945/1966, vol. 1: 265). It also requires that people agree to a *procedural* ethic rather than continue endorsing a substantive ethic of ultimate ends. Finally, at the collective level, this change corresponds to acceptance of the rule of law, which is the key element in the promotion of an open society.

In his account of the open society, Popper doesn't focus on specifying the ethical standards that induce obedience to the rule of law; nor does he analyze the mechanics of transformation of a closed society into an open one. Had he done so, I believe he would have noticed that there is "a catch," especially if one is to allow for a very short time-span for the transition from closed to open systems (i.e. the transition from an instrumental ethics, where the ends justify the means, to procedural ethics).

The catch seems to be the following: instrumental *rationality* (i.e. means–ends rationality, where the ends *dictate* the means) is fully embedded in open institutions such as science, the market, etc. And such instrumental rationality can be mistakenly associated with instrumental *ethics* (where the ends *justify* the means). The two are analytically different of course, but confusion is not unlikely. Thus a problem arises: should the difference between instrumental reason and instrumental ethics ever be obscured, it would make it actually *irrational* for any given individual willingly to adopt procedural ethics. For why should the rational individual forego the idea that one is right because one has the "right" ends? Why not ignore the equal rights of others when one is convinced of having, say, the best intentions?

If my concern is correct and indeed we see instrumental rationality and instrumental ethics unwittingly mixed up in people's minds, then there is a collective action problem (Olson 1965) involved in the transition from closed to open systems: for there seems to be no reason and no incentive for *rational* individuals to renounce the idea that the ends justify the means, and to adopt a different, procedural, ethics. (Hume's answer – that rule obedience is necessary because otherwise society would perish – doesn't seem to me to resolve the collective action problem, for it gives no reason to any one individual not to free-ride, i.e. not to count on *others* to obey the law while one seeks to get away with disobedience.)

But there is more: since liberal doctrine invites individuals freely to chose their own ends, and it actually *encourages* their self-interest, liberalism only compounds the problem. For an emphasis on self-interest makes it even *more* irrational for people to forego their individual ends for the sake of respecting the rights of others, or for the sake of complying with collective rule obedience (i.e. with the rule of law).

Does this mean that a secular *and* ethical *liberal* order cannot emerge *sui generis*, at least not in the course of one generation?[2] Or does this imply that absent recourse to a higher authority (such as that of religion), the only way to solve this problem is through a strong state that coerces people into rule

---

2 One is tempted to theorize that secular liberalism was possible only because society was already built on the basis of religious ethics. See also Max Horkheimer's notion of living on borrowed ethics, in the *Eclipse of Reason* (Oxford: Oxford University Press, 1947).

obedience? But if that were the case, the new order would no longer be liberal or be an open society!

So, what is to be done? The short answer may be perhaps to remind ourselves that engaging in a critical discussion about ethics, complete with education in what may be called the "ethics of reason," or the "ethics of freedom," ought not be entirely beyond the scope of the liberal project. Popper calls this "moral intellectualism," and reminds us that one of Socrates' fundamental ideas was that "moral excellence can be taught, and that it does not require any particular moral faculties, apart from the universal human intelligence" (Popper 1945/ 1966, vol. 1: 128). There is no reason for ethics to remain the province of religious fundamentalism or of conservative politics, since one can engage in it critically and with an open mind.

While the issue of "liberal ethics" is too vast for me to address in this essay, I will nevertheless try to tackle two of its aspects: (a) I will first give a brief account of how this problem plays in the post-communist context, and (b) I will attempt to derive from Popper's writings a minimal ethical standard of social interaction suited to the open society.

What I will not address, however, is the collective action problem embedded in the moral transition from closed to open society; nor will I discuss here the vexing issue of ethical rule enforcement. For even assuming that there is agreement on what I will propose as a "popperian standard" for moral decision-making, ethics is, by definition, the province of self-enforced norms, and thus it eludes traditional discussions of enforcement.

I realize that by focusing on matters such as "criteria for moral decison-making," or "rules of behavior" and "minimal standards of social interaction," I am on the verge of heresy, or, worse yet, of putting words into Karl Popper's mouth. For Sir Karl took particular pride in his anti-behavioristic, anti-psychological, rational approach to political philosophy. In spite of his methodological individualism, Popper was clearly reluctant to address the issue of ethics and of how individuals (should) make moral decisions. It is easy to see why: he must have thought it the height of presumption to offer rules for how one should behave, when the whole popperian project is predicated on individuals thinking freely for themselves without recourse to any authority, be it an enlightened one, such as his own.[3]

I will try to show, however, that what I believe to be a criterion implicit in Popper's approach to ethics is not only compatible with his emphasis on individual critical thinking, but is actually a good illustration of it, for the rule I will extract from his writings represents a general method by which one may decide *for oneself* what is "good" and what is not. This criterion for ethical

---

3 Another reason may also be Popper's reluctance to base decision-making on specific criteria – he devotes two important sections in the Addenda to *OSIE*'s second volume to refuting the need for criteria and principles.

decision-making is derived from a well-known traditional standard, over 2,500 years old, which preserves both individual freedom and value-pluralism.

From communism to the open society: when do ends *not* justify the means?

Who sets the rules in an open society? Since liberal individuals represent self-originating sources of value, the rules, including ethical ones, are to be set by individuals, with no appeals to a higher authority and no coercion. As noted above, the question "according to which criteria?" most clearly distinguishes open from closed societies. Closed societies operate according to the belief that the end justifies the means. Considering how harmful is this idea if one seeks to establish an open society (which is based on obedience to the rule of law), Popper's rather lax treatment of the difference between specific criteria is somewhat surprising. (See especially 1945/1966: ch. 9, note 6 for his discussion of means and ends.)

With the risk of caricaturing, I will illustrate below why a belief that the ends may justify the means is fatal to the establishment of an open society.

There is a myth in the West about the post-communist Big Bang – it circulates especially among economists dealing with reform. The idea is that in Eastern Europe, a new universe has been emerging from scratch. But not even in the economy is this an accurate perception, as many of the old private and institutional ties that preceded the collapse have remained unaltered and continue to permeate the new structures, even in the face of privatization and the transition to markets (Stark 1993).

The legacy of communism is not a moral *tabula rasa* on which one can build a whole new system from the ground up; the Berlin Wall did not collapse into a vacuum. On the contrary, one could say that, in certain cases, far from being the idyllic garden of Rousseau's uncorrupted good men in the state of nature, the region starts with a considerable handicap. This is so because communism was not merely a benign, a-moral system, but, rather, it was a system that actually encouraged immorality – by necessity – as a way to survive. Think of it this way: if property belongs to all, it belongs to nobody; then what's wrong in helping oneself since no one in particular is being harmed directly?

To focus on the problem, I will take a theoretical example and trace the moral quandary that an individual would now face if he or she had lived through, say, the last fifty years of the communist "Absurdistan" – as Vaclav Havel called it.

Imagine our friend to have been, in his youth (I'll assume a man so it's easier to picture him active in politics, for fewer women were militants at that time), a convinced communist, who genuinely believed in the Marxist–Leninist ideal of social justice and economic equality, and sought to establish it in, say, one of the East European countries. After the Second World War, the Soviet Army helps him and his comrades come to power. Our friend fights against the local "bourgeois reactionaries," jails many of them and even gives orders to kill a few – the Party demands it to consolidate its power. But he can justify this to himself: it's for a noble cause and for the common good. *The end justifies the means*, so his splendid intentions justify his crime! As the dominance of the Party becomes entrenched, however, idealism slackens. And as the socialist paradise seems increasingly remote, many people start to cut corners; our friend must now distort reality to avoid challenging the official dogma. He dislikes it but has no other choice, so he learns to lie about things large and small: from being an informant for the Secret Police, to cheating about fulfilling his job quota (or the Five-Year Plan), to lying to his children about his ideological convictions, and so on, in a never-ending waltz of double-talk and (self)-deception. Truth becomes irrelevant, or worse – it is a nuisance one needs to cover up. In addition, economic conditions are so harsh that he accepts bribes to make ends meet, and in turn he must bribe others to get anything done.

Then communism collapses, democracy and the market economy (the system that he was trained to hate, or at least to lie about) are becoming institutionalized, and, as our friend understands it, competition is now the name of the game – meaning, he has to stay ahead of the curve, no matter what. No more protection from the Party in exchange for his loyalty and obedience, no more shelter in the state-run sector where he worked for "everybody" (meaning for nobody in particular) and got away with doing nothing. Self-interest is now the new mantra and, after decades of publicly denying he had any interests of his own, the change is welcomed by him and his (former) comrades; they're ready to compete.

But the world that emerged from the ruins of communism is a lot more difficult to survive in than the (still) cozy West, where there is relatively low inflation, a safety net for the jobless, social security, a decent health system, banks one can trust, insurance that covers risk, justice that functions, and everything from hot running water to monthly salaries with which one can buy more than just a few loaves of bread. No such comforts are yet to be taken for granted in the wild capitalist jungle of the post-communist East. So, what's to keep our friend from, well, finding "unorthodox ways" to survive? Like taking a bribe or two (or more) to make ends meet, like lying on occasion when it suits him, or cheating from time to time to stay ahead of the curve? For it goes without saying that, a convinced atheist, our friend has little fear of God to mitigate his zeal; besides, society puts little pressure on him to change his ways. The legal system is still full of holes, the police and the tribunals are not yet efficient – or totally fair – and when they function policemen and judges are human too and subject to the same pressures to make ends meet as everyone else … In other words, much of the system still functions with the assumption that the ends justify the means. The main difference is that now the ends are not some lofty ideal and the "common good," but quite simply self-interest and survival of the fittest. Since self-interest is, after all, the liberal creed, nobody can be blamed, but now the question is: what – and who – gives our friend a moral compass?

I am not suggesting, of course, that reform communists are all corrupt while everyone else is perfect – far from it. There are as many uncorrupt, decent, and law-abiding former communists as there are corrupt and lawless liberals. The point is not to label people and to assign blame, the point is to try to highlight – even with the risk of caricaturing – some of the specific moral difficulties of the post-totalitarian transition.

Also, the point is to show that the issue of ethical change has no simple answers. The guiding principle of the open society – to minimize avoidable suffering – is of no real help in this particular instance, especially given the way it is stated (i.e. as a substantive demand). First of all, it is primarily intended for public policy at the macro-level rather than for individuals. And second, even if it did apply to individuals, it does not give them clear guidance for how to make moral choices. What is needed is a procedure, a criterion for moral decision-making that can be used in a variety of situations, that go beyond the substantive demand of reducing suffering (while incorporating this idea in the procedure itself.) Actually, Popper's negative utilitarianism, if taken literally, may, under certain conditions, have an adverse effect if applied in the former communist world, as it collides with the idea of transitional justice. Transitional justice involves retribution and restitution, both of which, at first, create additional social pain. For instance, application of the Popperian principle would prevent the adoption of laws such as those for the restitution of property, because in effect they initially increase rather than diminish over-all suffering.

In other words, liberal principles – and the principles of an open society – only work once we are *within* a liberal order, and once we are already in an open society framework. But they are not very useful in order to *create* such a society from scratch. They are, as Bryan Magee (see chapter 10) put it, a methodology for problem-solving, but not a way to initiate a social agenda, or to select and evaluate moral standards.

So who can tell our disoriented friend what to do? Who can suggest a way to solve his ethical dilemmas? He is bound to be lost; now that liberalism has made him a self-originating source of value, he might as well realize it: he's on his own! There will be little if any guidance from secular society. Quite the contrary, secular society, if anything, reinforces whatever negative inclinations he may have by encouraging him to think in terms of self-interest. And other than the moral guidance provided if, say, he joins a church (which, if fundamentalist, will re-establish a closed-society framework), there's little if anything in the public arena that can give him the tools to solve the myriad ethical dilemmas coming his way. Ideally, what's needed is for our friend to find a decision-making technique to solve his moral issues *alone*, without having somebody else's will imposed on him, and without subordinating the means to the ends of his actions. This is what the open society should help him do: engage in critical thinking about right and wrong, decide for himself what's "good" in accordance with what's right for others, reason and choose without appeal to a higher power and without the state to coerce him. In other words, he needs to sort, on his own, the good from the bad, the morally permissible from the forbidden, and the ethically necessary from the accessory, by using a criterion other than "the ends justify the means."

What tools has he got? What "technology" can he use for such (ethical) decisions? These are non-trivial matters since the institutions of the open society depend on our friend making appropriate moral choices, being law-abiding, respecting the sanctity of contracts, and so on. Without such respect for promises, contracts, and institutions, an open society cannot be implemented, and cannot survive.

The open society's *minima moralia*: criteria for an "open ethics"

In this last section I will explore the possibility of extracting a specific ethical stance from Popper's *Open Society*, and identifying a general rule of conduct to help resolve our moral dilemmas in a liberal environment.

While Popper devotes an entire chapter to condemning Marx's "historicist moral theory" (1945/1966, vol. 2: 208), he nevertheless seems reluctant to spell out a criterion according to which ethical dilemmas should be resolved so that what he calls "moral egalitarianism" (1966, vol. 1: 265) can be implemented in a meaningful way. If the ends (should) no longer justify the means, then how is one to approach moral questions? And if ethics is to be procedural rather than instrumental or substantive, how are moral decisions to be made? Even though Popper doesn't specifically address these issues, I believe that one can extrapolate from his approach to science and social engineering, and from his general discussions of ethics, to find a prudential rule that is compatible with the requirements of an open society, i.e. with value pluralism, individual autonomy, reason, freedom of thought, critical thinking, and rejection of authority.

In his insightful account of Popper's political theory, Jeremy Shearmur mentions that Popper fails to address the differences between private and public obligations, and therefore fails to discriminate among the various moral responsibilities we have towards one another (Shearmur 1996: 56). While I agree with Shearmur's assessment, I am not convinced that he's correct in criticizing Popper for "putting all … things into one basket" (ibid.: 56). I think that Popper doesn't have different criteria for public and private obligations for a reason: such difference would prevent the open society from functioning. It would either require that people be schizophrenic, and think one way in public and another in private (which is untenable), or it would require that the institutions of the open society be enforced by means other than those which private individuals would find acceptable (which is undesirable). Hence for the open society to exist, similar principles must govern both public and private obligations.

To my mind, for Popper, the necessity to help alleviate human suffering is *both* a matter of public policy and of individual concern. This is so not because he somehow fails to distinguish between the two domains, as Shearmur maintains, but because I believe that Popper implicitly posits a moral *continuum* between his public "negative utilitarianism" and the resolution of private moral dilemmas. The way I see it, this continuum resides not in the substance of what needs to be addressed (i.e. the reduction of suffering) but in the *procedure* by which one arrives at moral decisions. In other words, I believe that when he talks about "alleviating suffering" Popper uses this as shorthand for a specific method of moral reasoning that can be applied both in private life and in public policy.

Of course, I have no way to prove that my interpretation of Popper's implicit ethical project is correct – but all it takes is for someone to *disprove* it ... In the meantime, I am encouraged by Shearmur's reading of Popper as establishing a brand of "ethical objectivism in which there are close methodological analogies with his theory of knowledge" (Shearmur 1996: 94). I too believe this to be the case. I will try to make my intuition explicit by briefly reviewing some of the statements Popper makes about ethics, and then I will outline what I take to be an exercise in moral reasoning that yields a prudential rule, a specific standard for making individual moral decisions. Finally, I will show this ethical standard to be consistent with Popper's writings.

First, a reminder that Popper's primary concern is to protect the moral autonomy of individuals. There is no external authority that Popper recognizes as a source of ethics, and for good reason – that would rob individuals of their responsibility: "we must not accept the command of an authority, however exalted, as the basis for ethics. For whenever we are faced with a command by an authority, it is for us to judge, critically, whether it is moral or immoral to obey" (Miller 1985: 53).

Not only does Popper think that individuals should question authority, but they actually should themselves *become* ethical authorities: "We *create* our standards by proposing, discussing and adopting them," he says in the Addendum to *The Open Society*, volume 2 (italics in the original), (1945/ 1966, vol. 2: 385).

Also, Popper remarks that while we may indeed seek absolute standards, we are bound never to find one: "There cannot be a criterion of absolute rightness," he says, but adds:

> although we have no criterion of absolute rightness, we ... can make progress in this realm. As in the realm of facts, we can make discoveries. That cruelty is always "bad," that it should always be avoided where possible; that the golden rule is a good standard which can

perhaps even be improved, by doing unto others, wherever possible, as *they* would want to be done by; these are elementary and extremely important examples of discoveries in the realm of standards.

(1945/1966, vol. 2: 386; italics in the original)

The fact that there is no criterion for absolute rightness in the realm of standards mirrors Popper's attitude toward science, where absolute truth remains elusive yet we engage in progress toward it with each conjecture (and refutation) we make.

In addition to the idea that we make discoveries regarding moral standards just as we do in science, there are two other intuitive claims one can extract from Popper's argument, one of which is also noted by Shearmur: "[the] notion that there are absolute moral standards of which we may fall short – ... suggests the possibility of the application of [Popper's] fallibilist epistemology to ethics" (Shearmur 1996: 93). Indeed, I believe that this fallibilist (ethical) approach, which I will detail below, is Popper's key contribution to moral theory. Furthermore, Popper's statement that improving on the golden rule may involve foregoing *our* preferences for those of others intuitively points to a parallel between Popper's negative utilitarianism in public policy and a similar approach in private matters.

If a negatively stated rule is preferable to a positive one, then the question is: what would be a (private) ethical rule equivalent to Popper's (public) "negative utilitarianism?" Or, better yet, what is the standard Popper implicitly uses to derive his negative utilitarianism? As mentioned above, my intuition is that we can extract from Popper's writings a rule for decision-making that can be used regardless of where in the continuum between private and public it is to be applied.

There are two requirements that any such rule must have: (a) it must be a minimal standard, so that it can allow for maximum individual autonomy and discernment (i.e. for critical thinking); and (b) it must be procedural rather than substantive, so that it can be universalizable.

An obvious candidate is Kant's Categorical Imperative: "Act only on a maxim that you can at the same time will to become a universal law" (Kant 1994: xvii). Although Popper repeatedly praises Kant, he fails to explicitly endorse the Categorical Imperative as *the* standard for moral decision-making in the open society.[4]

The other "minimalist" candidate is the biblical golden rule: "Always so do unto others as you would want others to do unto you" (Matthew 7:12). For Popper, "individualism, united with altruism, has become the basis of our

---

4 One can speculate that Kant's Categorical Imperative may not have fit Popper's quest for a criterion because Kant's standard is formulated in the affirmative, rather than follow Popper's negative methodology. That may risk making the thought experiment proposed by Kant prone to possible illiberal applications.

western civilization" (Popper, 1945/1966, vol. 1: 102). But, in chapter 24, he warns against using a rule based on love as our criterion for ethics, by stating that "of all ... ideals, making people happy is perhaps the most dangerous one" (1945/1966, vol. 2: 237). Also, as mentioned before, Popper implies that there is a way to *improve* on the golden rule by doing to others as *they* would like to be done by (ibid.: 386). But the question is: how would we know? Especially when dealing with strangers or in situations where dialogue is not possible, how can we know what others would like?

I claim that even though we cannot *know* other people's preferences, we can use Popper's negative methodology to at least *eliminate* what we might reasonably expect others *not* to like. In other words, at a minimum, our decision-making technique about moral acts should seek to ensure that others do not dislike, or find repugnant, the things we do and which affect them. Thus in the absence of dialogue, and if we are without access to information about others' preferences, we need to try to *guess* what others may find offensive. However, second-guessing others is not always a sure-fire strategy to please them. Therefore we need to anchor our decision about what others may or may not like in a fixed standard that we can use to judge the various situations we find ourselves in. What we need is a minimal criterion for what other people may find offensive, a threshold beyond which we know not to go, because otherwise we may be harming them. But given that dialogue with those affected may not always be feasible, where could we possibly find such criterion?

I think that we can find it in ourselves. Quite simply, we can take ourselves – and our own dislikes – to be the measure of what *not* to do to others. Rather than trying to do to others as we *think* they may like (as the golden rule invites us to do), we should instead try to avoid hurting them. This we can do by using our own intuition of what we may find distasteful, in order to determine what we should avoid doing to others – in that way we remain respectful of what Isaiah Berlin calls their "negative liberty" (Berlin 1969).

In other words, instead of following the golden rule (to "do to others as we would like to be done by"), or Kant's Categorical Imperative ("to do only that which we could wish all others to do as well"), we turn away from what's permissible, and focus only on what to avoid. Thus we use as a criterion a "negative" golden rule ("Do NOT do to others what you would not want others to do to you"), or a negative Categorical Imperative ("DO NOT act in ways which you would not deem permissible for everyone else as well").

The question may arise if this change in enunciation, from a positive to a negative formulation, has substantive implications or is purely rhetorical. I will argue that the idea to *avoid* something that may be unsuitable, rather than to attempt to do what's "good," is as different in its implications as Popper's negative utilitarianism (to minimize suffering) is from the classical version, which commands us to maximize general happiness. In all situations, whether individual or collective, the idea is not to impose our preferences on others, or to second-guess what would make them happy, quite simply because we may be wrong in our assumptions about what others like. As George Bernard Shaw once said: "Do not do unto others how you would like to be done by, others may have different tastes!" From this perspective, one could argue that totalitarianism is the logical (and also the *patho*logical) conclusion of an "affirmative" ethical rule which makes it permissible to do unto others what one thinks is "good." Had the ethical standard been to *avoid* doing to others what one wouldn't like done to oneself, perhaps the face of history might have been different.

To summarize: in the absence of sufficient knowledge about how to act, a "negative golden rule" states that we shouldn't do to others what we wouldn't want others to do unto us. Such negative standard has us engaged in a thought experiment requiring not that we please others, but that we avoid hurting them. Thus when we put ourselves in the place of those who are likely to be affected by our actions, we ask ourselves: would we find it acceptable, from *that* position, to be the recipient of those actions? If yes, the chances are that others might think the same and welcome our acts (unless we are a truly peculiar creature of totally bizarre inclinations.) If not, we should abstain from acting for fear we may hurt them.

I believe this method for moral decison-making to be faithful to the Popperian spirit in several ways. First, it requires critical thinking and makes use of falsifiability – we advance in our knowledge of what's right by trial and error. We do not claim to be an authority on what's "good" or what "should" be done in particular cases. There is no absolute "ought" we are required to abide by, merely an "ought not" that prevents us from doing to others the harm that we would not like to see done to us.

As a way to improve ethical standards, this negative golden rule, just like Popper's scientific methodology, calls for (ethical) conjecture and refutation. It works as follows: as we're about to act, or to make a moral choice, we first conjecture that what we are about to do is good. But to test the validity of our claim, we attempt to refute it by applying what might be called the "acid test of self-infliction": how would *we* react if we did to ourselves whatever we plan to do to others, or if someone else did that to us? If the answer fails to deter us from the action, then we may proceed, the standard holds but only in this situation. In other cases, the appropriateness – or "truth" – of the standard needs to be tested again. Thus each new situation calls for new conjectures and new tests of their refutation.

Second, this approach to ethics adapts Popper's idea of piecemeal engineering to the smallest possible "piece": the level of the individual and his or her moral decisions. Popper writes: "Men believed God to rule the world. This belief limited their responsibility. The new belief that they had to rule it themselves created for many a well nigh intolerable burden of responsibility" (1945/1966, vol. 2: 24). Whether they like it or not, men (and women) are thus responsible for "engineering" the world they live in. The question is: How are they to acquit themselves of this obligation? Popper writes: "It is our duty to help those who need our help, but it cannot be our duty to make others happy, since this does not depend on us, and since it would only too often mean intruding on [their] privacy ..." (ibid.: 237). And also "the attempt to make heaven on earth invariably produces hell. It leads to intolerance" (ibid.: 237). From this, two ideas follow: (a) that each of us is responsible, through each of our decisions and actions, for indirectly engineering the collective fate – in other words society is shaped by the sum total of all piecemeal *ethical* engineering done by its members. And (b) that each of us can be responsible only for our own happiness, not for that of others. The most we can do for others is to avoid inflicting on them any pain.

Third, by using a negative methodology, the negative golden rule remains consistent with Popper's other negative claims. Here we can observe the continuum I mentioned above between public and private: the same decision-making technique that asks us to avoid inflicting pain to others (instead of catering to what we believe to be their happiness), also requires that, in matters of public policy, we forego the greatest happiness and concentrate instead on avoiding people's suffering. I realize that Popper is very explicit about making a moral distinction between the two, pleasure and pain. He says: "there is, from an ethical point of view, no symmetry between suffering and happiness, or between pain and pleasure... [H]uman suffering makes a direct moral appeal, an appeal for help, while there is no similar call to increase the happiness of a man who is doing well anyway" (1945/1966, vol. 1: 284). This objection however cannot be raised against my claim that there is a continuum between public and private. The difference Popper talks about is one of kind between the effects of positive versus negative rules: increase happiness versus avoid suffering, but the continuum exists in either case, depending on which scale one evaluates one's actions – in this case the negative one. Popper's call to alleviate whenever we can the suffering of others is an extension of the negative golden rule because the same reasoning applies to private and to public matters: since we would not want others to allow us to suffer, we should not remain indifferent to the suffering of others either.

Does this emphasis on our own standards make the negative golden rule subjectivist? Does it trap us into moral relativism? I believe not. For one thing, even though we take our own likes and dislikes as the measure of what is "good" (of what should be avoided), this is only a "crutch," as it were, in the absence of better information about the tastes of others or the likely impact of our actions on them. In the absence of appropriate knowledge, it is a way to avoid, or minimize, negative unintended consequences. If, as Protagoras suggests, man is the measure of all things, then we need a representation of that measure (1945/1966, vol. 1: 190). We can only really know ourselves, not others, and as such, we stand in, as it were, for all those we do not know but who are likely to be affected by us. Is trying to represent others presumptuous? I believe not: even though there is indeed an infinitely large variety of tastes in human nature, the things that we find truly repugnant fall, it seems, into a much narrower and more universalizable range. But I do not see how a *negative* criterion could be accused of subjectivism, because even though we judge each case given our own perspective for what's acceptable and what's not, the procedure we are embarked on at the meta-ethical level is clearly universalistic – and universalizable. The thought experiment we are invited to undertake highlights this universal idea: not only are people likely to find the same things abhorrent – violence, pain, suffering, hunger, poverty, dishonesty, etc.; but since we are all equally rational, we are equally likely to engage in the same exercise and come up with similar results. Thus, if we all apply the same rule, others are equally likely to avoid causing *us* the kind of pain they wouldn't like to suffer from us. Popper stresses that we all share a common rationality, which he describes as the "rational unity of mankind" (1945/1966, vol. 2: 225). The negative golden rule as a general criterion of ethics underscores this idea.

Also, Popper highlights another aspect of rationality which, I believe, belongs to this prudential rule of conduct. The negative golden rule is predicated on the idea of (inner) dialogue. Popper writes: "Rationalism is ... bound up with the idea that the other fellow has a right to be heard, and to defend his arguments. It ... implies the recognition of the claim to tolerance ... One does not kill a man when one adopts the attitude of first listening to his arguments" (ibid.: 238). He further adds "Kant was right when he based the Golden Rule on the idea of reason ..." (ibid.: 238). Reason implies objectivity, and, as Shearmur reminds us, for Popper, objectivity "is best secured through inter-subjective testability" (Shearmur 1996: 96), which means through dialogue. Here too, the rule matches Popper's approach.

Furthermore, the mental experiment which consists in substituting one person's dislikes – ours – for those of others who are potentially affected by us, in effect treats others "as if they were us," i.e. with the same respect we deem to deserve for ourselves. In other words it compels us to treat others as ends in themselves, in the same way we consider ourselves to be ends. This emphasizes the idea of "moral egalitarianism," of which Popper is a strong defender: "I hold, with Kant, that it must be the principle of all morality that no man should consider himself more valuable than any other person. [T]his principle is the only one acceptable ..." (Popper 1945/1966, vol. 1: 256).

Finally, this negative golden rule seems particularly suited to what Popper calls a "society that has lost its organic character" (ibid.: 174), in other words, an open society. For Popper such a society is an "abstract society" (ibid.: 174), and could be caricatured as a society where "men practically never meet face to face ... [Where they] have no, or extremely few, intimate personal contacts, ... [and they] live in anonymity and isolation" (ibid.: 174f.). A rule that is applicable equally to all, whether they are near or far away, intimate friends or total strangers, and that doesn't require our having a privileged relationship with our fellows (such as love, or respect, or admiration, all of which are fickle and can one day disappear), is perhaps the most suitable standard by which to make moral decisions in an "abstract" society.

Could a negative golden rule be what Popper implicitly had in mind as a rule of conduct for the open society? I think so, but it is difficult to do more than speculate, and I do not wish to second-guess Popper more than I have already done. But I believe the following passage in the Addendum to be illuminating. He writes:

> How do we learn about [moral] standards? How, in this realm, do we learn from our mistakes? First we learn to imitate others (incidentally, we do so by trial and error), and so learn to look upon standards of behavior as if they consisted of fixed, "given" rules. Later we find (also by trial and error), that we are making mistakes – for example that we may hurt people. We may thus learn the golden rule; but soon we find that we may misjudge a man's attitude, ... his aims, his standards; and we may learn from our mistakes to take care *even beyond the golden rule.*
>
> (1945/1966, vol. 2: 390; emphasis added)

I believe this supports my conjecture – but perhaps someone is ready to refute it.

A few things remain to be said on this subject, and the first is: even admitting that I may be correct and that, (a) a negative golden rule is indeed the "right" standard for the open society, and (b) that Popper himself (implicitly) thought it to be so, how does this address the moral dilemmas posed by the post-communist transition?

The honest answer is – it does not. Or, at least, not automatically or directly. A rule, in and by itself, does nothing to change people's attitudes. This is especially the case with a rule of ethics which is valid only if self-enforced. And there is no way to oblige people to adopt it, nor should there be any, as a society that coerces ethical obedience, no matter how subtly, can no longer be open. The self-enforcement of such a rule is strictly a matter of individual choice and conscience. However, people's choices can be educated, and their conscience developed. Open, critical discussion, and the constant questioning of fundamental moral issues is the best way to develop the individual's faculty to be both critical, but also *self*-critical (1945/1966, vol. 2: 387). The education system has a key role to play in giving children early on a forum to address moral and ethical issues. Popper reminds us that one of the fundamental tenets of Socrates is his theory that moral excellence can be taught, and that it does not require any particular moral faculties, apart from the universal human intelligence (1945/1966, vol. 1: 128). Thus the negative golden rule can be discussed and practiced from an early age, starting in the home, and continuing in the classroom, the office, the marketplace, the public place – in short, in each and every daily interaction, whenever there's a choice to be made which may affect others.

However, if open institutions depend on specific principles and ethical standards, if, furthermore, ethics depends on education, and if education depends on political will, then the sobering thought may be that, in the absence of a concerted political effort to change not just the institutions but the ethical criteria themselves, the post-communist transition may not necessarily lead to an open society. On the contrary, it may lead to a Hobbes' war of all against all and to his subsequent *Leviathan*, rather than to Locke's civilized, limited government.

Thus, to go back to the issue raised at the beginning of this essay, it is not a change in institutions *per se* which automatically results in the adoption of liberal values, but, rather, a change in individuals' way of thinking and of making moral choices which also results in different institutions.

One of the interesting features of the negative golden rule as a decision-making standard is not only its perfect reflection of the liberal doctrine and its espousal of individual freedom and value pluralism, but also the fact that it is an ethical criterion represented in every one of the world's religions – from Zoroastrism to Confucianism to Hinduism to Judaism to Islam. It has been implicitly preached, if not exactly practiced, around the world for over 2,500 years,[5] (Swidler 1994: 55). This raises an obvious question: if versions of the negative golden rule have been around for so long in so many parts of the world, why haven't these societies become open? I believe, again, that the answer lay in education, in its willingness to help the development of critical thinking, and in its encouragement of open dialogue about ethics. These are political issues rather than religious concerns. Furthermore, knowing the rules of one's religion does not also guarantee their respect. Respect and internalized rule obedience can come only from a profound awakening of one's individual

---

5 The following religious figures explicitly endorse a form of the (negative) golden rule: Zoroaster (628–551 BCE): "Do not ever do unto others that which is not good for you" (Gathas, 43.1); Confucius (551–479 BCE): "Do not to others do what you do not want done to yourself" (Analects, 12.2.), and "what I do not wish others to do to me, that also I wish not to do to them" (Analects, 5.11); Mahavira, the founder of Jainism (540–468 BCE): "A man should wander about treating all creatures as he himself would be treated" (Sutrakri-tanga 1.11.33), and "One who you think should be hit is none else but you. Therefore neither does he cause violence to others nor does he make others to do so" (Acarangasutra 5.101–2); Buddha (563–483 BCE): "Do not hurt the others with what makes you suffer"; Mahabharata, the Hindu poem (third century BCE): "Do not do to others what you do not wish done to yourself; and wish for others too what you desire and long for yourself – this is the whole of Dharma" (Mahabharata, Anusasana Parva 113.8); Rabbi Hillel (approx. first Century BCE): "Do not do to others what you would not have done to yourself – this is the heart of the Torah, all the rest is commentary" (Btalmud, Shabbath 31a); Jesus of Nazareth: "[W]hatever you want men to do to you, do also to them …" (Matthew 7:12). "And just as you want men to do to you, you also do to them likewise." (Luke 6:31); Mohammed (seventh century AD): "The noblest religion is this – that you should like for others what you like for yourself; and what you feel painful for yourself, hold that as painful for others too" (Al Q'uran); all cited in Swidler (1994).

conscience, and such awakening only happens when one develops the faculties of reason and critical thinking. Unfortunately, these faculties are rarely encouraged by religion, which much prefers dogma to criticism. Therefore religion, although it can be supportive of individual morality, cannot be the proper tool to teach what in effect is an ethics of reason and an ethics of freedom – including freedom from the constraints of organized religion. The open society, in order to maintain itself open, therefore has no choice but to undertake the task of articulating, for its own benefit, such moral education: it has to promote an ethic that's simple to follow and is applicable in private as well as in public life; an ethic that maximizes the assets of liberalism (especially its respect for value pluralism), while minimizing its costs (such as atomization and lack of social cohesion). It can do that by proposing a standard, such as the one discussed, that's both common to all individuals, yet is compatible with differing individual creeds and personal values. To paraphrase John Rawls (1996), such a moral standard will create an (ethical) "overlapping consensus," in which various comprehensive moral doctrines can coexist peacefully.

Even a rule as simple as the negative golden rule, if consistently applied, can have enormous social consequences, for it fosters tolerance and promotes the institutions of an open society, such as freedom, pluralism, and the rule of law. Take for instance our hypothetical friend from the beginning of this essay: perhaps, in his youth, he might still have become enthralled by Marxism. But before zealously allowing his good intentions to determine what's "good" and dictate what he could do to others, he might have wondered whether he would have welcomed the same thing done to himself. He might have thought: "Would *I* want others to tell me what to think or do? Would *I* allow them to dictate their will and to suppress my freedom, even assuming that the world might eventually benefit from my sacrifice?" On the answer to such questions may ride the fate of generations, for such piecemeal ethical engineering might have yielded, for instance, a political construction quite different from the Marxist–Leninist one.

Perhaps this criterion of ethics which all individuals in the open society can share in common, yet which puts no constraints on their ability to use their judgment, and, on the contrary, actually encourages them to exercise critical thinking, can be called a standard of "*open* ethics," without this idea representing a contradiction in terms.

REFERENCES

Berlin, Isaiah. 1969. *Four Essays on Liberty*. Oxford: Oxford University Press.

The Holy Bible. 1985. New King James Version, Gideons International, Edinburgh: Thomas Nelson, Inc.

Kant, Immanuel. 1994. *Ethical Philosophy*. Indianapolis: Hackett Publishing Company.

Miller, David. 1985. *Popper Selections*. Princeton: Princeton University Press.

Olson, Mancur. 1965. *The Logic of Collective Action*. Cambridge, Mass.: Harvard University Press.

Popper, Karl. 1966. *The Open Society and Its Enemies*, volumes 1 and 2. Princeton: Princeton University Press.

Rawls, John. 1996. *Political Liberalism*. New York: Columbia University Press.

Shearmur, Jeremy. 1996. *The Political Thought of Karl Popper*. London and New York: Routledge.

Stark, David. 1993. "The Great Transformation? Social Change in Eastern Europe," *Contemporary Sociology* 21 (3): 299–304.

Swidler, Leonard. 1994. "Towards a Universal Declaration of a Global Ethic," *Dialogue and Humanism* 4(4): 51–64. Center of Universalism, Warsaw University, Poland.

10

WHAT USE IS POPPER TO A PRACTICAL POLITICIAN?[1]

Bryan Magee

Some years acquire symbolic status, and one such year is 1968. All over Europe and the United States university students exploded into violent rebellion. Insofar as this would-be revolution had an ideology it was unquestionably Marx-inspired, even if the Marxism was not always orthodox. It so happens that in the years 1970–1971 I was teaching philosophy at Balliol College, Oxford. And because of Oxford University's system, almost unique, of individual tuition for undergraduates, this meant I found myself in a continuing one-to-one relationship with bright students who were in the throes of revolutionary fervor.

Arguing with them was enormously illuminating for me. It seemed as if the more intelligent they were the more passionately Marxist they were – but also the more affected they were by intellectually serious criticisms of Marxism, which usually they were hearing for the first time. It was when they found themselves unable to meet these that they revealed where their fundamental motivation lay. This was not usually a positive one of belief in Marxist ideas. Still less was it commitment to communist forms of society, which usually they had been defending without knowing anything about the reality of them. The motivation was usually negative: it was inability or refusal to come to terms with their own society as they saw it. Psychologically, this was nearly always at the root of their attitude.

Basically the chain of cause and effect between their ideas seemed to go something like this. They longed to live in a perfect society. But only too obviously the society in which they found themselves contained serious evils. So this form of society had to be rejected. A particularly interesting point here is the fact that, because what they demanded was perfection, they thought that if anything was seriously wrong then the whole must be rejected. If, say, newspapers reported cases of old and poor people dying of hypothermia in winter because they had no heating in their homes the students would say savagely "There's something sick about a society that lets old people freeze to

1 First published in A. O'Hear, *Karl Popper: Philosophy and Problems*, Royal Institute of Philosophy Supplements, 1996.

death in the winter." If there were reports of students unable to take up university places because of an inability to get grants they would say "There's something fundamentally rotten about a society that refuses to educate people unless they've got money." It was virtually a formulaic response, of the fixed form: "There's something fundamentally rotten about any society in which x happens," with x standing for any serious social evil. If anything at *all* was seriously wrong, the whole of society was sick: unless everything's perfect everything's rotten. Such an attitude could rest only on utopian assumptions. And it quite naturally made those who held it receptive to a holistic as well as systematic social critique of the only society they knew. It also led most of them to suppose, erroneously, that there must be something somewhere that was infinitely better: since, plainly, things were not perfect here, they must be perfect somewhere else – or, at least, people somewhere else must be trying. Criticisms of communist reality were nearly always met by the counter-accusation that things were just as bad here, if not worse, and at least the communists were striving to realize a moral ideal, which our cynical and self-interested politicians were not.

These attitudes display several errors of a fundamental character to which intelligent people in general are prone when they think about politics. Instead of starting from what actually exists, and trying to think how to improve it, they start from an ideal of the perfect society, a sort of blueprint in the mind, and then start thinking of how to change society to fit the blueprint. If they cannot see any practicable way of getting from reality to the blueprint they may be tempted then to think in terms of sweeping reality away, in order to start from scratch, in order to realize the blueprint.

Karl Popper's ideas are a marvellous antidote to such illusions. First of all he is insistent on its being an inescapable fact that wherever you want to go you have to start from where you are. Even the most cataclysmic revolution is an attempt to achieve certain ends, a way of trying to change society as it actually is into a different form of society that is preferred. And as the history of revolutions illustrates, existing society never is swept completely away: huge and important features of it always persist into the successor society, usually to the bafflement and chagrin of the revolutionaries. As a way of achieving desired social change revolution is exceedingly cost-ineffective as well as ineffectual. First and foremost, large numbers of people get killed, or are made to suffer appallingly in other ways. Second, desirable as well as undesirable social fabric is destroyed. Third, unrestrained violence on a large scale is uncontrollable when accompanied by a breakdown in the social order. Fourth, because it is uncontrollable the kind of society that emerges from it is nearly always one which the revolutionaries themselves say is quite different from what they wanted.

All forms of political thinking that start from blueprints of what is desired are anathema to Popper, and rightly so. All modern forms of society are in a state of perpetual change, and as time goes by the pace of this change gets faster, not slower. If we were to set ourselves the task of actualizing the most ideal blueprint, and then succeeded in actualizing it, even then change would not just suddenly stop. Marx and Engels thought it would – thought that with the realization of their perfect society history would come to an end. But nobody now believes this. Change will go on. So from the very moment we actualize our blueprint reality will start moving away from it and turning into something else. So the real political task is not to actualize an ideal state of affairs that can then be preserved for ever. This is the task to which the greatest political thinkers of the past, such as Plato and Marx, addressed themselves, but in reality it is not even an option. The real political task is to manage change.

As part of the process of perpetual change, people's aspirations and priorities perpetually change. So again, there too, even if we were able to start out with an ideal blueprint, and to succeed in our approach to it, as we worked toward it people's wishes would start moving away from it, so that even before we achieved it scarcely anybody would wholeheartedly want it. Something close to this has only too obviously happened in the late twentieth century with the ideal of socialism under its classic definition of public ownership and centralized planning of the means of production, distribution, and exchange – an ideal which earlier in the century powerfully motivated millions of intelligent and well-meaning people, yet to which now scarcely anyone subscribes.

There is a need for perpetual revision of aspirations and goals, and this is inimical to the whole idea of a blueprint. Blueprints are fixed, static: if they changed unceasingly they would not be blueprints. They are therefore at best a source of never-ending problems, given the reality of permanent social change, and only too often they are a source of tragedy. Because they are fixed, peoples' attitudes towards them become fixed: they become objects of quasi-religious commitment and belief. And because they are seen as ideally desirable, political opponents who actively try to prevent them from being realized come to be looked on as wicked people who must be stopped, perhaps even removed from the scene altogether; and their elimination is seen as fully justified, indeed demanded, morally. Blueprints thus lead to rigidity, fanaticism, and through them to anti-rationality in many forms. The man with a blueprint usually knows he is right; and because of his utter certitude he feels justified in eliminating opposition by whatever means may be found necessary.

Popper's recommendation is that what we should eliminate are blueprints – eliminate them from our thinking entirely. Instead of basing our approach on an imaginary state of affairs that does not actually exist and is never going to exist, he recommends that we start from the social reality in which we find ourselves, and that we examine it critically to discover what is wrong with it, and to see how it may be improved. From that starting point he proposes what might be called a methodology for the management of change. I would like to go through this proposed method step by step.

First of all we are required to formulate our problems with care. That means, among other things, not taking for granted what they are. We have to ask ourselves what precisely are, say, the main problems that face us in the field of primary education? What, precisely, are the main problems that face us with the treatment of teenage offenders against the law? What, precisely, are the main problems that face us in our relations with the United States? And so on and so forth.

There will, legitimately, be differences of opinion about what the problems are, before one has even begun to think in terms of solutions, and these differences should be thoroughly debated. It is of the utmost importance to get diagnosis right before one proceeds to cure, otherwise the proposed cure will be the wrong one, not effective, quite possibly harmful. So a lot of time and trouble and thought and work needs to go into the identification and formulation of problems before one attempts to move forward from that position.

Once a problem has been identified and clearly formulated, the next step is to consider alternative possible solutions. At this stage especially there can be opportunity for great boldness, and also for imagination and ingenuity, for freshness of perception and vision, for unexpected initiative. Usually it is here, if anywhere, that creative politics comes in.

But of course many if not most of the proposed solutions would not actually, if tried, work out very well in practice. As soon as you start to do something, anything, unexpected snags arise. Even in the most apparently sensible undertakings measures take longer than expected, or cost more, or prove to be administratively cumbersome, or alienate some of the individuals involved, or have unfortunate side-effects.

It is a matter of great practical concern that these drawbacks should be minimized by being foreseen and avoided. So proposed solutions need to be critically examined and debated, with the explicit object of bringing their faults to light before they are turned into reality. The more effective the criticism at this stage, the greater the saving in time, economic resources and human unhappiness, so a debate of this kind is not an abstract, airy-fairy matter, but a hard-headedly practical one. The proposals whose effective criticism is most desirable, because most fruitful, are those of government, because these are the ones that are put into practice on the largest scale, and with the most powerful backing, and with the greatest effect on people's lives. Full and free critical public discussion of proposed government policies is therefore essential if avoidable large-scale error is indeed to be avoided: without such discussion there will inevitably be more, and more costly, public-policy disasters than there need to be.

And of course there will be mistakes anyway. Even after a great deal of misplaced expectation has been eliminated by critical discussion, and the proposals thus critically improved are put into practice, things will still go wrong. Our actions have unforeseen consequences. So there is a need for practical as well as theoretical vigilance. After a policy has survived critical discussion and been put into practice, a critical eye needs to be kept on how it is actually working out, with a view to catching the first sign that is not working as hoped. At this stage the most important thing is not to be seeking reassurance that all is well, but the opposite, to be on the alert for the possibility that things are not going as they should. This requires the practical monitoring of public policy in action, and for that to be effective people need to be free to criticize not only a government's proposals but also its deeds. Again, the sooner harmful practices are identified the greater the saving will be in time, re-sources, and human unhappiness. Governments that forbid public debate and criticism of their activities are bound to persist in mistaken, costly and harmful practices for much longer than they otherwise would; and being government activities these mistakes will usually be on a large scale.

It should always be remembered that the debate surrounding policies and their implementation may bring to light errors not only in them but also in the process one stage further back, the formulation of problems: we may come belatedly to see that our initial formation of our problem was wrong. Indeed, Popper remarks that we seldom really understand a problem fully until we have tried to solve it and failed.

This, in its barest outline, is the methodology recommended by Popper to the practical politician. Some people may say it is embarrassingly obvious. I only wish it were. You do not need to be a very attentive reader of the serious press to realize that this is not how real-life politics is for the most part con-ducted. And as some one who was a professional politician for nearly ten years I can assure you that the thought processes involved do not come easily to many politicians; indeed, some have serious difficulty in understanding them even when they are explained. If Popper's principles seem obvious to a phi-losophy-oriented audience it is because they are so rational, so congruent with situational logic. That is a powerful recommendation for them, but alas, it has not yet brought about their general acceptance or even comprehension. The task of actively promoting them still requires adherents.

Other critics may object that the whole approach is too cautious and therefore too slow. We haven't got time for all that talk, they may say: it's a luxury we can't afford. To this I believe the best reply is that of all possible political methods this is the one most likely to maximize the extent to which change remains under rational control. Attempts to short-circuit processes of criticism are almost bound to lead to more error, and therefore more cost, and also more in the way of unintended consequences. There may indeed be more *change*, but disconcertingly much of it, too much, will not be in the required direction. This turned out to be one of the systematic short-comings of centralized planning, and led in practice to its becoming almost invariably associated with systematized lying. Of course one cannot go on talking for ever. Decisions have to be made. But a debate that is genuine discussion and not just waffle or delaying tactics, although it may take time now, will save more than time later on.

The approach advocated by Popper is a broad recipe for effective and successful problem-solving. As such it has a general application to most practical affairs, not only to politics but to administration in any form, and also to business. People familiar with his philosophy of science and his more general theory of knowledge will have noted already that it instantiates his formula for problem-solving in those fields:

$$P_1 \rightarrow TS \rightarrow EE \rightarrow P_2$$

where P_1 is the initial problem, TS the trial solution proposed to this problem, EE the process of error elimination applied to the trial solution, and P_2 the new situation thus arrived at, with its new and sometimes unexpected problems. In fact the relationship between Popper's methodology of politics and his theory of knowledge is so close that it is worth our going on now to look at some specific features that they have in common.

First, Popper regards himself in both fields as addressing not a static or stable state of affairs but a process of change, and he sees the main challenge as being how to manage change, in one case the growth of knowledge, in the other ongoing social development. In both cases he sees the demands this makes on us as consisting above all else of problem-solving. In both cases, therefore, he thinks we should start from the careful analysis and understanding of problems, and not leap straight away to what is in fact the second stage, the proposal of trial solutions.

In politics solutions, real or attempted, are normally called policies. Every reputable political or social policy is a proposed solution to a problem; and we always need to be clear about the problem before we can propose the solution. We must always be able to ask of a policy: "To what problem is this the solution?" If there is no problem to which a given policy is a solution then the policy is superfluous, and therefore harmful, if only because it consumes resources to no purpose. Policies which are not solutions to any identifiable problem are part of the common currency of so-called practical affairs. Committees are especially good at producing them. I have stopped many a committee meeting dead in its tracks by asking the question: "To what problem is this the solution?" The whole notion that you can start with policies is deeply erroneous, and very damaging in practice. One of the forms it takes is starting from a blueprint, because of course a blueprint is a proposed solution; but it takes many other and more mundane forms. It is essential to start from *problems*, and to arrive at the formulation of each policy only as a solution to a problem.

According to Popper, in both politics and the growth of knowledge, criticism is the most effective agent of desirable change, and must therefore be not only free but welcomed, and acted upon. We can never be in a position to know that we have got things right; our formulations and policies are always open to improvement; therefore any notions of certainty or unquestionable authority are not only out of place but damaging. The best we can *do*, like the

151

best of our knowledge, is the best only for the time being, and in the prevailing circumstances. It is always, in principle, improvable, and therefore should always be subject to critical discussion.

In practice this attitude ought to breed a respect for political opponents, and a willingness to learn from them. In all the democracies I know, politicians lag behind the public on this matter. They would be more, not less, popular with their electorates if they were more willing than they are to admit error, and they would also be more, not less, popular if they were more willing than they are to admit that their opponents are quite often right.

The Popper approach constitutes a programme for practical and rational improvement, and the usual word for that in politics is "reform": so it is a methodology of reform. But it leaves open the question of how quick or slow reform should be, the even more important question of how radical it should be, and the most important question of all, namely what it should consist of. This makes it an approach that can be adopted by anyone on the political spectrum between those who want no change at all and those who want revolution. What this means in practice is that it can be adopted by anyone committed to democratic politics: so it is also what you might call a methodology for democracy. It so happens that the youngish Karl Popper who wrote *The Open Society and Its Enemies* in the late 1930s and early 1940s had always been left of centre, and throughout the whole of his adult life up to that point a strongly emotionally committed social democrat. But like so many people he moved to the right in middle age, and by the time of his death would have been accounted a conservative by most people – though to the end of his days he continued to regard himself as a liberal in the classic sense of the word, meaning someone who puts individual liberty first among the political values. My point is that his basic approach is one that can be adopted by anyone committed to democratic politics, from the extreme democratic left to the extreme democratic right, which indeed was the gamut that Popper himself passed through.

Having said that, though, the point has to be made that the Popperian approach sits most comfortably with a left-of-centre position, the sort of position Popper himself occupied when he produced it. This is because it gives rise naturally to a radical attitude toward institutions. It is not only policies that have to be seen as attempts to solve problems: institutions do too. A country's education system is its solution to the problem of how to educate its young; its armed forces are its solution to the problem of how to defend itself; its health services are its solution to the problem of what public provision to make for those of its citizens who need medical help; and so on and so forth. Just as in the case of policies, an institution that is not a solution to any problem is superfluous – indeed, it is that condition that renders institutions obsolete. And because an institution is a practical solution to a problem, so long as it has a real function it is capable of being more effective or less, more satisfactory or less, more comprehensive or less, more expensive or less, more popular or less, and so on. The Popperian approach involves subjecting institutions to a permanently critical evaluation in order to monitor how well they are solving the problems they exist to solve – and involves moreover a permanent willingness to change them in the light of changing requirements. I have always taken the famous dictum of Jesus of Nazareth "The Sabbath was made for man, and not man for the Sabbath" to mean that we should bend institutions to fit human beings, not human beings to fit institutions; but this is at odds, I do believe, with some of the basic attitudes common to political conservatism, which include a reverence for institutions as such, a deep-seated unwillingness to change them, and a readiness rather to let their requirements override personal considerations. There is no logical incompatibility, but there is, I think, a certain psychological uncomfortableness in combining a Popperian approach to the requirements of institutional change with a typically conservative emotional attachment to existing institutions. The only kind of conservative with whom the two can sit comfortably together are those of the radical right, politicians like Margaret Thatcher, whose approach to traditional institutions was in fact highly disruptive.

The permanent monitoring of institutions to see if they are *not* performing as required, and the permanent monitoring of the implementation of policies to see if they are having undesirable consequences, are activities – and reflect a cast of mind – that come much more readily to radicals, of left and right, than they do to traditional conservatives. They also run counter to the way people working in institutions, especially those with authority, tend normally to behave. The normal tendency is to cover up organizational and administrative failures as much as possible, and to resist facing even to oneself the fact that one's activities are not having the desired effects. The Popperian approach, which requires one actively to seek out failures and shortcomings and do something about them, calls for a degree of intellectual honesty from politicians and administrators, as it does from scientists, that does not come to them at all easily, and constitutes a disconcerting personal challenge. What provides the incentive to meet this challenge is the higher success rate that results from doing so.

In fact a thoroughgoingly problem-solving approach has many practical advantages, perhaps even more in politics than in science. It is far easier to get agreement on problems than on solutions, and a government that starts from the problem – let us say, to take a small but emotive example, the problem of what to do about the number of homeless people sleeping rough on the streets of London – and then shows itself open to alternative possible solutions will probably have not only a higher degree of practical success than one that starts with the answer, in other words a policy; it will also enjoy more support and goodwill, even from those who disagree with what it eventually does. In a democracy a great deal of electoral advantage is to be had from a problem-solving approach, because people will feel that they have been brought in.

153

And of course, if I may be forgiven for stating the obvious, a problem-solving approach directs one's attention to problems, and makes doing something about them the first priority. It protects one from being seduced into trying to build Utopia; and yet it does not easily allow one to relapse into complacency or inactivity. One's energies are channelled not into constructing ideal models but into removing avoidable evils. Popper encapsulates the first rule of thumb he recommends for public policy in the words "Minimize avoidable suffering." Psychologically it is a different approach from that of crusading for ideals, to which so many political activists are dedicated: it is more practical, and nearly always more fruitful. In any case the two are not necessarily incompatible. I am not opposed to idealists as such, but I do regard them with the gravest of suspicion. It is a fact that social evils have been perpetrated by idealists in our century on a simply stupendous scale that includes the deliberate murder of tens of millions of men and women and the herding of tens of millions more into forced labor camps (I am thinking not only of the Soviet Union but also of China, where the numbers involved may have been greater). These things could not possibly have been done by people who had adopted "Minimize avoidable suffering" as their guiding principle. But they were done by idealists, and condoned all over the world by other idealists, more often than not with a sense of moral self-righteousness accompanied by savage denunciations of anyone who criticized what they were defending.

A point Popper makes which I stress more than he does is the unavoidability of unintended consequences. I stress them because they often dominate practical politics – as they soon came to do in all communist societies, for example. An awareness of them also immunizes us against enthusiasm for any form of centralization, especially centralized planning. To anyone engaged in practical affairs, business as well as politics, they are of never-ceasing importance. Only on someone divorced from reality can they fail to impinge.

Political lessons to be learnt from Popper are not confined to the problem-solving approach and its method. He has certain large-scale perceptions about politics that seem to me right and important although unfashionable. For instance, he perceives clearly that the societies in which we in the West are living in the 1990s are by all real (as against ideal) standards – that is to say by all the standards of past experience – exceptionally non-violent, as is the international scene as a whole. He also sees that for the great majority of men and women in the democratic West life is better now than it has ever been before, not only materially but in the most important non-material ways, for example health, education, and cultural opportunity. He therefore sees clearly that the cultural pessimism so fashionable today, when intellectuals and artists are saying on all sides that we live in a uniquely terrible and violent time, presents more or less the opposite of the truth. I suspect that the illusion it represents has been brought about partially by the collapse of the historicist, progressivist illusions that were held earlier in the century by a great many of the same people, and to which Popper was equally opposed. On the face of it, it is peculiar that so many individuals who for decades believed with a kind of religious intensity that everything was getting better are now equally certain that everything is getting worse. But both attitudes are holistic and uncritical, and meet what seem to me primarily religious emotional needs. The fact is that the liberal democracies of the West are the only large societies in the whole of human history in which the great majority of the people have enjoyed not only material prosperity and literacy but also what have come to be known as fundamental human rights. This is a very recent historical phenomenon, and it is a wonderful thing. Even so, there is no contradiction at all between seeing this clearly for what it is and at the same time trying to improve these societies, and for that purpose adopting a radical and essentially critical stance in their political and social affairs. It happens to be the position I myself have always occupied, independently of Popper, and it is what first drew me to his work, before I knew anything about his epistemology or his philosophy of science.

Another overall perception of Popper's which I share is that equality of outcomes is not a desirable social goal. It took me a long time to learn this lesson, and when I did it was not from Popper but from my poor constituents in East London. They were almost entirely without social envy, which I came through them to realize is a largely middle-class phenomenon anyway. They wanted a better deal for themselves – better wages, better houses, better schools for their children, and so on – but had no desire to pull down anyone who was better off. On the contrary, they actively rejected any such attitude; it ran counter to some of their most heartfelt aspirations, more often for their children than for themselves. And they saw it as incompatible with elementary personal freedom. They were right in this. And it was also Popper's view. He once said that if a form of socialism could have been discovered which was compatible with personal freedom he would still be a socialist.

Another general attitude of Popper's that I loudly applaud is his hostility to the tyranny of fashion in all its forms – the idea that we have to do certain things, or do things in certain ways, because these are the 1990s, and that we really have no choice, in that anything else is contrary to the spirit of the times, and therefore inappropriate, perhaps even inauthentic. This error is at its most predominant and destructive in the world of the arts, but it operates in politics too. In Britain after the Second World War we had years of uncritical commitment to Keynesian economic management followed by uncritical commitment to monetarism; we had an uncritical belief in nationalization followed by an uncritical belief in privatization. Town planners guided by what they took to be the spirit of the times devastated the centers of many of Britain's most beautiful towns during the 1960s and 1970s, and corralled the poor of the inner cities into tower blocks. Anyone who opposed these developments at the time was denounced as conservative or reactionary, fuddy-duddy, out of date. Popper has always believed in either fighting or ignoring such tides of opinion. He sees them as forms of what another kind of philosopher would call "false consciousness," and as ways of evading responsibility for our own decisions and our own actions. Insofar as we go along with them we are enemies of our own freedom. We can do *whatever* we can do, and it is up to us to do the best we can.

One of Popper's specific proposals that I think has great merit is that it should be accepted internationally as a fundamental principle that no existing frontier is to be changed except by peaceful negotiation. The point here is that nearly all the national frontiers in the world were established by force, usually either imposed on the vanquished by the victors in war or imposed on colonized peoples by imperialist powers; therefore if the fact that a frontier has been imposed without the consent of one of the parties is to be accepted as an excuse for that party to use violence to get it changed there would be justified wars breaking out all over the world all the time, several on each continent. This cannot be acceptable to the international community now. Existing frontiers, constituting as they do actually existing political reality, must be regarded by the United Nations as operative no matter how they were arrived at, and must be guaranteed by whatever international peace-keeping forces there are, unless a majority of those whose frontiers they are is wish to change them by peaceful means.

Up to this point I have been endorsing Popper's approach and commending it to you. And the truth is I do believe it provides working politicians with rules of thumb of the utmost usefulness. But it does have, inevitably, limitations and shortcomings. The chief limitation is that, being a methodology, it is almost entirely about method and not about content. The most pressing question facing the individuals who have to take important decisions is nearly always "What should we do now?" Everyone else can stand back from that question and then criticize the way things are done but the decision-makers themselves cannot. Only rarely does the Popperian approach help them toward an answer. This fact has recently come to the fore in the former communist countries of Eastern Europe and the Soviet Union. To an extent rare in history they have found themselves with opportunities to build a new society that is radically different from the one they had before. Popper's philosophy offers them first-rate guidance about how to do things, but very little about what to do. What kind of local government, if any, do they want: at what level, how constituted, and with what powers? What kind of education system do they want, what sort of schools, how organized, by whom, teaching what? How much welfare state do they want, and in what areas – and how much can they actually afford: how is it to be administered, how funded? It is questions like these that constitute most of the content of large-scale practical politics.

In any case, most politics is not large-scale. When I became a Member of Parliament and began spending my days in the House of Commons among hundreds of other MPs, I was struck by the fact that, among themselves, they scarcely ever discussed the sort of political or social questions thrashed out in pubs and debating societies, like are we in favor of the return of the death penalty, or censorship, or nationalization. The questions that held them in thrall were much more like: "If we raise the widow's pension by half a percentage point where are we going to find those extra millions of pounds?" They would have differing views about such questions, and would argue heatedly, but these mostly were the sorts of questions they would be arguing about. And it is inevitable that these are the sorts of questions that day-to-day government has to concern itself with. It is seldom that Popper's work offers much guidance with them.

This in itself is not a criticism of Popper, because he is not talking to us on that level. From a philosopher a politician must expect strategic, not pragmatic, guidance. What I am drawing attention to is not a shortcoming but a limitation. It is, however, one that practical politicians are likely to be a lot more conscious of than other people.

Practical politicians are only for a very small part of the time concerned with putting principles into practice. Most of the time they are struggling to make the best they can of difficult, messy and uncontrollable situations. I will give you an example of this that involves a conflict between me and Popper personally. I have already mentioned his conviction that the international community should impose an iron refusal to allow existing frontiers to be changed by force, and have given his reasons for it. Well, when the military junta then governing Argentina invaded the Falkland Islands, for which Britain was responsible in international law, and *de facto* war began, he telephoned me at the House of Commons in great passion, wanting me to urge the British government to declare war formally on Argentina. I refused. What I said to him went roughly as follows. "I agree that the Argentinians absolutely must be made to leave, by negotiation if possible but by force if necessary. And I will vote for the use of force if there is no other way. But I want to get them out with the minimum possible harm to everyone concerned, and I see this as a damage limitation exercise. There happens to be a sizeable British community living permanently in Argentina that consists of tens of thousands of families, many of whom have been there since the nineteenth century. They have their own schools and other institutions, as well as their own homes, businesses, and professional practices. If we declare war on Argentina, the Argentinian government may well intern them and confiscate their assets. Their whole world will be destroyed, and in many cases their individual lives will be ruined. I believe we can get the Argentinians out of the Falkland Islands without that happening – though only if we don't declare war."

Popper, always willing to sacrifice himself to a principle, was willing to sacrifice others too, and would not agree with me. Not only did he continue to telephone me angrily throughout the Falklands war, always urging the same course of action on me; he continued to bring the subject up with me for the rest of his life, always maintaining that he had been right. I am convinced to this day he was wrong – and not only because what I wanted to happen did in fact happen. I fully acknowledge that it might not have done. But I am convinced that we were right to try. I re-emphasize that I was always completely in agreement with Popper that in no circumstances should Argentina be allowed to get away with the forcible annexation of the Falkland Islands. He and I differed only about how they were to be made to leave. But on this we differed profoundly. It was not the principle that was in dispute but the way it should be put into practice. Popper wanted commitment to the principle to be publicly proclaimed in a formal act: I saw this as unnecessary to the actual implementation of the principle and almost bound to be seriously damaging. So I saw my own approach as essentially practical and his as essentially theoretical – but far too theoretical, culpably so, too little concerned with the actual lives of individual men, women, and children. And I have to say, as an intellectual and academic myself, that I see this fault as all-pervading in the attitudes of intellectuals and academics to political and social matters, and as being an extremely serious, often debilitating fault. Also, having been a professional politician as well, I find the sense of personal superiority to politicians so commonly expressed by intellectuals and academics unfounded and misplaced, self-deluding.

This story of a clash between a political philosopher and a professional politician illustrates a point of profoundest importance. I do not believe that there are many people who hold Popper and his work in higher regard than I do; and I knew him well personally. As a professional politician I made conscious use of his methodology, and found it of extraordinary practical usefulness and fruitfulness. Yet any individual who, if only by his vote in an assembly, has to take responsibility for executive political decisions, is likely to find himself unable to put Popper's principles – or anybody else's principles, for that matter – into practice in a way that the originator of the principles would wholly approve of. This is because practice has unavoidable and compelling exigencies which theory can never encompass, and which those who are solely theoreticians seem only rarely to appreciate – and never fully to understand. But that would be a subject for a different paper.

11

THE POLISH CHURCH AS AN ENEMY OF THE OPEN SOCIETY

Some reflections on post-communist social-political transformations in Central Europe

Andrzej Flis

In *The Open Society and Its Enemies*, first published half a century ago, Karl Popper distinguished two kinds of economic-political systems: closed societies and open societies. The former have a semi-organic nature and place submission to authority among the highest values; the latter are abstract and impersonal entities that, by their very nature, "set free the critical powers of man" (Popper 1984, vol. 1: 1). Closed societies are permeated by the tenet of the primacy of the collective over the individual. Open societies, on the contrary, are marked by a belief in human initiative and the affirmation of individualism. Closed societies deny the interest of the "human individual as individual" while acknowledging only his interest as a "tribal hero." Open societies grant their members the right to personal decisions and free choice as long as they do not violate the freedom of others (ibid.: 190).

In the foreword to the Polish edition of this book, written just after the collapse of the Soviet Union, Karl Popper stressed that he had introduced the term "open society" as a synonym for the "not very fortuitous term 'democracy'" (Popper 1993, vol. 1: 1). The essence of democracy, he stated, is political freedom and its opposite is despotism, a system as old as civilization. "Under despotic governments," the author wrote, "we are terrified and have no right to responsibility for our own deeds. This means that we are stripped of our humanity. Moral responsibility is, after all, part of our humanity" (ibid.: 1).

For nearly half a century, Poles were stripped of part of their humanity by the totalitarian communist system that drew its ideological legitimation from Marxist doctrine. Before the malignant spread of the communist system over Central Europe, this doctrine had already become the object of Sir Karl Popper's passionate criticism. "The expectation that Marxism would become a major problem," Popper noted in 1950, "was the reason for treating it at some length" (Popper 1984, vol. 1: 1).

The Poles stubbornly resisted the communist authorities for nearly half a century, laboriously widening their margin of freedom. The dates 1956 (the loss of power by the Stalinist faction in the communist party as a result of workers' demonstrations in Poznań), 1968 (student protests), 1970 (a general strike on the Baltic coast), 1976 (strikes in Ursus and Radom), 1980 (the rise of "Solidarity") and, finally, 1989 (the definitive overthrow of the communist system) mark successive stages in the struggle of civil society against the totalitarian state. This struggle had already begun during the Second World War, prior to the establishment of the communist system, with the heroic, two-month-long Warsaw Uprising, doomed to defeat even before its initiation on 1 August 1944, because of the cynical attitude of the Western Allies.

Like other institutions and social groups, the Catholic Church was suppressed by the Polish United Workers' Party throughout the period of communist dictatorship and came out on the side of the political opposition, demanding the introduction of a democratic system in Poland. To the amazement of most observers, conditions for such a development arose in 1989 when the first postwar non-communist government was formed as a result of the Round Table agreement. The head of this government was Tadeusz Mazowiecki, a Catholic journalist and one of Lech Wałęsa's advisors. It is therefore hardly strange that many Poles then expected the Church hierarchy to support the "Solidarity" government in its efforts to transform Poland into a democratic state and to lend its authority to the difficult task of shaping new political patterns different from those that made up the sad legacy of several decades of totalitarianism. However, things turned out otherwise. Poland was launched down the road leading back to an ideological state. The bishops decided to fill the post-Marxist doctrinal vacuum with Catholic fundamentalism. They undertook the task of transforming Poland once again into a closed society – this time, a theocratic one. In its claims to be the leading force of the nation, the Polish Episcopate appeals to "democratic" arguments, to the supposed will of the majority, a will that, in view of the hierarchical and monarchical organization of the Church, somehow cannot be made manifest within its own structure.

Leaving aside its original, etymological meaning of "rule by God," theocracy can be understood in two ways. First, as political domination by the clergy and the abolition of the difference between religious and secular authority (as in pre-communist Tibet or today's Iran). Second, as a political system in which the division between the two orders is preserved, but in which the clergy demands that the state compel individuals to observe religious norms (as in medieval Europe). In this second instance, sin is not only a violation of the divine commandments, but also a misdemeanor punishable by the secular administration – and the clergy, the repository of supernatural law, sits in judgment of that administration. In this second instance the clergy becomes something of the order of a *super-authority* or, to put it another way, an authority over the authorities, since only the clergy *knows* what is good and what is evil, and the clergy alone, thanks to the competence it enjoys, has the *right* to assess whether man-made law agrees with supernatural law and to evaluate the observance of that law by all actors in public life, including the state administration.

Beginning in August 1990 with the introduction of religious instruction in public schools – despite current law[1] and an initially negative stand by the Mazowiecki government – the Catholic Church has followed a scenario for the transformation of Poland into a closed society. Further steps in this process have been the addition of new impediments to divorce, the anti-abortion legislation, and the campaign of hysteria that preceded its passage, the December 1992 Radio and Television law that made respect for "Christian values" obligatory for both public and private broadcasters, rules forcing soldiers to take part in "field masses" and other religious observances,[2] the attempt to force the *Sejm* to ratify a Concordat that is unfavorable to the state, the pressure on the Constitutional Commission of the National Assembly to clericalize the Constitution,[3] and finally the increasingly aggressive attacks on the policy of integration in the European Community.

There are many reasons behind the Church's success to date in its efforts to transform Poland into a closed society. They can be categorized fundamentally as negative and positive. The negative reasons are above all carryovers from the communist regime, which will continue for some time to be a burden on the fate of Poland: the lack of a democratic political culture, the weakness of the state apparatus, and a poorly functioning party system that, with a few exceptions, is made up of small political groupings engaged in ceaseless factional conflict. Among the positive factors, the institutional might of the Church is paramount. Thus, in a situation where approximately thirty parties are fighting for parliamentary seats, the well-developed Church hierarchy naturally becomes the most powerful actor in political life. Furthermore, the Catholic Church is the only centralized organization in Poland, resting on the principle of unquestioning obedience and furnished with abundant material resources, that has branches in every corner of the country and whose highest authorities

1 The *Instruction* of the Minister of National Education, dated 3 August 1990, on the introduction of religious instruction to kindergartens and public schools was unconstitutional and in conflict with three legal statutes.

2 In the *Soldier's Prayerbook* (1994), Brigadier General Kazimierz Tomaszewski, second in command of the Warsaw Military Region, instructs his subordinates: "It would be inadmissible to set any such precedent as exclusion from an honor company for reasons touching differences of religion ... Refusal to follow the standard is a refusal to carry out an order ... Participation in the Ceremonial Roll Call at a Field Mass is a duty, and if you are an unbeliever or a member of another faith, you may refrain from active participation in prayers. Only carry out the commands that are given to you without any public display of the fact that you are dissatisfied" (*Gazeta Wyborcza*, 31 December 1994–1 January 1995).

3 The issues here are above all, although not exclusively, the introduction of an invocation of God in the *Preamble* of the future Constitution, the abolition of the principle of the separation of Church and State, and the acknowledgment of Christian values as the foundation of public life.

enjoy complete freedom from social oversight. It is this *institutional* power of the Church that makes it the dominant force in political life and gives it the strength to close Polish society against the will of most of its members. In such a situation of many small parties, few politicians are able to resist the demands of a Catholic hierarchy that itself lies beyond the scope of public opinion and can therefore systematically carry out the actions that it has planned in advance, needing only to adjust them on the tactical level to the changing balance of forces in parliament.

We are witnessing a paradoxical reversal of roles in the Poland of the nineties. "Now," as Wojciech Lamentowicz notes, "we have to protect democratic values not so much from a powerful, authoritarian state, but from a powerful, authoritarian Church. The Church, which before had been the defender of the people, has become the new obstacle to self-expression" (cited in Hockenos 1993: 247). This is happening because the Catholic hierarchy has undertaken the effort to transform Poland into a confessional state and, by exerting constant pressure on the state authorities, is trying to raise religious norms to the status of laws that must be followed by all the citizens of the state regardless of their convictions.

Several years ago, this fundamental policy by the Polish Church compelled Adam Michnik to formulate a warning against the impending "Iranization" of the country. That term does not reflect the essence of the problem. Iran is a theocracy in the direct sense of the word, while Poland is threatened by indirect theocracy, in which the authorities are secular in the formal sense but subservient to the religious hierarchy. In Iran, the clergy openly exercises authority in the state, both legislative and executive, and bears the political consequences. Things are different in Poland. The leaders of the Church exert influence on political life from behind the scenes without holding any public office. Thus, from the formal point of view, it is not the Church hierarchy that promulgates such unpopular laws as the ban on abortions or tax exemptions for the clergy, but the politicians who in the final analysis must answer for their decisions before the electorate. This is *authority without responsibility*, a situation that is fundamentally demoralizing and which constitutes a great threat to the future of Polish democracy.

The *division* of authority from responsibility is accompanied by the progressive extension of ideology throughout the state. The Polish state is thus gradually ceasing to be a territorial organization representing the general interests of its citizens, and slowly being transformed into "the secular arm of the Church," into an institution that represents the mass of believers and leads them toward future salvation with the help of criminal sanctions. The logical consequence of this type of system is the subjugation of all spheres of public life to moral control by the government, over which the Church stands as supreme arbiter and highest court.

The progressive extension of ideology throughout the state, as enjoined for several years by the Church hierarchy and extremist Catholic movements, can be seen not only in the efforts to make "Christian values" a supreme constitutional principle, but also in the insistent attempts to transform the specific – by its very nature – language of religious fundamentalism into the objective means of public communication and a generalized conceptual system serving to describe the world. Thus, demands for the separation of Church and State are called "relegating religion to the catacombs" and the idea of treating Catholics and non-Catholics equally is called "persecution of believers." Opponents of the omnipotent clergy become "enemies of God," tolerance is "the acceptance of evil," and abortion "the killing of children."

When the current *Sejm* began working on the liberalization of the anti-abortion law that had been forced through the previous parliament under concerted Church pressure, the suffragan of Łowicz, Bishop Józef Zawitkowski, addressed the parliamentary delegates during a sermon that was broadcast on national radio, in the following words:

> If there have been too few crematoria, concentration camps and crimes against my nation for you, then sign this new act of mass murder! Just don't use the same hand to sign the Concordat with the Holy See. Take your example from the other capitals where the sins of Sodom and Gomorrah are legal. Then you'll be progressive. They'll welcome you to Europe with applause. But God will burn this city![4]

The words of the suffragan of Łowicz were not an isolated outburst by a high member of the Church hierarchy. The language of Bishop Zawitkowski has been heard throughout the country for several years, as the accepted means by which the Catholic clergy communicates with the outside world: Polish society and its democratic, secular authorities. "In Poland," said Father Czesław Bartnik at a diaconate conference in December 1991,

> against the background of the City of God we are beginning to see … the *regnum diaboli, civitas diaboli*, a society in service to the anti-Christ, making for itself the theme of history with its blasphemous liturgy and its black notoriety for sin, crime and what is anti-human. The *civitas diaboli* likes to hide itself under the screen of the *civitas saecularis* – the innocent secular society. Its ideal is the secular in opposition to God. Its light is the darkness of sin.[5]

This Catholic newspeak hardly differs in essence from the communist newspeak disseminated by the media during the *ancien régime*. Its goals are, first, to neutralize its political opponents at the initial stage of stating their own interests,

---

4 *Gazeta Wyborcza*, 9–10 July 1994.
5 *Gazeta Wyborcza*, 14–15 November 1992.

and second, to lend moral legitimacy to the physical and administrative compulsion used against those opponents when they try to act. This Catholic newspeak is a language of aggression and hatred directed against non-Catholics who demand equal rights and oppose discrimination. As sketched by Bishop Zawitkowski and Father Bartnik, the collective portrait of the non-Catholic is not a picture of a partner in dialogue or even of an opponent, for an opponent deserves some respect. It is the portrait of an enemy. An enemy has nefarious intentions and his arguments are false by their very nature. He says one thing (demanding an "innocent secular society") and does another (fights against God). He cunningly conceals his true aim (wallowing in sin) and the sources of his strength (a pact with Satan). There is no discussion with an enemy. He must be unmasked, driven out of society and destroyed. Otherwise, the enemy will destroy the Fatherland and all God's people.

The desire to transform the state into the secular arm of the Church, so very characteristic of the Catholic hierarchy in Poland after communism, is hardly anything new. On the contrary, this type of Church–State relations has a long history that reaches back to the medieval period and functioned as a *de facto* constitutional model until the French Revolution, and as a *de jure* model until the mid 1960s, when it was abandoned as a doctrine by the Second Vatican Council. The present efforts by the clergy and religious fundamentalists to impose a confessional state on the Poles, however, appeal to a different ideology from what was used in the past. This is no longer the *theological* legitimation forged in the medieval period, according to which all power derives from God and the bishops, his representatives on earth, enjoy the right to supervise the secular authorities. Rather, this is a *quasi-democratic* legitimation: the Church hierarchy represents Catholics; 95 per cent of Poles are Catholics; therefore the clergy is the natural leadership of all true Poles – ergo, an attack on the Church is an attack on the nation.

The bishops have resorted time and again to this secular, *quasi*-democratic argumentation in their political campaign to transform Poland into a confessional state. For instance, demanding that the *Sejm* introduce religiously inspired censorship of radio and television in 1992, they posed the following rhetorical question:

> Whom do the delegates to parliament represent if, in a country with a decided Christian majority, they reject a proposal to adhere to the Christian system of values in the mass media? ... Can the highest state authorities remain passive and indifferent when the religious feelings of the citizens are insulted? Do some secular circles, unfriendly to Christian culture, have the right to eradicate and ridicule Christian values and the values of Polish national culture?[6]

6 *Komunikat 289. Konferencji Plenarnej Episkopatu Polski.*

It is worth noting in these remarks the linking of Christian values with national values, referring implicitly to the stereotype of the *Catholic* Pole that has been propagated indefatigably by the disciplined ranks of the clergy and the religious fundamentalists. This linking is intended to suggest that everything that is good for the Church is *ex definitio* good for the state, and everything that harms the Church also harms Poland. This simple rhetorical figure inevitably recalls the ideological formula served up to Poles by the former communist regime: whatever is good for the party is good for the nation, and whatever harms the party weakens the nation. Both these constitutional constructions have in common features Popper identified with a closed society: they put the interests of the collective above the interests of the individual, they do not result from mature reflection and critical thinking, nor do they tolerate criticism or substantive discussion, and, finally, they replace the force of argument with the argument of force.

Appealing to the supposed will of the majority as a means to legitimize theocratic claims borders on the ironic in the case of the Polish Church, which has no scruples about scorning democratic institutions, including the institutions of direct democracy, when they come into conflict with "Christian values." This can be seen particularly clearly in the case of the statement by the bishops in May 1992, when the Episcopate not only opposed a national referendum on the admissibility of abortion, but went on to suggest that such referenda could lead in the future to "other unworthy deeds," including concentration camps.[7] The bishops' anti-democratic stance finds ideological backing in the teachings of the present Pope, especially in his encyclical *Evangelium Vitae*, which is an attack on the basic rules of the democratic system – especially on the authority of parliament and the majority. *Evangelium Vitae* rejects *expressis verbis* the principle that Thomas Jefferson called "the idea of a republic" – *lex maioris partis*, and it calls the supporters of abortion, contraception, and euthanasia (who include the European Parliament) the representatives of "the civilization of death."

In its claims to be the leading force of the nation, the Polish Episcopate appeals to "democratic" arguments, to the supposed will of the majority, a will that, in view of the hierarchical and monarchical organization of the Church, somehow cannot be made manifest within its own structure. What is more, the very criterion of the Christian majority is essentially undemocratic. The 95 percent of the Poles about whom the clergy and the religious fundamentalists so eagerly speak are not Catholics or Christians, but merely the people

---

7 This equilibristic leap of logic utilized the following reasoning: "Voting for the legalization of the destruction of human life not only violates human law, but also offends the whole natural order. The possible admission of such voting could in consequence lead to other unworthy deeds, such as euthanasia or depriving ill people of life as lacking social usefulness. The most radical form of the questioning of the right to life according to the foregoing criteria was, as we know, the concentration camp." See *Odezwa biskupów polskich w sprawie referendum na temat życia nie narodzonych, z 2 maja 1991 roku*.

who have been *baptized* – incorporated in the community of the faithful *de jure*, as infants, decades ago, without their own knowledge or consent.

If being a Catholic is defined by use of the criteria of church law, then it turns out that Catholics are a *minority* in Poland. Thus, according to data published by the Main Statistical Office and the Catholic Mission Society, less than 42 percent of Poles define themselves as "regularly practicing."[8] The significance of this figure is enhanced by the fact that a *majority* of Poles hold views at odds with the official position of the Church on such important questions of conduct as the ban on contraception (68 percent), the ban on abortion (56 percent) or the ban on premarital sex (53 percent).[9]

The most damaging factor for the "democratic" legitimation of the clergy's theocratic claims, however, is the widespread approval of a state that is neutral on questions of conscience, as declared by 75 percent of Poles, and the even stronger disapproval of the Church's engagement in politics (81 percent).[10] These data show clearly that the overwhelming majority of Poles regard the Church solely as a *religious* institution and do not see it as their political representative. Furthermore, Catholics, or at least a significant number of them, fear the Church as a political force. "In the interviews that I have conducted," says Hanna Świda-Ziemba, "many responses contained an element of fear: the Church can take away our jobs, can harass us, can make the life of the most average family miserable."[11]

Fear of the Church as a political institution explains why, in a country that is 95 percent Catholic *de jure*, the parties of the left that derive from the communist political system won an overwhelming victory in the last parliamentary elections in September 1993 and captured the presidency in November 1995. This fear also demonstrates the falsity of the *quasi*-democratic legitimation to which the Church so readily appeals in its efforts to build a confessional state. "Poland is perhaps the only country in the world," writes Paweł Smoleński, "where it seems to us that we live in accord with God, and at the same time there is no agreement with his earthly servants. Therefore everyone ... who takes a firm stand in the discourse with the Church automatically scores points."[12]

In the last parliamentary and presidential elections the winners were the heirs of those political forces that created a closed society of the communist type after the war. This happened, in large part, because the post-communists, previously opposed by a grass-roots social movement, now appeared as the main opponents of the campaign to transform Poland back into a closed society – this time, of the clerical-Catholic type. In short, the former commu-

---

8 *Kościół katolicki w Polsce 1918–1990*, Warszawa, 1991, p. 166.
9 The percentage of Poles supporting these prohibitions is, respectively, 17 percent, 29 percent, and 26 percent. The data were collected from a nationwide sample by the Center for Public Opinion Research in November 1992. See *Polityka*, 5 December 1992.
10 Ibid.
11 *Gazeta Wyborcza*, 28–29 October, 1995.
12 Ibid.

nists seem today to be more credible democrats than the Catholic right, despite the unquestioned merits of the latter in overthrowing the communist system in 1989.

The fact that the right did not manage to win even a single seat in the last parliamentary elections, despite the unequivocal support of the Church, signals the lack of consent by the preponderant majority of society for the continuation of the program of Christianizing Poland by legal-administrative means. This tendency has not changed as shown by Lech Wałęsa's defeat in the presidential elections at the hands of the post-communist, Aleksander Kwaśniewski.

On 19 November, the day of the parliamentary elections, Cardinal Józef Glemp, the Primate of Poland, expressed his opinion that the country was choosing not so much between two candidates as between two systems of values: Christian and neo-pagan.[13] "If Kwaśniewski is elected," the secretary of the Episcopate, Bishop Tadeusz Pieronek, had stated several days earlier, "this would mean a defeat for the mission of the Church."[14] The bishops of the Kielce diocese prayed, "Lord, do not permit Poland to be led into the next century by a president who does not acknowledge the Cross, even when our churches are full."[15] Despite the hysterical Catholic propaganda and the dramatic appeals from the clergy, that is exactly what happened. The Catholic Church suffered another painful political defeat.

Poles oppose not only the transformation of religion into a state ideology, but also, and this is immensely significant, making it the basis of morality.[16] This much is acknowledged by a representative of the clergy, the sociologist and priest Władysław Piwowarski. "The great majority of Catholics," he writes, "are characterized by what is known as selective religiousness, which is an ongoing tendency."[17] His diagnosis bodes nothing good for the Church's political intentions, which in the future – as at present – will have to be realized on the basis of democratic institutions. These institutions, no matter how vulnerable they may be to overt or behind-the-scenes pressure from the Church hierarchy, cannot in the long run ignore the mass preferences of society. This fact was clearly demonstrated in the most recent parliamentary and presidential elections.

The chances for the Church's political expansion are therefore undercut by the very nature of Polish religiousness: it is ritualistic, ceremonial, folk-spectacular; in the sphere of the experience of faith it is declarative and superficial, if not downright empty! Religion, as Father Piwowarski states, is not a

---

13 *Gazeta Wyborcza*, 20 November 1995.
14 *Tygodnik Powszechny*, 15 November 1995.
15 *Rzeczpospolita*, 10–12 November 1995.
16 According to surveys carried out by the Center for Public Opinion Research in the summer of 1995, only one-third of the respondents accept the view that religion should become the basis for moral renewal in Poland after communism. See *Rzeczpospolita*, 19 September 1995.
17 *Polityka*, 11 May 1991.

personal value in Poland. "The proof of this is the fact that only a small percentage of Catholics (approximately 15 percent) deepen their faith either through the institutional Church ... or through religious communities."[18] In such a situation, it is hardly surprising that religious fundamentalism enjoys no significant social support in Poland and that only 9 percent of the population accepts the engagement of the Church hierarchy in political life.[19]

Nor is this all. The chances for the political expansion of the Church are also being weakened by the general social transformations of recent years. Thus, with the fall of communism, the need for the Church's protective-integrating role disappeared in Poland. After decades of subjugation, society recovered its freedom, becoming pluralistic as it gained a voice in its own affairs and became able to pursue the realization of its own needs in an unfettered way. Together with the fall of the communist system, the Polish Church ceased to be a surrogate for a sovereign state and became one of many organizations making up the overall institutional system. To these changes is added the ongoing process, which began as long ago as the 1960s, of the disintegration of the canons of national culture based on aristocratic, Romantic and Catholic patterns and the tendency to replace them with a pluralistic culture containing pronounced cosmopolitan and hedonistic elements. This process has wiped away the bases of the traditional Polish identity, shattered the authority of the Church hierarchy – as both a religious and a national institution – and transformed the worldview and aspirations of ever-wider social groups, especially the young, city dwellers, people with secondary and higher education, and the more affluent strata. In short, the extensive systemic transformation has gradually caused the Polish Church to lose the support of the most important social groups, the very groups that in large measure will determine the future of the country. In this context, a comparison with Spain is unavoidable – a state in which, more than half a century ago, the Catholic hierarchy undertook the task of creating a new, closed society on the ruins of the Republic, as noted by Karl Popper in *The Open Society*.

The victory of General Franco in the Civil War in 1939 opened amazing possibilities to the Spanish clergy. Excluded from public life by the anticlerical, democratic governments of the Republic, it secured a dominant position in all spheres of public activity in the fascist state. The Catholic religion was elevated to the rank of state ideology and the status of a central ingredient of Francoism. This marriage of Catholicism and fascism was reflected institutionally. Church dignitaries sat as full members in the highest organs of the state: in the government, the *Cortes*, the Regency Council. In Franco's Spain, the Catholic hierarchy quickly established its full control of schooling, the press, publishing, the cinema, and, in practical terms, all other institutions of

18 Ibid.
19 Data from the Center for Public Opinion Research, November 1992. See *Polityka*, 5 December 1992.

public life. Nevertheless, despite enormous determination and commitment of resources, the attempt at creating a perfectly Catholic society in total obedience to divine and church law ended finally in utter defeat. Today's Spain, after all, is one of the most secularized countries in Europe.

Utilizing its impressive organizational potential and the power of the structures of the Francoist state, the Church managed to establish and maintain for several decades a tight control over the bodies and minds of the Spaniards. And yet the moral-religious evolution of the Spanish people followed a completely different direction than what was intended. The socio-economic transformation that took on a particular dynamism in the 1960s crushed the foundations of the post-Republican order. It was superseded by an industrial, urbanized society becoming more and more closely integrated into Western Europe. To this process were added the disintegration of the traditional canons of national culture and the dissemination of a consumer lifestyle. All these changes have led to the present marginalization of religion and the Catholic Church in Spain.

The criticism of Spain voiced by Pope John Paul II in 1991, when he accused the country's inhabitants, and especially the young, of rejecting the faith of their ancestors and submitting to the slavery of consumerism, materialism, and hedonism, echoed around the Catholic world. The successor of the present Bishop of Rome will have ample reasons to level similar words at Poland in twenty years' time.

REFERENCES

Hockenos, Paul. 1993. *Free to Hate*. New York: Routledge.

Popper, Karl R. 1984. *The Open Society and Its Enemies*. London: Routledge.

——— 1993. *Otwarke społeczeństwo i jego wrogowie*. Warsaw: PWN.

12

LIFE AFTER LIBERALISM

Adam J. Chmielewski

Polish readers of *After Virtue* in 1995 will doubtless be apt to reject this account of Western modernity as American or British readers were in 1981. But they have of course very much the same interest as those earlier readers in deciding whether its central theses are true or false. For Polish culture too was formed in part by a range of influences from the French, German, and Scottish Enlightenments – I think of philosophers as various as Stroynowski, Staszic and Kołłątaj – and by a variety of Polish reactions to them. But, more than this, in that openness to the prevailing Western modes of thought and practice that has followed the collapse of the Soviet empire, there is evidence of a willingness to embrace just those positions of which *After Virtue* is most severley critical. If *After Virtue*'s diagnosis of contemporary modernity is to some significant degree correct, then what it asserts must hold too, to some extent at least, of Polish modernity.

(MacIntyre 1995)

In 1989 we all became liberals. And history had ended. Or so it seemed then. Now, however, after a handful of years has passed since the transformation began, it is more and more apparent that not all of us feel like that anymore. But then there were precious few exceptions to this rule and in these I shall not be much interested here. I am more interested in a liberal state of mind that possessed the intellectuals in the former communist countries when the constraints of the totalitarian regimes were shattered and freedom took the long awaited rein into its invisible, yet – let us be frank – ruthless hand. In what follows I shall refer briefly and in a somewhat random way to the theoretical forefathers of this attitude.

It is interesting to reflect questioningly upon the justifiability of the wholesale conversion to liberalism that took place amongst intellectuals in Central Europe. At least one reason for questioning it should be obvious to any critical thinker: the sheer number of the conversions is bound to make one suspicious about their honesty. Another reason to assume a somewhat reserved attitude toward this social, quasi-religious phenomenon, is that some of the new believers – neophytes is the word – were until quite recently, in their majority, supportive – sometimes with equal, if not excessive, zeal – of a wholly different socio-philosophical outlook and, as it then appeared reasonable (and quite often profitable too), claimed to be capable of proving the poverty of liberal social arrangements. Despite its professed and apparent rationality, the conversions bore an evident religious character. The new opium of intellectuals took a form not dissimilar to the Enlightenment's rational religion. It made one feel as if the only way of being for a rational man was to be a liberal, as if there were some historical necessity in adopting the theory of liberalism and employing it in practice.[1] These features of the suddenly reborn liberalism justify the above usage of the expression "liberal state of mind" since it has the advantage of referring to the emotional rather than reasoned state of a person. Indeed, the initially enthusiastic liberal movement was very strong in that its dogmas were being fervently accepted. At the same time it was, however – as is the case with most enthusiasms – rather vague in content. In what follows I shall first point out a certain vagueness in the doctrine and practice of liberalism, then I shall refer to its more precise theses which, as I shall argue, are philosophically unsound.

An interesting way to consider the rationality of the multiple intellectual conversions, and some accompanying phenomena, is to see them in the context of claims of the notorious *Four Essays on Liberty* by Sir Isaiah Berlin, recently published in Polish. This book is widely known for its formulation of the concepts of negative and positive liberty and is being treated by some of the new Polish liberals, and not only them, as one of the volumes of the "holy scripture" of the final and unquestionable liberal truth.

Isaiah Berlin is an historian of ideas, a distinguished master of this discipline. This fact cannot easily be separated from his treatment of liberalism and its enemies, so I shall begin by recounting briefly general views of history that can be read off from Berlin's writings. Under the influence of the eminent Oxford historian and philosopher, Robin G. Collingwood, Isaiah Berlin came to think that a study of a historical period, or a person from the past, is always guided by a set of historically determined principles and assumptions regarding the very process of research and its subject, adopted prior to the conduct of the study. Explanation and analysis of the basic concepts and categories that introduce an order into human experience must thus have an historical dimension.

The great change in European thinking began, according to Berlin, in the first half of the seventeenth century. Giambattista Vico and Montesquieu

---

1 Whoever would not willingly come to the newly reassembled flock of true believers could thus rightly be considered irrational, a deviant, not so much reasoned with as treated. There are two kinds of deviations in need of a therapy, a very repugnant one, professed by "post-communists" (considered for propaganda reasons as virtually indistinguishable from old-time communists), and another one, also – though perhaps less – repugnant, adopted by the right-wing thinkers.

published their works then; later still, thinkers like Herder and Hamman became famous. Berlin considers this period in the history of Europe to be an historical era during which took place the inception of a new trend in European thought that marked an end of the domination of the universalist philosophical ambitions – traditional European monism. Radical pluralism appeared on stage, and along with it were born – or revived in a new form – many other numerous and powerful doctrines: irrationalism, voluntarism, relativism, nationalism, populism, Romanticism, later still fascism, and existentialism. Amongst the newly conceived ideas there was also the idea of liberalism. All these – not infrequently contradictory – doctrines, ideas, and concepts were the offspring of the Enlightenment.

In *Four Essays* Berlin takes as his target a number of fundamental issues of social philosophy, most prominent of them being various forms of historical determinism, according to which all human actions are determined by external factors and according to which, as a result, man cannot be considered the proper agent, possessed of autonomous, individual intentions or projects which he or she embodies in his or her action, and that he or she cannot properly be held responsible for their deeds.

Another basic question debated by Berlin is the concept of "negative" freedom, as distinct from the "positive" freedom. Contrary to universally held opinion, Berlin does not argue exclusively for negative and against positive freedom. He demonstrates some appreciation of positive freedom too, a measure of which he thinks to be a precondition enabling negative freedom to function at all. However, Berlin makes it all too plain that these two forms of freedom are not identical and need to be kept conceptually apart.

Negative freedom can be measured by the number of avenues of conduct that are open to individual human beings, capable of autonomously deciding their own lot in everyday dealings as well as in a long-term perspective. They do so by means of acts of free will, exercised fully by them only when not interfered with. Interference of some sort can be counted as a limitation of human freedom in the negative sense. Thus negative freedom is a freedom *from* something. As Quentin Skinner, remarking on Berlin's *Two Concepts of Liberty*, put it:

> Liberty itself is to be understood … essentially as non-interference, as absence of constraint upon the pursuit of our chosen ends so far as this is compatible with the peaceful enjoyment of a like freedom by all … Our aim must rather be to secure a cordon of rights around us, and to insist that the demands of social life should be minimized, and that our rulers must never trespass beyond these boundaries.
>
> (Skinner n.d.: 2–3)

Despite his reserved appreciation of positive freedom, Berlin devoted a considerable amount of space in his book to showing that a definition of freedom as a freedom *to* something, freedom to exercise some rights, or freedom to benefit from privileges, is as a rule prone to lead to conditions foreign to any conception of freedom whatsoever.

The late Sir Karl Popper, in one of his books, has expressed the conviction that the world of the Western liberal democracies is perhaps not the best of all possible worlds, yet it is certainly the best of all *existing* worlds (1963: 369).[2] He believed in the values of the Western social world, which he took to be an epitome of the open society he defended, to the extent that in his great book *The Open Society and Its Enemies*, he even claimed that "tribalist exlusiveness and self-sufficiency could be superseded only by some form of imperialism." Perhaps he was right, but he also significantly claimed that one cannot sacrifice any generation for the sake of the uncertain and indefinite happiness of future generations. This was, as we all know, continually and deceptively done by communists who always insisted on temporary sacrifices that were to pay off very soon, or just a bit later, and, as a result, we had continuously to tighten our belts, for the benefit of future generations.

Liberals in Central European countries, who, against communists, often employed Popper's argument about the immorality of present sacrifices for future uncertain benefits, did not make the same mistake; instead, they argued for immediate satisfaction of long-frustrated needs. Indeed, if the doctrine of liberalism has any essence at all, one of its elements must be the postulate for ever-increasing consumption, satisfaction of ever-increasing needs and the ceaseless creation of new ones. In so doing, however, the liberals were paying heed much more to the satisfaction of their own private needs than to those of the general public. This was also in agreement with the liberal doctrine – at least as it was interpreted – since again, as Popper among others said, all attempts toward establishing universal happiness have inevitably ended in establishing hell on earth. Another consequence of this conviction was that people were to pursue their own happiness the way they saw fit and were capable of, using the newly regained freedom according to their own abilities. No one was to tell them what they were to do with freedom. But also no one was obliged to help anyone else anymore. Those who were so stained by the corruptions of communism as to be incapable of benefiting from their newly obtained freedom, should – as one of the leading Polish liberals said – be ashamed of their poverty.

Such pronouncements and such a practice are in striking contrast with sobriety and even-handedness of judgment displayed in his writings by Sir Isaiah.[3] Berlin's prose promotes an attitude which makes it more difficult to think that there always is one, final answer to human dilemmas in their daunting variety;

---

2 Sir Karl repeated these words in a conversation with me, six weeks before his death.

3 One wonders, could this be another expression of the perennial discrepancy between theory and practice?

that a man, if he wishes to preserve his freedom, must be capable of living according to precious few principles and rules, prohibitions, and enjoinments, and that these skimpy rules are usually all we have at our disposal when coping with contingencies, grave and minor problems of everyday life.

Following this train of thought one is inclined to ask whether we are not sometimes forced to accept fluctuations and changes even of these very few guidelines and principles that are left intact by rational scrutiny and the tests of practice. Are we not sometimes forced to disregard them when the principles are, in turn, upset by the contingencies of reality, or are too simple to provide guidelines in the face of the intricacies of always impredictable social practice? Are we not sometimes bound to live our lives according to no principles whatever?

If this is so, does it not apply to the principles of liberalism itself? One can point to an all too obvious fact: that even the attractive principles of liberalism, known in and through the practice of the Western liberal democracies – those of criticism, rationalism, freedom of speech, freedom of assembly, democratic vote – when conjoined with lack of sympathy, sensibility, imagination regarding other people, with dogmatic temper or lack of manners, personal dishonesty or egotism, excessive zeal or apathy, are sometimes prone to turn into monstrous and frightening contradiction of themselves, all the more dangerous since veiled in tempting and seductive rhetoric. Not infrequently liberal politicians are tempted to use their own rhetoric to cover their ineptitude, their misbehavior or indecision, or their doubts, or qualms, if they still have any. These problems, appearances to the contrary, not only belong to the political practice of liberalism, but also create a very urgent, yet still unsatisfied, demand for theoretical ways of solving them.

A major difficulty which some people see as preventing them from acquiescing in liberalism lies in the fact that liberal theorists often treat the practical life of existing societies as interesting only to the extent to which it conforms with their principles. Where it does not, it is usually disregarded or is reinterpreted into conformity with them by way of a radical conceptual change, or is forced into conformity with them in practice. The liberals of Central and Eastern Europe have done this continuously for the past couple of years. Without much success, though.

Social and political practice leaves one uncertain as to what exactly the doctrine of liberalism is. The problem is usually dealt with in an ostensive way by saying that liberalism is what Western countries (not all of them, however) do in their economic and political practice. Disregarding for present purposes the problem of whether it is possible to transfer and deploy in a relatively short period of time their experience into the post-communist countries, one may with a great justification ask the question whether the practice of the liberal Western democracies is at all capable of giving us an unequivocal answer to the question of how to reorganize our social life. To be a Western liberal is to be a libertarian as far as the economy is concerned, conservative regarding property, and an opportunist in the sphere of morals. The few short years of freedom have already brought about tendencies that bear exactly these features; perhaps one should treat them as a sign of proceeding maturation of our young democracy in Poland. This of course may be taken as a favorable phenomenon, yet it is apparent that such policies do not seem to be as effective as hoped for by their proponents, and more importantly, by the population affected.

Berlin seems to be aware of some of the dangers of an uncritical liberal attitude since he writes: "Those who endure the defects of one system tend to forget the shortcomings of the other … [I]n resisting great present evils, it is as well not to be blinded to the possible danger of the total triumph of any one principle. It seems to me that no sober observer of the twentieth century can avoid qualms in this matter." One can justifiably say that it is exactly those snares in which Polish liberals found themselves entangled. Having won the historical battle against the totalitarian regime – somewhat by default, and partly thanks to a wholly unliberal populist movement – they thought that this victory is an evident sign of their infallibility. It is well deserved, and – most importantly – they do not need to do anything else to continue to stay at the helm of the ship of state, since, according to the theory, from now on, only the social and economic laws were to rule society by their invisible hand, and only these autonomous laws were capable of shaping it into the desirable, rational, and final form.

Liberals, it seems, have committed this mistake by instinctively adopting the stance expressed not so long ago by Professor Francis Fukuyama who, in the wake of the fall of the communist evil empire, pronounced the End of History. Indeed, it seemed as if History, wandering and hesitating aimlessly all too long, having tried out all the items in the inventory of possible political systems, has finally asserted that only the liberals were right. It is thus quite understandable that in the opinion of liberals there was not much else to do; the ascent to power was taken by them as a well-deserved gratification, not as a demanding service, hard work, a duty, a strenuous effort toward radical reform of the whole society, but as a long delayed pay-off.

It is not insignificant to remind ourselves in this context of Karl Popper's convincingly formulated, though not necessarily sound, arguments against the idea of social engineering. As is well known, he vehemently argued against holistic social engineering and his arguments were widely accepted by the rank-and-file of the opposition movements in Poland. Holistic social engineering was thought to be a feature peculiar to the Marxist revolutionary holistic social philosophy. As a result, virtually none of the opposition groups worked out their own comprehensive, original plans for a new Poland since, in a very peculiar sense, *there was no need for that*. The needed blueprint of new political arrangements was unquestionably taken to be already formulated in the theory of liberalism and embodied in its practice; and one of its elements seemed to be an explicit prohibition of any holistic projects of social reform.

More than that, reform was to take place, as it were, by itself, provided that the rational forces of human activity were given their proper outlet and were free to operate. Rationalism of human arrangements cannot be a product of rational human effort, being too complicated to be grasped by limited and fallible human minds.[4] Moreover, liberals obviously could not possibly have adopted the very practical attitude for which they criticized their historical rivals, the communists. Thus Popper's argument against holistic planning was in fact understood as a form of a prohibition of a well-thought out comprehensive, overall reform.[5]

It is not surprising, then, that it took only two years for liberals to lose all the popular support they had, and to vitiate their activities by a bitter internal power struggle, all in the disgraceful air of corruption. Ironically, popular support was given instead to post-communist parties, historical successors to political parties which denied the nation its freedoms for five decades. Liberals were taken by surprise by this result and subsequently, by acting deeply offended, revealed that they did not learn anything from their mistake, and found themselves very close to political extinction – which seems quite imminent, at least in Poland.

Thus, in order to establish what liberalism really is, one should perhaps do better by disregarding ideological statements of Popper's and Berlin's, and looking to the voluminous theoretical formulations of the doctrine. But also

4 As Edmund Burke said in his *Reflections on the Revolution in France* (1910/1964: 84), "Politics ought to be adjusted, not to human reasonings, but to human nature, of which the reason is but a part, and by no means the greatest part." And also: "We are afraid to put men to live and trade each on his own stock of reason; because we suspect that this stock in each man is small, and that the individuals would do better to avail themselves of the general bank and capital of natures and ages." The similarity of the Popperian attitude to Burke's is a basis for frequent assertions about Popper's conservatism.

5 It is wholly understandable in this context that Professor Leszek Balcerowicz, a former Communist Party member and subsequently chief Polish liberal reformist, confessed in a conversation with President Yeltsin in 1992, that they, Polish liberal reformers, including himself, were too optimistic in assuming that as soon as the fiscal mechanisms of reform were in operation, the managerial staff and the employees of the state-owned plants and factories would accommodate to the new economic circumstances *by themselves* (!). From the perspective of the past few years it seems quite astonishing how it was possible for any discerning person to come to the conclusion that the huge, "manually-operated" socialist economy, inefficient by its design, would suddenly revolutionize its own nature and become a lively and efficient capitalist organism. This telling example is, among many things, a proof that false consciousness, caused by adulation of any theory whatever, is equally blinding and dangerous to communists and liberals alike. The immediate result was, as far as Poland is concerned, over three million people out of work and a 40 percent fall in material production output. Now, everyone more or less agrees that unemployment was inevitable, but it is at least arguable that it could have been quite possible to keep it somewhat, or – depending on perspective – considerably, lower. None of the liberals, including Balcerowicz himself, would listen to such suggestions or criticism. Infallibility is far more common than one might otherwise have thought.

in this respect one's task resembles the hunting of the snark, a beast which is characterized by the fact that it exists only in the imaginary, not the real, world. Liberal politicians differ immensely from each other, yet – however difficult it is to imagine – liberal theorists differ between themselves even more. It leaves us in doubt as to what are the necessary and sufficient conditions of being a liberal and the issues, after many decades of debate, still seem far from being settled. If it is an exaggeration to say that liberal theorists themselves are not quite sure what it takes to be a liberal, the exaggeration is only a slight one.

Out of Berlin's four essays on liberty, the most interesting is the *fifth*, i.e. the extended "Introduction" documenting a small proportion of the critical debates stirred by the appearance of the *Essays* in 1969. In this "Introduction" Berlin tries to answer a variety of charges against his concept of determinism and the distinction between positive and negative freedom. His answers do not seem – particularly from the point of view of standards of Oxford philosophy of language – to be satisfactory or convincing. Irrespective of their philosophical soundness, irrelevant in this context, they reveal an even more important feature: they reveal these "unquestionable values" whose acceptance seems a condition not only of being a liberal, but also of being human:

> Could it be the case that if the evidence of the facts should go against us, we should have to revise our ideas, or withdraw them altogether, or at best concede that they – these propositions if they are propositions – hold only for particular societies, or particular times and places, as some relativists claim? Or is their authority shown by philosophical analysis which convinces us that indifference to freedom is not compatible with being human, or, at least, fully human – whether by human beings we mean the average members of our own culture, or men in general everywhere, at all times? To this it is sufficient to say that those who have ever valued liberty for its own sake believed that to be free to choose, and not to be chosen for, is an inalienable ingredient in what makes human beings human; and that this underlies both the positive demand to have a voice in the laws and practices of the society in which one lives, and to be accorded an area, artificially carved out, if need be, in which one is one's own master, a 'negative' area in which a man is not obliged to account for his activities to any man so far as this is compatible with the existence of organized society.
>
> (Berlin 1969: lix–lx)

There always is a big problem with any undisputed and inalienable claims since different people, equally valuing their own freedoms, usually take very different values as undisputed and inalienable, disputing and denying at the same time to others their values and rights. Indeed, it seems as though if you search long enough, you will find a hedgehog in every fox. Some say that all human beings, despite all their differences and disagreements, have something in common. Others say they do not. Who is right? Who is able to answer such a question? And, most interestingly, is the philosophical doctrine of liberalism capable of solving this problem?

The dispute is concentrated around the issue of the human self and its nature. Berlin's most fundamental conviction is that a man is an autonomous, individual human being, capable of an irreducibly free choice. It seems, however, that Berlin cannot defend such a claim without supporting it by an additional claim of a transcendental source of the human being's humanity – a claim which is otherwise criticized by him. If Berlin rejects the Kantian idea of an absolutized autonomous individual and his freedom of will, along with the claims of historical and social relativism, as he does, he faces a difficulty in answering a very interesting philosophical question: *where do the autonomous individuals come from?*

The finality of the assertion of the existence of autonomous human individuals not only does not solve any interesting questions but, more importantly, prevents one from asking them. It is exactly the greatest weakness of Berlin's liberalism, and not only his, that he does not address the issue of the social, cultural, historical process of the constitution of the human self. It seems that liberalism, by ascribing the fundamental and final status to its own claims concerning the human self, is forced to turn a blind eye to a vast philosophical domain and imposes too severe a constraint on its own scope. This results in depriving liberal claims about the human self and its freedom of much of their interest. Liberal doctrine, just because it sees human individuals as "irreducible" and as non-constituted, as final constituents or atoms of the society, prevents itself from considering the questions of utmost philosophical importance – the issue of the constitution of human self and the sources of its freedom.

The "I" for a liberal seems to be just a peg on which to hang anything an individual wishes to. The liberal self has no history, has no sources, has no origin. This enforced transcendentalism, adopted out of fear of relativism, makes liberal theoreticians turn their back on the problem of the social construction of the human self, and eventually leads them to some kind of voluntarism and emotivism. As Professor MacIntyre observed:

> From the standpoint of individualism I am what I myself choose to be. I can always, if I wish to, put in question what are taken to be the merely contingent social features of my existence. I may biologically be my father's son; but I cannot be held responsible for what he did unless I choose implicitly or explicitly to assume such responsibility. I may legally be a citizen of a certain country; but I cannot be held responsible for what my country does or has done unless I choose implicitly or explicitly to assume such responsibility.
>
> (MacIntyre 1984: 220)

The most interesting question is however how an individual acquires his or her ability to wish, to act, to choose, to consider, in the first place. We are left in the darkness, by Berlin as by any other liberal writer, regarding this issue. We can understand better this important and not at all accidental omission by remembering the main features of the communitarian concept of the human self, so different from the one adopted by liberal writers. In order at least to glimpse the vast problematic we can quote from MacIntyre again:

> I am born with the past; and to try to cut myself off from that past, in the individualist mode, is to deform my present relationships ... What I am, therefore, is in key part what I inherit, a specific past that is present to some degree in my present, I find myself part of a history and that is generally to say, whether I like it or not, whether I recognize it or not, one of the bearers of a tradition.
>
> (Ibid.: 220)

All these and related considerations must be alien to a liberally minded philosopher which regrettably deprives his theoretical efforts of much interest, and is equally true of Berlin's as well as of Rawls's and Nozick's – or Richard Rorty's – liberal utopias.

Another, though in many ways connected, problem with Berlin's argument is that his distinction between negative and positive freedom seems to be delineated too sharply, which prevents him from realizing that the negativity and positivity of freedom consist in one, unitary, inseparable and dialectical social and historical process of acting and being acted upon by a variety of factors on various levels of social interaction. The crudest version of the doctrine of determinism claims that in nature as a whole everything can act upon the man, but for some reason in this perspective man and man only remains an element condemned to inactivity, whose movements are caused by forces external to him. The error of determinism thus understood is evident and consists in treating the human being as an unjustifiably distinguished creature. Even though Berlin seems to be aware of the possibility of such an error, he often expresses himself as if he understood determinism in such a crude way.

Despite all these reservations, Berlin's work is one of the most honest documents of the liberal reflection in the twentieth century. This stage of liberal thought seems to belong already, however, to the past, since liberal theory has been formulated and reformulated in a variety of new ways, particularly by Rawls, Nozick, Walzer, Dworkin, and others. Berlin's work can be treated as a course one has to attend in order to understand the present, and pass on to the next stages of history. Unfortunately, it is not seen like that by new liberals in Poland who are unwilling to accept any criticism of Berlin's, Popper's, or anyone else's, for that matter, formulations of liberalism.

All of us have struggled for the best of existing worlds, as promised by Popper. We have been told that we shall enter the promised land by striving for the negative, not positive, freedom, which meant for us freedom from restraints imposed hitherto on speech, movement, and association. The immediate result, however, was not what we expected: great privileges have become available to few only, while at the same time the vast majority of people were freed from their daily bread, jobs, hope, dignity, and experienced helplessness. Yet the liberals have not been waiting too long with an explanation for this result and hastened to supply a justification of this state of affairs by pointing to the fact that a liberal economy and politics are compatible with equality of opportunities, but not with equality of achievements. On the other hand, their own achievements turned out to be quite baffling to some of the leaders of reform. As Vaclav Havel wrote:

> The return of freedom to a place that became morally unhinged has produced something that it clearly had to produce, and therefore something we might have expected. But it has turned out to be far more serious than anyone could have predicted: an enormous and blindingly visible explosion of every imaginable vice. A wide range of questionable or at least ambivalent human tendencies, quietly encouraged over the years and, at the same time, quietly pressed to serve the daily operation of the totalitarian regime, has suddenly been liberated, as it were, from its straitjacket and given a free reign at last. The authoritarian regime imposed a certain order – if that is the right expression for it – on those vices (and in doing so 'legitimized' them in a sense). This order has now been broken down, but a new order, that would limit rather than exploit these vices, an order based on a freely accepted responsibility to and for the whole of society, has not yet been built, nor could have been, for such an order takes years to develop and cultivate. And thus we are witnesses to a bizarre state of affairs: society has freed itself, but in some ways behaves worse than when it was in chains.
>
> (Quoted in Himmelfarb 1993: 549–50)

Having freed themselves from the duty of creating a design for the new society, and absolved themselves from the necessity of hard work, the leading liberal reformists predictably formulate a theoretical attitude which is to justify their lack of leadership.

There thus cannot be any element of surprise in the fact that the promoters of liberal change have lost their credit so soon and were, paradoxically, ousted from their public offices, at least in Poland, with an air of disgrace. Another reason possibly accounting for their failure was that they ascended to power too quickly, and were not prepared, nor able, to rule rationally on their own, because they did not think such preparation to be necessary.

Thus our practical experiment with liberalism has been, so far, a bitter lesson in realism. We have to draw all the lessons from this we can, if only to learn that there are no ready-made recipes for happiness. Perhaps awareness of the fact that all recipes are fallible, even those coming from the best of all existing worlds, will motivate us to take a more creative attitude toward our societies and ourselves, will make us realize that we should trust our own judgment instead of waiting for ready-made advice. After all, only we know best what is in our own interest and what is not, do we not?

Liberals, as is well known, like to give advice. One of them, John Gray, told Poles that they should have been following (my own formulation), instead of more or less pure Popperianism, an ideology of "Berlinized Popperianism".[6] Perhaps he was right. But in his latest interview given to a Polish journalist,[7] Isaiah Berlin, commenting on this advice, said: "I cannot tell Poles – take some from me, and some from Popper. I do not think there is any need for you to read Popper or me. One has to follow one's normal moral instinct. I do not believe that the experience of communism has abolished in people the awareness of what is right and wrong. This knowledge survived … "

It seems, then, that the question, is there any life after liberalism? – particularly an intellectual one – should be answered, contrary to dogmatic liberals, in the affirmative. In this life there is, among others, an important place for everything liberals fight for. But not only for this, since man does not live on freedom alone.

REFERENCES

Berlin, Isiah. 1969. *Four Essays on Liberty*. Oxford: Oxford University Press.
Burke, Edmund. 1910/1964. *Reflections on the Revolution in France*. London: Everyman.
Himmelfarb, Gertrude. 1993. "Liberty: one very simple principle?" *The American Scholar*. Autumn: 549–50.
MacIntyre, Alasdair. 1984. *After Virtue*. Notre Dame: University Press of Notre Dame.
—— 1995. "To the Polish readers of *After Virtue*." Preface to the Polish edition of *After Virtue*, June 1995. Warsaw: PWN.
Popper, Karl R. 1963. *Conjectures and Refutations. The Growth of Scientific Knowledge*. London: Routledge & Kegan Paul.
Skinner, Quentin. n.d. "Two rival traditions of liberty and citizenship." Unpublished essay.

6 "Koniec ery liberalizmu" ("*The End of the Liberal Era?*"), Znak, Kraków, 1992/5.
7 "*Nil desperandum*", *Odra* 1994/6, p. 14.

13

THE NOTION OF THE MODERN NATION-STATE: POPPER AND NATIONALISM

Joseph Agassi

A brief historical background

The literature on the history of nationalism is unsatisfactory. It repeatedly exudes a profound sense of frustration. The frustration is due to the fact that the matter is highly controversial, yet the arguments in it are rather obvious; hence, it is not depth but subtlety that is needed here. Much that is said in this context is uncontested; it is unclear what is contested. In such cases the introduction of some historical background information usually suffices to clear the air; not so in the study of nationalism: studies of its origins repeatedly involve confusions of different items that come jointly. Nationalism is a theory about the nation, and an attitude toward it. The attitude includes at least a sense of national identity. This sense is close to patriotism, yet the two differ, since the one is a modern phenomenon and the other is ubiquitous. Patriotism is a kind of altruism, one that individuals choose to develop within the bounds of their societies, be these tribes or nations (in the old or the modern sense of the word). Nationalism, however, is group egoism.

Can patriotism be a form of nationalism? This is contested. The crux of the matter is international conflict. Being group egoism, nationalism is itself a source of conflict, since every international conflict of interest invites nationalists but possibly not patriots to defend their side. It is conflict that raises the question in the first place. Hence, those who overlook it are out of the debate even when they claim to support both nationalism and, say, socialism. (See Agassi 1984.) The advocacy of international conflict was the rule in the early modern nationalist ideology, including that of Johann Gottlieb Fichte (Russell 1934: 356–61) and Georg Wilhelm Friedrich Hegel (Popper, 1957b: 37, 58, 65, 68–9). They are followed by cohorts of social philosophers up to and including Martin Heidegger (Popper 1957b: 77–8). Their teaching is inflammatory; it consists of demagoguery and promises of a great destiny designated for their own nation, making it superior to all others. This is a secular version of the doctrine of the Chosen People. It has added to international conflicts, especially to World War I and the enthusiasm for it (see Russell 1934: 24). This kind of nationalism is often termed "chauvinism"; it will not be discussed here.

The characterization of modern societies as nation-states is generally taken for granted. So is the praise for patriotism. Some oppose all nationalism, viewing it as chauvinism, and thus contrary to the siblinghood of humanity. Mikhail Bakunin, for example, stated this satisfactorily (Maximoff 1953: 324). It is hard to see how peace-loving thinkers can disagree with him on this. Indeed, many writers have expressed opinions very similar to his; conspicuous among them are Karl Marx (see Russell 1934: ch. 20), Bertrand Russell (1946: 580, 696) and Karl Popper (1957a: 288; 1957b: 50, 51, 381). Yet anti-democrat Prince Metternich took democracy to be nationalist (Kissinger 1964: 209) and liberal Ernest Gellner took early nationalism to be liberal (1983).

Is anti-chauvinist nationalism consistent? Usually it is not. But can there be a consistent anti-chauvinist nationalism? What has prompted the use of the label "chauvinism" for evil nationalism is the hope that nationalism can be benign. Can nationalism be benign? Can it discard the doctrine of the Chosen People? What is "benign nationalism" good for? These are the questions of this essay.

Demagoguery aside, chauvinism is a doctrine of the national destiny. It may be replaced with a doctrine of destiny that is hopefully in harmony with the siblinghood of humanity. Karl Marx replaced the national destiny with that of the working class. On the other hand, the doctrine may be rejected in all versions. Karl Popper showed that it is inherently wicked. His critique of a national destiny is couched in his critique of the more general theory behind it, that of a general plan of history, the doctrine of historical inevitability that he called "historicism." Historicism, he said, cannot harmonize with any liberal political philosophy (Popper 1957b: 275).

Can nationalism survive the rejection of historicism? Will we then have a liberal version of nationalism? Will it be of any political use?

The leading liberal Herbert Samuel said "yes," He said (Samuel 1937: ch. 13) against the doctrine of destiny that it invites prophesies that are used as inflammatory materials. Prophesies, he added, especially inflammatory ones, tend to be self-fulfilling (ibid.: 176). Yet he supported nationalism, as he saw in variety a good for its own sake (ibid.: 181). He recognized the selfishness of nations, but he added that egoism should not be abolished: it should be balanced with altruism: nations as individuals have duties both to themselves and to others (ibid.: 182). Is this a version of liberal nationalism or is it the liberal recognition of the very existence of nations and support of their specific cultures? This is a difficult question. So one first may ask, why bother with it? Is there a need for a liberal version of nationalism? What should the difference be between classical anti-nationalist liberalism and liberal nationalism, and why should it matter?

Nationalism without essentialism

Karl Popper is a leading opponent of nationalism. His major contribution to political philosophy is his proposal not to legitimize some governments but to put them all under democratic control. Hence, whether the state is national or not matters only to the extent that this makes it democratically controllable and controlled. Western democracies are normally viewed as nation-states; is this view correct? Popper said, this view is false: we do not know what nations are and the idea of the national state is reactionary and he even puts the word "nation" in quotation marks (1957a: 288–9; 1957b: 51, 318). Ernest Gellner disagreed: he described the rise of nationalism as the intended increased egalitarianism through the abolition of aristocratic privileges, and as the intended increased liberalism through the spreading of the national culture that can be used as a democratic system of communications (1974: 142, 153).

The doctrine of destiny is a variant of the doctrine of the Chosen People; that doctrine rests on historicism, which, in its turn, rests on essentialism, which, in its turn, now leads to irrationalism. Popper bolstered the siblinghood of humanity by storming these doctrines, separately and jointly and by refusing essentialist definitions, as being either confusions or mere hypotheses.

Initially, essential definitions belonged to the rationalist accessories: they were supposed to improve our understanding of things that we already have some idea about, such as schools, fields of study, science, and nations. Yet essentialism is an error. Definitions are verbal and so they cannot help us understand the world, but we may make hypotheses about the peculiarities of the world. Such is Popper's claim that what characterizes science is the critical attitude. His peculiar attitude to essentialism lies not in his just critique of it but in his striking alternative to it. In characterizing schools, fields of study, science or nations, we describe (hypothetically) not essences but living traditions or institutions. This way petrified essences are replaced by flexible items, open to empirical examination and to improvement through critical assessment.

Traditions and institutions, said Popper, are hypotheses in the sense that they can be criticized and improved. The road to their improvement is making hypotheses about them and criticizing them. Popper's criticisms of some current hypothesis about science, for instance, suggest that efforts to enhance the critical attitude in science may help improve it. The same can happen to nationalism, I suggest. This, Popper did not say, mainly out of indifference to it (see Agassi 1993: 239).

Traditions and institutions do not depend on essential definitions. Like any other criticism, anti-essentialism will not kill entrenched traditions, however valuable it is as criticism. This is best illustrated by the story of nationalism: it is historically given; and so it survives criticism (hopefully in improved versions).

What is a nation? Popper said, we do not know (1957b: 51). This may be unproblematic, as when the President of the United States of America speaks to the nation in the traditional State of the Union address. Established nations are unproblematic. In the nineteenth-century debates raged about the essence of the nation; obviously they reacted to problems concerning national aspirations. They were couched in terms of definitions, and this determined their character to a large extent: aspirations led to the uncritical endorsement of confused theories that describe the stages of growth of a society, and in the nationalist version one of these stages is "nationhood." Popper rejected all theories of stages as essentialist and historicist. His critique should prevail. But as the debates left their marks on history, they are hard to ignore. What should be put instead of the theory of nations, nationalism and nationhood?

The need for group affiliation is ever present and in the modern world the said group is usually the nation. Popper recognizes this need for group affiliation, but he is hostile to it, seeing it as collectivist (Popper 1957a: 288; 1957b: 65–6). Perhaps; nevertheless, it is important to know under what conditions and how governments should cater to that need.

This need is suspect, as it is linked with the national destiny. Popper's criticism of destiny should prevail. Yet the actual experience of a shared destiny is often real and reasonable. It is inherently political, as it is the perception of common interests shared by sufficiently many people to create a surge of a sense of national unity. This is a general fact, blatant in the less fortunate nations, but it erupts from time to time even in advanced nations, and then it causes surprise, especially among the anti-nationalists.

The rationality of a shared destiny is obvious: as Ben Franklin said in his autobiography: "we are the thieves who must hang together lest we will hang separately." Albert Einstein was as much a cosmopolitan as anyone could be. He opposed all versions of nationalism; but under the pressure of circumstances he yielded and supported the Zionist cause, as one he found just. And he was grateful for this change (Einstein 1954: 190). Popper condemned Zionism because of its indifference to the local population and because of its revival of Hebrew (Popper 1957a: ch. 24, n. 54). These are now accomplished facts; the latter – revival of Hebrew – is beneficial, and the former – indifference to locals – is shameful and still in need of rectification. But this rectification is hopeless unless it is effected without threatening Israeli nationalism.

My suggestion is in this vein. The idea of nation-building invites attention. It appears in the charter of the United Nations Organization. Though it is a part of the UN's program for decolonization, it never attracted much attention, in political research or in practice. Under what conditions can the rise of a nation be beneficial (with democracy and liberty as criteria) and how can these conditions be realized? This is an interesting and useful question. The same should be said of existing nations: not about their rise but about their growth – the growth of national unity should be similarly examined. In both cases the need for group affiliation should be used for the improvement of the human condition. Combating it is useless and worse.

This program is in tune with Popper's teachings. He regrettably identified nationalism with its essentialist–historicist variants, and thus with chauvinism. This is a one-sided view of history. Gellner's book on nationalism (Gellner 1983) corrects it: he describes the early history of the nationalist movement as egalitarian. My aim is to go further and suggest that Popper's drive for egalitarianism suffers from a shortcoming: the way to boost egalitarianism is not by ignoring nationalism, much less by opposing it, but by steering it in the right direction.

National discrimination Israeli style

The liberal tradition discusses the state, not the nation. And this has a great advantage: the modern state is much better delineated than its nation. Citizenship is as well delineated as the state: the state determines its citizenry and sets procedures for granting and removing citizenship. Here is a significant principle that is curiously not written in any constitution: nationality equals citizenship. All and only the citizens of a state are members of its nation. (This oversight is particularly odd, since, as the *Encyclopaedia Britannica*, 1911, article on Nationality, tells us, this was the early use, in international (private) law, with no tinge of nationalist ideology.)

This principle delineates nationality almost as clearly as citizenship. It is not a perfect delineation, as it leaves unclear matters of dual citizenship and of the diaspora. But then these are (or should be made) marginal. Pluralism can take care of diasporas by delineating them non-politically: they are then viewed as sub-cultures. This is not the case of national minorities, which are political, and politically discriminated against. Popper denies this view in his idealized view of the multi-national empires (Popper 1957a: 158; 1957b: 50, 55–8; see also Popper 1976, section 21 and Hacohen 1996: 471). There are two obvious ways to prevent national discrimination: by adoption of the principle that all citizens belong to the nation or by denouncing nationality.

The denunciation of nationalism, particularly when it is just (i.e. when it is directed against chauvinism) gives political thinkers and practitioners headaches: it is counter-productive. The headache can be cured by identifying the nation with the citizens, with the general public, so that the nation's opinion is its public opinion, the citizens' opinion, and then the consensus is what most citizens endorse. All this seems trite; it is and should be trite. The question is, why then does the headache persist? Should the trivial view remove it?

My own concern in this matter stems from a problem about my own national identity, I am an Israeli. My Israeli passport officially testifies that I am a citizen, yet I am bound by Israeli law to carry an official identity card, and that card ascribes to me, equally officially, Jewish nationality. Officially I am also ascribed a religious affiliation, also Jewish. My choice in this matter is limited.

In 1949, when identity cards were first issued, I was a soldier, and I was required to fill a questionnaire. I was not allowed to fill it myself: another soldier did it for me. I wondered why, but found out at once. I said, nationality, Israeli, religion, none. The other fellow wrote, nationality, Jewish, religion, Jewish, nodding his head wisely as I protested. At the time this disturbed me a bit, but it did not seem to matter. This was a great mistake on my part, as I have learned from Hillel Kook, alias Peter Bergson, who fought in vain against the Allies' indifference to the Holocaust and for a secular Hebrew republic. (See Agassi 1981.) To that end he stressed the difference between (the Israeli) nation and (the Jewish) congregation. In Israel the two are systematically conflated. Consequent to all this, Israeli non-Jews are treated as a national minority, and thus as second-class citizens. This raises insoluble internal problems and impedes the peace process.

Matters in Israel regularly worsen in that respect: there is now a new Israeli law that bars from office anyone who does not agree that Israel belongs to the Jewish people at large, rather than to her citizenry. This law is sometimes called "the Miari Law," after a non-Jewish Member of Parliament who allegedly represented the Palestine Liberation Organization there when it was still illegal to communicate with its members. As that organization is now officially recognized, the Miari Law may be revoked. Yet there is a catch here: a discussion in parliament about it should be possible, but it is not, since those who oppose the law are excluded.

The Miari Law will be void when Israeli citizenship and nationality are one. The nation as a whole being largely Jewish should be of little political concern then, and invite no political interference – as required by the principle of the separation of church and state.

The principle of separation of church and state is an ancient Christian doctrine. Russell says that its popularity was due to the influence of St. Augustine (Russell 1946: 360). Machiavelli, the pioneer modern political thinker, reaffirmed it. Montesquieu and others copied it from him. It was first implemented in the United States and in Revolutionary France. England and Denmark have different models of a state-church, with the monarch as the head of the church, as suggested by Hobbes and Spinoza. The difference between the different constitutional solutions is often overlooked. And quite rightly so, since they all aim at the avoidance of religious discrimination, and this aim was achieved sufficiently successfully in the West. So it seems that a solution can be found without bumping into the headache concerning nationality. Is this so?

Not quite. Though Israel is and should remain Jewish for the foreseeable future, her being Jewish regrettably differs from France being Catholic. The principle of separation of church and state allows for Israeli citizens to choose their religious affiliation as they wish; it allows Israel to prefer Jews to others as new immigrants. Yet the wording of the famous Israeli Law of Return and its application violate this principle. The law says that every Jew has the right to immigrate and become a citizen. This invites the state to adjudicate on the question of affiliation to a religious community: the debate over who is a Jew permeates Israeli politics and vitiates it by imposing backward religious practices on a modern population. Also, immigration is almost entirely restricted to Jews. (Requests for naturalization are left to the discretion of the minister of the interior, who always refuses.)

The practical consequences of the Miari Law concerning the ownership of the state are not studied; it frustrates the normal desire to live in peace and prosperity, on the pretext that our historic task is to prepare a shelter for some future Jewish refugees.

One-fifth of Israel's citizens are non-Jews. They are Arabic-speaking and mostly (two-thirds) Muslim. They are second-class citizens because the nationality of almost all Israeli citizens is either Jewish or Arab. Religious discrimination is ubiquitous in Israel. Non-Jews are seldom allowed to bear arms, and the better jobs are bonuses for ex-soldiers. Also, non-Jews are not allowed to own land in predominantly Jewish towns; most of them live in their old, crowded places, whose local governments are maltreated. Their education system is separate and unequal. Official policies discriminate openly, as does the campaign for Judaizing the Galilee, for settling Jews in areas densely populated by indigenous Muslims.

Discrimination by creed and by gender was repudiated in Israel's Declaration of Independence. This document plus some constitutional laws serve as a substitute for a Constitution. A constitutional law safeguards the equality of women, yet they are discriminated by law through the relegation to religious courts of all family matters. Women are barred from religious court sessions. So they cannot serve there as witnesses or judges.

Individuals hostile to religion challenged the status of Jewish nationality in the Israeli Supreme Court. They lost: the court rules that the terms "Jewish" and "Israeli" are synonyms for the purpose of registration. Hence, Israeli non-Jews are not registered as Israelis. Some of them tried to change their Arabic first names to their Hebrew equivalents. They were refused. The courts rejected their complaint that this constitutes discrimination.

Reform or destroy nationalism?

The current Israeli response to the proposal to separate state and church rests on two items: the Law of Return and the Miari Law. Either precludes the separation. But this is an excuse: the wording of the Law of Return should be modified to grant the right of sanctuary to all those persecuted as Jews, regardless of their religious background. As to the Miari Law, it is undemocratic: as the government is accountable to citizens, the country belongs to them.

Regardless of the relations between church and state, discrimination is wrong. Being inconsistent about discrimination, Israeli law cannot fight it. Political and educational measures should be taken to that end. Philosophical attitudes to this practical matter vary. Some of those who are hostile to nationalism view it as inherently evil and recommend its abolition. The spirit of compromise alone should lead to the recommendation that it should be tamed; also, tamed nationalism may be very useful for the reduction of discrimination.

There is here a parallel (and an overlap) between nationalism and utopianism: Popper's objections to both rest on some historical records. But the record is no guideline; also, it is incomplete. Ian Jarvie has stated (Jarvie 1987) that utopianism need not suffer the defects rightly depicted by Popper (mainly utopian engineering, which he rightly condemned as irresponsible). He also noted that some responsible, liberal thinkers, who did contribute to progress, were guided by some utopian visions. (It was modernist utopianism, largely that of Francis Bacon, that ushered the modern world.) Gellner did the same regarding nationalism (Gellner 1974, 1980, and 1983): one may be a nationalist without endorsing collectivism: early nationalism came to abolish aristocratic privileges.

Popper's objection to utopianism and nationalism is expressed in psychological terms: he denounces them absolutely, rather than conditionally. This sharply differs from his qualified denunciation of religion and of socialism. He attacked only illiberal religions. He also said, though all socialist regimes are illiberal, they *could* be liberal. Could this not be said of nationalism? Not, of course, if it is nothing more than the doctrine of the Chosen People. But if it is more than that, then we could reject that specific doctrine and endorse the rest. This rest is the need for a sense of affiliation, but not only that. Under what conditions is nationalism admissible, then?

Classical individualism takes societies to be complexes of individuals; classical collectivism takes individuals to be parts of collectives. Popper denied both doctrines. So I have ascribed to him the affirmation of the existence of individuals as well as of collectives (Agassi 1987). And then nation-states may serve as ample evidence for the possibility and viability of liberal nationalist traditions. They are, after all, some of the most liberal states around. One might deny that they are national, of course, and in the chauvinist sense of the word they surely are not. This is why liberal thinkers are so often exasperated by the fusion of liberalism and nationalism: they consider it obviously inconsistent. But all inconsistencies are easily removable by modification, at times with reason.

The philosophic import of the matter is this: non-utopian reduction of discrimination is piecemeal engineering, and the starting-point is at home. Popper said, the starting-point is the worst case. This is not always practicable, but the worst case at home is. And what makes the cases at home more amenable to improvement is the concern of the public with local affairs. This concern is nationalist at heart.

It is no accident that nationalism was fueled by the wish of religious minorities to be treated as equals. Some of them had little success (the originators of Irish nationalism, who were Protestants); others were luckier (the Jews of Italy who served Italian nationalism). The practical matter is more significant than the philosophic one, as it is imperative to fight religious discrimination. In Israel the way to do this is by instituting the separation of state and church, and the way to effect this separation is by appeal to the Israeli sense of national identity rather than by teaching that nations in the chauvinist sense do not exist. The move in Israel toward religious fanaticism is caused by the frustration of the national identity: since it is confused with a religious identity it seems reasonable that the one will be reinforced by reinforcing the other.

Nationalism and patriotism

Since nationality is generally admitted as a modern phenomenon, there is some leeway in examining its historical roots. Of course, it is easier to seek its roots in illiberal traditions as they abound. Moreover, since liberalism is rooted in egalitarianism and nationalism implies the preference of the interest of one's own people, Popper's equation of national sentiments with tribalism is reasonable. Yet it is no clinching argument. Moreover, an illiberal *history* does not mean the movement is illiberal, or else all old institutions, particularly religious ones, should be deemed illiberal, yet there are liberal religions, even militantly liberal ones. The same is true of nationalism. This is often rejected on the ground that liberal nationalism is inconsistent. But then liberal religion is too. Monotheism was an advocacy of the siblinghood of humanity and drew its strength from this, yet it also came as the doctrine of the Chosen People.

The dispute over nationalism then is not historical at all; it is theoretical and practical. Can liberal nationalism be consistent? Can it serve good causes?

According to Popper, nationalist feelings infiltrate liberal strongholds and sabotage their liberalism. Also, and more importantly, being psychological, feelings are irrelevant unless group-cohesion is achieved through psychology alone. This idea is a dangerous myth, says Popper rightly: the surmise that cohesion needs a boost may lead to the imposition of conformity. Imposition is harmful; group-cohesion that develops freely or voluntarily is usually lauded – as patriotism. Is it ever needed?

This question was not asked until the nationalist movements were well under way. It was first answered in the nineteenth century by Prince Metternich, the reactionary inventor of the word "reaction" and the first who contrasted liberalism with nationalism: one need not heed the liberals, he said, since they are not patriots; they cannot be patriots, he added, since they are cosmopolitans. These are harsh words. Even an anti-nationalist from Bakunin to Popper can agree that liberals can indeed be patriots, and even better patriots for their liberalism. Patriotism need not be hostile to foreigners, yet nationalism, being group egoism, too often is. As nationalism is often used to incite to war, it is then not patriotic, since the love of country should lead to the love of peace.

Nor need patriotism be nationalistic, as it is a general form of love of one's country and country folk, be they a nation or not. Moreover, not all members of the nation need be patriots, and it is even an error to identify patriotism with the sense of national identity or unity. Yet the sense of national identity, according to what Metternich said, clashes with cosmopolitanism. To identify with humanity, it suggests, is to refuse to identify with the nation.

Does cosmopolitanism exclude patriotism? This question has two parts. First, is liberalism cosmopolitan? Second, are cosmopolitanism and patriotism mutually exclusive commitments? The reason for splitting the question is simple: it is *a priori* obvious that liberalism need not be cosmopolitan: it can be confined to the nation alone. This is, for example, the faith of all liberal isolationists in the United States of America.

Liberalism is egalitarian, and cosmopolitanism is the wish to be a citizen of the world. Taken literally, cosmopolitanism is a fiction: the world is not a single state, and for the present it cannot be. Yet there is a simple connection here: it is no accident that all liberal science fiction writers describe the future regime of our globe as a liberal United Earth. But this is merely to admit that liberalism cannot as yet be practiced thoroughly and systematically.

To declare oneself a cosmopolitan, then, is not to describe a political fact but to express a political sentiment. Does it exclude the sentiment of the patriot? The cosmoplotian sentiment is that of the Enlightenment: the siblinghood of humanity, the universalistic concern, namely, the concern for the whole of humanity. Patriotism is the concern for one's own country (be it a nation-state or not). They may but need not be mutually exclusive. Patriots undertake some concrete duties towards their own people. Cosmopolitans are committed to some vague duties toward humanity at large. This may offer great comfort to those who wish to be freed from firm commitments in favor of vague ones. This need not be so, of course, since if one takes seriously any duties towards humanity at large, then one has undertaken a tremendous burden, much larger than patriotism can impose. My example for this is Bertrand Russell. His concern for humanity placed on his shoulders the matter of nuclear disarmament. Whether he was right or not in his proposal of a policy of unilateral unconditional nuclear disarmament is not the issue here. At issue is the tremendous burden which he undertook, which is seldom found among those who are concerned with the whole of humanity and who disregard concern for their own people. In any case, it seems clear that Russell did not find concern for humanity in any way in conflict with the concern for his own people: he was a patriot, even though he never confessed to patriotic sentiments. Why?

Russell was proverbially shy. Yet in his autobiography he does reveal very deep feelings; he even reports the feelings he had on the worst day of his life. It was the day World War I was declared, Trafalgar Square was then full of jubilant people, and he roamed the square feeling most lonely and miserable (Russell 1968: 16). Was he concerned only with the fate of his own people, or of humanity at large? This is a silly question, and yet cases of international

191

conflict impose a choice between the interests of one's own nation and humanity. Thus, perhaps nationalism dictates volunteering to fight a war even though it was an error to start it. Russell did not consider this option. He went to jail as a conscientious objector.

Liberal nationalism

Consider an international conflict, say, war. Nationalists will fight for our interest and cosmopolitans will incline toward a pacifist position. There is a just national war. The Israeli war of independence is an example. It was a war for survival, and so all nationals had to enlist. Popper said that the Zionist movement was chauvinist and led needlessly to this tragic situation. So be it; should Israelis have capitulated or fought? Was it wrong on their part to declare independence?

Liberals do recognize a just war. Consider an unjust war, then. War is unjust when not the neighbor but we are the aggressors. This was the case with Israel's invasion of Lebanon. What should liberals do in such a case? What will patriots do? Both the liberal and the patriot should oppose aggression, even when their own people commit it. This is right even on pragmatic grounds. Russell, and other intelligent pacifists, declared pacifism in the national interest of every nation. Again, the question here is not, was Russell right in his political proposals; it is, are patriotism and liberalism mutually exclusive?

Popper asserted that a liberal can be a patriot, and he was right. He discussed this in more detail in an early publication of his (Popper 1927), when he still wrote on educational matters. He spoke there of the sense of love of *Heimat*, of one's place or home or homeland. He did not like it but recognized its positive educational value. His concern, it seems, was then to suggest that it can be used positively and that it is wiser to pursue it positively than to combat it. (See Hacohen 1996: 470.) My view of nationalism, especially of the sense of national identity, is quite similar to that. Whereas patriotism is hard to analyze, the sense of national identity is obvious. It can hardly be doubted that Russell himself had a very strong sense of national identity, though he scarcely ever found it necessary to dwell on it.

Cosmopolitan liberal feelings may conflict with a sense of national identity, as nationalism is selfish. So they should be harmonized with each other in the spirit of compromise, as advocated by Samuel (see above); it was defended, though not endorsed, by the American theologian Reinhold Niebuhr (1932: ch. 9). He found it wiser to demand that politicians follow the national interest as selfishly understood rather than the public interest at large as understood by good liberals. Wise national political action, he added, is hopefully in accord with the interest of the neighbor too, not in contrast to it. Wise political leaders, he suggested, should use the sense of national identity and interest for the better by disseminating the idea that the establishment of international harmony is in the long-term national interest. Only through the education of the common people, he suggested, can democracy hope to replace the short-term interest with a longer-term one.

This moves the discussion to harder questions; as conflict is inevitable, the questions are real. One nation's interest may conflict with the most benevolent act of another: the interest of a grain-producing nation is hurt by another's act of donating some grain surplus to alleviate the hunger of a poor nation. This is a very unpleasant fact and it raises the question in a totally new context. Yet the context imposes on us some vision of internationalism, and it is important to see that internationalism is not cosmopolitanism.

The example just noted is not too difficult, and it is regularly solved through negotiations. The United States adopts one attitude toward pollution in negotiations with Mexico and the opposite attitude in negotiations with Canada. (In the south it suffers from pollution that comes across the border but in the north its position is reversed.) This is clearly a matter of selfish interest and it is generally assumed that it will be solved with no violence and not too much injustice. But when the rich countries close their gates to immigration it is clearly not a liberal but a selfish move. It is clear that opening the gates of the rich countries to all immigrants will cause damage without solving the problems that lead to mass migration. Nor is it easy to recommend a more liberal policy. What is done is to recommend as much openness as possible, especially to political refugees, and even some sacrifice, and to reduce the gap between rich and poor nations by offering incentives to prospective emigrants to stay and help improve matters at home.

I do not know Popper's position regarding such matters. These are international conflicts that will not vanish even if nationalism will. Nor is it reasonable to expect governments to act against the interest of their citizens. It is reasonable, however, to harness the national sentiment to help the nation become more generous and more aware of the national need for altruism. This is the solution suggested by Reinhold Niebuhr.

The advocates of public assault on nationalism obviously must give up hope of entering political life. This makes anti-nationalist politics shallow (Weiler 1995: 54). The option to oppose nationalism but to keep quiet about it is not serious. The other option is to have no opinion about it. This is very hard when nationalism is common in the politics of all countries, and in most of them it is of the illiberal sort, that does have to be opposed. Effective opposition happens by recognizing the legitimate need of the ordinary citizen for affiliation, and the obvious fact that the logical choice will be to affiliate with the nation. A philosophy is defective if it bars honest, critically minded, and qualified thinkers from entering politics. This clearly invites a reform of Popper's political philosophy. But difficulties abound. For instance, most politicians these days belong to some religious denomination not sincerely but for practical reasons. This is wrong and it should trouble philosophy, since both the recommendation to prevaricate and the demand to stay out of politics are wrong. I do not know what can be done about this here and now.

Conclusion

The discussion on nationalism is central today for intellectuals who wish to contribute to politics: chauvinism has either prevented them from this for too long, or, worse, it made them contribute negatively. Popper's observations on the ill effect of the Hegelian tradition regrettably still stand. The cause of it is simple: not to be involved in one's own nation forces one to stay out or to partake in a very limited way and preferably in utopian projects. In particular it blocks intellectuals from partaking in the struggle against evils at home, since their protests are dismissed as insensitive to the complexities of national issues.

Discrimination has had a religious component since time immemorial. In modern times this component has lost some of its popularity. And then other components became predominant, such as xenophobia and skin color. Israel is sensitive to the discrimination of Jews in modern Europe. When it became uncomfortable to justify it by reference to religion, it was justified by reference to culture. A leading contributor to this attitude was Richard Wagner, who blamed the Jews not for anything religious or moral or political, but for their taste in music. The cultural excuse for discrimination soon turned into racism. This is the story of the secularization of anti-Judaism, of the invention of anti-Semitism. In Israel it is common dogma that anti-Semitism is identical with anti-Judaism: wherever religion is secularized, the disposition is strong to play down the process of secularization.

The discrimination that is practiced in Israel today is not so much by religion as by religious affiliation: religion is not very strong in Israeli society, whose founding fathers were confessed atheists. (Admittedly Israeli politics pushes the population increasingly toward religion, but this is derivative.)

The point then is that there are many grounds for discrimination, and they all amount to the same: the excuses for discrimination are and should be dismissed by every liberal thinker without further ado. Popper was the first to ask, what should the liberal attitude be to excuses for discrimination that happen to be valid? Suppose that Germans are racially superior to Jews and Gypsies. Will that make their discrimination against them right? No, says Popper, discrimination should be in favor of the inferior, not *against* them. This is noble; is it practical? Shaw said, no. He said: dying individuals will sacrifice everything to prolong their lives; society will not: social resources should be better managed.

For example: nuclear war would increase the numbers of birth defects beyond limit. Civilized societies would then be unable to offer all victims the benefits they enjoy today. The same trouble is already present when the civilized world faces enormous migration pressures. There is a general view that if discrimination against foreigners were lifted, then local advantages would vanish without benefiting others. This is not different from the argument against Marxists: taking money from the rich will not improve matters. And it is this kind of consideration that, these days, boosts xenophobia: unskilled workers in one nation find a common cause in fighting the import of cheap labor, and they hope that chauvinism will help this fight. Israel is in this position, in addition to the chauvinist craving for land. This is a matter of national interest, and it cannot be addressed without reference to nationalism.

The discrimination by religion is the focus of all this, as the Israeli and Palestinian non-Jews are mostly manual workers feared as competition and under a pretext that is a mix of nationalism and religion. It is useful to separate the different factors – religious, political, and economic – as well as the liberal and illiberal strains of Israeli nationalism. This should be done in a sincere effort to improve matters as long as peaceful improvement is possible. Nationalism should harmonize with the siblinghood of humanity: national concern should boost it.

REFERENCES

Agassi, Joseph. 1974. "The last refuge of the scoundrel." *Philosophia* 4: 315–17.

—— 1977. *Towards a Rational Philosophical Anthropology.* Dordrecht: Kluwer.

—— 1981. *Between Faith and Nationality: Towards an Israeli National Identity* (in Hebrew). English version, 1988, New York: Gefen.

—— 1984. "Nationalism and the philosophy of Zionism." *Inquiry* 27: 311–26.

—— 1986. "Will Israel ever become a nation?" In Alpher 1986.

—— 1987. "Methodological individualism and institutional individualism." In Agassi and Jarvie 1987: 119–50.

—— 1991. *The Siblinghood of Humanity: Introduction to Philosophy.* Delmar, NY: Caravan Press.

—— 1992. "Hobbes in contemporary Israel." *International Problems: Society and Politics.* 31: 17–25.

—— 1993. *A Philosopher's Apprentice: In Karl Popper's Workshop.* Amsterdam and Atlanta GA: Editions Rodopi.

—— 1997. "Celebrating the open society." *Philosophy of the Social Sciences* 27: 486–525.

—— 1999. *Between Faith and Nationality: Towards an Israeli National Identity.* New York: Gefen.

Agassi, Joseph and I. C. Jarvie (eds). 1987. *Rationality: The Critical View,* Dordrecht. Kluwer.

Alpher, Joseph (ed.). 1986. *Nationalism and Modernity: A Mediterranean Perspective.* New York: Praeger.

Amsterdamski, Stefan. 1996. "The Significance of Popper's Thought", *Proceedings of the Conference Karl Popper: 1902–1994.* Poznan Studies in the Philosophy of the Sciences and the Humanities 49.

Einstein, Albert. 1954. *Ideas and Opinions.* New York: Crown.

Encyclopedia Britannica. 1911. Vol. 19.

Gellner, Ernest. 1974. *Contemporary Thought and Politics.* London: Routledge.

—— 1980. *Spectacles and Predicaments.* Cambridge and New York: Cambridge University Press.

—— 1983. *Nations and Nationalism.* Oxford: Blackwell.

—— 1996. "Karl Popper – the Thinker and the Man." In Amsterdamski 1996: 75–85.

Hacohen, Malachi. 1996. "Karl Popper in exile: The Vienna progressive imagination and the making of the open society." *Philosophy of the Social Sciences* 26: 452–92.

Hellwig, Monika K. 1976. *The Eucharist and the Hunger of the World*. New York:

Jarvie, I. C., 1987. "Utopia and the architect." In Agassi and Jarvie 1987: 227–43.

Kissinger, Henry. 1964. *A World Restored*. New York: Universal Library.

Maximoff, G. P. 1953. *The Political Philosophy of Bakunin*. New York: Free Press.

Niebuhr, Reinhold. 1932. *Moral Man and Immoral Society*. New York: Scribners.

Popper, Karl, 1927. "Zur Philosophie des Heimatsgedankens." *Die Quelle* 77: 899–908.

—— 1957a. *The Open Society and Its Enemies*. 3rd edn, vol. 1. London: Routledge.

—— 1957b. *The Open Society and Its Enemies*. 3rd edn, vol. 2. London: Routledge.

—— 1957c. *The Poverty of Historicism*. London: Routledge.

—— 1976. *Unended Quest: An Intellectual Autobiography*. London: Fontana.

Russell, Bertrand. 1934, 1962. *Freedom versus Organization: 1814–1914*. New York: Norton.

—— 1946. *A History of Western Philosophy*. London: Allen & Unwin.

—— 1968. *Autobiography*, vol. 2. London: Allen & Unwin.

Samuel, Herbert. 1937, 1939. *Belief and Action: An Everyday Philosophy*. Harmondsworth: Pelican.

Weiler, Gershon, 1995. "Reason and myth in politics." In I. C. Jarvie and N. Laor (eds), *Critical Rationalism, the Social Sciences and the Humanities*, vol. 2, *Boston Studies*: 162, 41–57.

14

IS THERE CAUSALITY IN HISTORY?

Cyril Höschl

My theme is that time acts as a condition limiting the possibilities of science and creating the absolute horizon of our ignorance, and this differs from science to science because of differences of time scale in the subject matter.

The philosophical work of Sir Karl Popper differs strikingly from others by its wideness of scope. It covers, among other things, the methodology of science, logic, political science, history, probability theory, psychology, and the histories of science and philosophy. Sir Karl has many followers working in very different disciplines who, consequently, do not always understand each other. What might be called "the Prague appreciation of Sir Karl" was initiated by medical doctors, with a weak philosophical background, who were interested primarily in his thoughts regarding the self and its brain. But analytical philosophers, mathematicians, sociologists, and political scientists in Prague were interested in what George Soros, in his address at the Central European University, called "a totally different aspect of his work."[1] But despite his wide-ranging philosophical interests, Sir Karl's thought shows considerable consistency, closely related to his "clarity, beauty and kindness." What is the reason for the *prima facie* thematic breadth of his work? In my opinion it is the inability of scholars like me to match his universality and his exceptional capacity to apply general ideas in seemingly independent areas. Let me share with you the rather private delight that I experienced in discovering a common denominator in Sir Karl's notes on induction and demarcation of science (Popper 1980; Popper and Eccles 1977) on the one hand, and his fight against historicism (Popper 1957) in political science on the other.

First, I will briefly describe the initial conditions of my hypothesis. Let us assume, in accordance with Popper's philosophy, that induction does not work and that it will lead, *sooner or later*, to a dead end. So general theories cannot be derived from individual events. But they can be refuted by individual events, because these can contradict the description of facts.[2] This implies that the

1 The Open Society Prize. The ceremony held at the CEU, Prague on 26 May 1994. In Memoriam Karl Popper in Prague. CEU&3.LFUK, Prague, 1995, p. 34.
2 The theory always comes before the fact: the fact either disproves the theory or not. It never happens the other way round. Science always uses deduction.

predictive power of induction is time-limited. Popper's example with swans (Popper 1980) is a good illustration. Popper tried to find a demarcation line between science and pseudoscience, or, to put it differently, between critical thinking and dogmatism. He was inspired in this by Einstein, who stated at a lecture in Vienna in May 1919 that it would be necessary to forsake his theory of relativity if observation did not find the changes in the red shift that he predicted would be caused by gravity. That was Popper's stellar hour: science in fact puts forward hypotheses that it is possible to test. In Popper's terminology, "possible to test" means "possible to falsify," possible to disprove. If somebody says, for instance, that all swans are white, and I show him a black one, then he has two possibilities: either to correct his original statement, which represents the scientific approach, or to say that the black one is really not a swan.

Popper calls the latter response "the immunization of a hypothesis." One who immunizes a hypothesis against any kind of falsification can always claim to be "right," but this is why Popper cites Einstein's statement of how to refute his hypothesis as an example of the genuine scientific attitude. A scientist, for Popper, is someone who, like Einstein, is able and willing to give a description of circumstances in which his hypothesis would be refuted. For instance, psychoanalysis is an example of a pseudoscience. If you go to see a psychoanalyst, and she treats you and you then feel better, she will say: "You can see now that it works, you are feeling better already." But if you feel worse and do not want to continue the treatment, she will say: "Now you are in the expected stage of resistance and this proves that everything has worked as it should." Marxism also immunized itself in this way, remaining unshaken after *history disproved* its postulates one by one.[3]

Now I have italicized the temporal references printed here – *sooner or later* and *history disproved* – in order to emphasize that science always leaves a theory open for falsification in the future. That is why induction does not work on a long-range scale. It may seem obvious that the sun will rise tomorrow morning. But there is no guarantee that this is true for days $D_{(1,\ldots,n)}$, where $n = \infty$. Similarly, the hypothesis that all swans are white can be regarded as true *until* someone shows us a black one. This is why Popper argues that scientific method is a permanent confrontation of theories with facts. Science, in other words, works by permanent attempts at falsification. And falsification occurs

---

3 One little postscript to this: Popper distinguishes between honest and dishonest immunization. An honest immunization defends a theory by expectations that can themselves be falsified. When, for example, Newtonian physicists claimed that there must be another planet beyond Uranus because they could not explain the deviation of its course from Newton's calculation in any other way, they immunized their theory of the movement of cosmic matter. But this immunization was itself falsifiable. And when methods of observation improved, they were found to be right. Their immunization contributed to the search for and eventual discovery of Neptune. Dishonest immunization, on the other hand, makes it impossible to falsify any hypothesis. According to Popper, the unscientific is everything that is not falsifiable.

as a result of deductive, and not inductive, inference. It occurs when the facts contradict the theory.

But now comes the crucial moment. Scientific trials arranged to falsify hypotheses are feasible only on a time scale that is comparable with a human life. If we accept Popper's rejection of induction as scientific method, then we have to conclude that the scientific approach is not feasible on very large time scales. Natural laws make it possible to predict events.[4] But where the falsification of theories is missing, it is also impossible to discover laws. This is the case with large time horizons. This is the reason why Darwin's evolutionary theory is not really a theory of biology, but rather a history of nature. Simply put, it has virtually no predictive power.[5] Astronomy is another example. It can test predictions only on a very limited time scale. Despite, or should I say due to, the incredible differences in the age of the light which draws in the sky the picture of a far-away universe, scientists can project time into one "current" moment or "cinema picture." But they cannot predict any significant new event in space, not even the appearance of a supernova or the extinction of a star. On the other hand, the gravitation laws enable us to predict short-term events, like the free fall of a stone, or tomorrow's sunrise. Time acts as a condition limiting the possibilities of science and creating the absolute horizon of our ignorance.

The order of scientific disciplines sorted according to their achievements (practical applications, number of publications, progress over the centuries, etc.) correlates well with the size of the time scale with which they deal (see table 1). There are, however, some exceptions and complications, when, for example, rapid scientific achievements in technology can be applied to "long-time" disciplines like astronomy and geology. The speed of the processes that are studied also plays a role. The second important factor is the degree of complexity of the system that is studied. According to F. A. Hayek (Hayek 1952), there is no chance that the human brain[6] could understand a system that is more complex than itself. But human society represents just such a system. And Hayek suggests that, in fact, the only way in which we can bring order into chaos is to let it arrange itself (Hayek 1990).

History, as a subject of scientific method, shares both of these handicaps. It studies an incredible complexity of billions of interactions among individuals. And it does so on a time scale that is too large to be studied using scientific trials. Popper's rejection of historicism[7] is therefore a logical consequence of his rejection of induction and of his demarcation of science from pseudoscience.

---

4 The term "prediction" (to predict = to tell in advance) is related to "correlation," "causality," and "forecasting."

5 Not one new species has been predicted since evolutionary theory was introduced.

6 "If the human brain was so simple that we could understand it, we would be so simple that we could not." Emerson Pugh.

7 Historicism, according to Popper, says that we have a chance to discover laws that would enable us to predict history. Historicism, in other words, sees an analogy between historical and natural sciences.

Table 1

Discipline (in order of progressiveness)	Time scale of studied events
Electronics	milliseconds
Nuclear physics	< seconds
Chemistry	seconds
Biochemistry	seconds – minutes
Molecular biology	minutes
Physiology	minutes – hours
Pharmacology	hours – days
Biology	years
Medicine	lifetime
Humanities	tens – hundreds of years
Historical and political sciences	hundreds of years
Evolutionary biology	thousands of years
Geology	> thousands of years

Finding a law that makes prediction possible may be closely connected with the discovery of a cause. And the presence or absence of a cause may have significant predictive power. But my question is: "Can there still be causes of historical events, if scientific method is not applicable in history, and there is, therefore, no possibility of predicting them?"

There is a well-known tendency to mistake prediction for causality in contemporary science, as predictors are often suspected of being the cause of the events that they predict. Causality means that all phenomena occur as consequences of other phenomena. But the relation of two or a few phenomena (their "correlation") is always a rough abstraction. There are at least two types of "causes": crucial stimuli and conditions. The influence of crucial stimuli in history is not falsifiable in properly designed trials because of the extremely large time periods to be tested. The conditions are permanently changing, so their influence can hardly be detected. Human and animal purposes complicate matters. Taking the subjectivity of animals into account, it is preferable to talk about a *reaction* rather than a consequence. And as the period of time between "cause" and "consequence" gets longer or irregular, the correlation often becomes fuzzy and difficult to find. Purpose, moreover, is an *important feature* complicating the one-way temporal direction of causality.

Aristotle in *The Physics* (1; 2, VII, 198a) saw four main kinds of causes: substantial (Latin *Causa materialis*, Greek AITIAI HYLÉ); formal (Latin *Causa formalis*, Greek AITIAI EIDOS); moving (Latin *Causa movens*, Greek AITIAI TO KINÉSAN); and purposeful (Latin *Causa finalis*, Greek AITIAI HU HÉNEKA). This understanding of order was replaced in the eighteenth century by the mechanistic materialists Holbach (Holbach 1770) and La Mettrie (La Mettrie 1747), who, following the discoveries of Galileo and Newton, understood causality in the mathematical sense as a transfer of energy from one body to another. But this idea of causality is not applicable

200

in history. And it was then criticized by the empiricists, who stressed that cause is nothing but habit. According to Hume, the only reason to infer causality between two events is their constant temporal conjunction. And were it so, causality could not be distinguished from correlation. But this kind of causality is also not applicable in history, since history emerges in singularities, and significant correlations are between typical or repeatable events. After Hume, Immanuel Kant (Kant 1912–23) postulated that things-in-themselves are in principle unknowable; that what we really study is nothing but the world of phenomena; that reality cannot be built on custom alone; that causality is one of the categories of our mind; that we tend to chain up events and to formulate laws; and that causality is valid only in the world of phenomena, as opposed to the world-in-itself. But were it so, there would not be causality in history but only phenomenological investigation. Positivists such as Auguste Comte and John Stuart Mill then formulated four methods for discovering causality:

1   the method of identity (e.g. of two phenomena)
2   the method of difference (missing phenomenon 1 accompanied by absence of phenomenon 2)
3   the method of grouped changes (if it is not possible to remove a phenomenon, the changes are correlated)
4   the method of residuals (stepwise exclusion of several phenomena; suspect cause can be hidden in the remaining ones).

But the crisis of modern science warns us not to overestimate this understanding of causality. It makes us aware of the limits of reductionism even in natural science: we can search for causal relationships at certain levels of knowledge, but we are not able to find them among different levels, e.g. the psychological (mind), the biological (body), and the historical (society).

That is why contemporary science is openly searching for "markers," as opposed to causes. Markers have predictive rather than explanatory power. Four main types of prediction can be seen to emerge:

1   a tautological (for example, "duration and severity of illness" predicts "bad prognosis")
2   a heuristic ("fishing"; it often emerges as a "correlation" on endless sheets of print-out, with multiple regression analyses not primarily testing a specific hypothesis; it is characterized by the statement "we have also found ..." which can be also understood as "we have caught ... ")
3   a logical (models; e.g. the prediction of steady-state plasma drug concentrations accomplished by obtaining two blood samples after a single test dose)
4   an irrelevant one (mistakes; errors, e.g. when measuring normal volunteers using tools pertinent for pathology).

But tautological predictors are not causes. And heuristic predictions need an amount of data that is not, because of the time required, obtainable in the study of history. In addition, heuristic power does not prove causality. And logical models are not applicable in history. So I am afraid that the only type of prediction frequently used in history (4) is the irrelevant one.

We can, I think, conclude that since the methods used in natural science do not apply to the study of history, historical prediction is in practice far less reliable than in natural science. If there is causality in history, we have no tools to discover it.

REFERENCES

Aristotle. 1980. *The Physics*. London: Heinemann.
Hayek, F. A. 1952. *The Sensory Order*. Chicago: University of Chicago Press.
—— 1990. *The False Conceit. The Errors of Socialism*. 3rd edn. London: Routledge.
Holbach, P. H. D. d'. 1770. *Système de la nature ou des lois du monde physique et du monde moral*. London.
Höschl, C. 1993. "Prediction: nonsense or hope?" *British Journal of Psychiatry* 163 (suppl. 21): 46–54.
Kant, I. 1912–23. *Kritik der reinen Vernunft*. In *Werke*, ed. E Cassirer. 11 vols. Berlin: Reimer.
La Mettrie, J. O. de. 1747. *L'homme machine*. Reprinted Princeton: Princeton University Press, 1960.
Popper, Karl R. 1957. *The Poverty of Historicism*. London: Routledge & Kegan Paul.
—— 1980. *Unended Quest. An Intellectual Autobiography*. 5th edn. Glasgow: Fontana/Collins.
Popper K. R. and J. C. Eccles. 1977. *The Self and Its Brain*. Heidelberg, Berlin, New York: Springer.

15

MATCHING POPPERIAN THEORY
TO PRACTICE

Fred Eidlin

What Popper offers us isn't just a bunch of useful ideas, but also an ethics. Joseph Agassi has even called Popper's philosophy "the new religion" (1982: 242). Tom Settle, argues that "Popper's philosophical thought is unified by a structure of interconnected problems posed by his moral views" (1982: 116).

For Popper, the search for knowledge, for absolute truth, was not a game. It is not by chance that words like "hope," "courage," respect," "duty," "faith," "humanitarianism," even "love," occur so frequently in his writings. His anger at Hegel is due not only to the intellectual support Hegel allegedly provides for totalitarianism, but also to his alleged pollution of the intellectual atmosphere, to his alleged hindrance of the search for truth (see, for example, Popper 1966: 78–80 and 393, also Popper 1976b: 294–8). In Popper's view, to carry on and promote the search for the truth is a moral obligation. This helps us to understand why, although Popper condemns Hegel and the likes of him, he admonishes us to respect simple, ignorant people as potential sources of truth. Mortal sins for Popper are pretentiousness, dishonesty, and unclarity.

As a student, I spent too much time being bored. When I became acquainted with Popper's philosophy in 1975, I thought I could now look forward to a life of intellectual adventure, not only in the application of Popper's ideas in my own research, but also in exchanges with other scholars inspired by Popper.

After all, Popper had explained a good part of my boredom. Genuine inquiry, in his view, is not on topics or subjects; it is driven by live problems. Much of what counts as scholarship is boring because it is not problem-driven. Even the great Aristotle might at times be given to dry fact-gathering and systematization. Moreover, even if a scholar has a problem, he might be difficult to understand because he has failed to express himself clearly. Even a scholar with as great a reputation as Hegel could be opaque, not because he was profound, but because he sought to hide his own confusion from his readers.

The revolutionary potential in Popper's philosophy, though by no means universally recognized, has been appreciated by many. Bryan Magee, for example, draws our attention to the major influence Popper has had on individuals of first-rate significance in their own fields – how his philosophy changed the way they did their work. William Bartley contends that "the gulf between Popper's way of doing philosophy and that of the bulk of contemporary professional philosophers is as great as that between astronomy and astrology." If Popper is right, Bartley wrote, then "the majority of professional philosophers the world over have wasted or are wasting their intellectual careers" (1982: 269).

What is this revolutionary philosophy?

I am not thinking of Popper's many useful ideas and his important contributions to substantive debates in several fields. It is possible to discuss and even develop upon most of these without being at all infused with the spirit of his philosophy. Many have borrowed ideas from Popper without making the slightest mention of where they came from. Some have even taken ideas from Popper and presented them as anti-Popperian ideas.

What I have in mind are Popper's behavioral prescriptions for inquirers, and the views about knowledge underlying these prescriptions. For example:

We are ignorant, very ignorant indeed!

> Thus a scientist may be a great and most admirable discoverer; but still he does not know: he is far from being a super-human authority. He must submit to criticism; and very likely he will be superseded … It may be well for us to remember that, while differing widely in the little bits we know, or rather guess, in our infinite ignorance we are all equal.
>
> (Popper 1978: 2)

All people are possible sources of truth – even simple, uneducated, ignorant, dogmatic people. Therefore, the *rationalist attitude* can only be: "I may be wrong and you may be right, and by an effort we may get nearer to the truth" (Popper 1966: 25).

Truth is hard to come by! It is difficult to get at the truth. Truth is not manifest (Popper 1965: esp. 27–30). It can be very hard to break the fetters of what we think we already know. Moreover, it is not enough simply to find the truth and expose it for all people of good will to recognize it. You may have to work very hard to make yourself understood to others. You will still often be misunderstood, even by listeners and readers of good will.

Knowledge has many sources, but none is justified. With every step forward we discover new and unsolved problems. Where we thought we were standing on firm and safe ground, in fact, all things are insecure and in a state of flux (Popper 1976a: 87).

Do I have a real problem? There are so many urgently important problems that we have no excuse to squander our efforts on insignificant research. The mere fact that people in my discipline are doing something is no reason to do it. Disciplines do not exist, but are merely administrative units of great convenience to university administrators. "There are no subject matters; no branches of learning – or rather of inquiry: there are only problems and the urge to solve them" (Popper 1983: 5). We should not believe in "fashions, trends, tendencies, or schools, either in science or in philosophy … [F]ashions can have only one serious function – that of evoking criticism" (ibid.: 7).

Is my problem formulated clearly enough, so that all my readers know what is going on? What makes it a problem? Why is it important?

Have I reconstructed the problem situation clearly enough? Would representatives of opposing positions recognize my reconstruction as a faithful representation of their positions? Before criticizing these opposing positions, have I tried not only to represent them faithfully, but also to strengthen them, so that I am criticizing them in their strongest versions?

Have I formulated my hypotheses or problem solutions clearly and sharply enough, so as to make it as easy as possible for my listeners and readers to recognize the difficulties bound up with them? Have I myself tried to detect the weaknesses in my proposed solutions? Have I remembered that it is better to propose risky hypotheses that are false than less risky hypotheses which, although they may be more plausible, say less about reality?

Have I really tried as much as I could to benefit from criticism? Have I done everything possible to understand why my critics are not satisfied with my views? Although it may often be very difficult to understand my critics, I should be thankful for their efforts. As Popper writes (in his answer to Lord Boyle), "serious rational criticism is so rare that it should be encouraged. Being too ready to defend onself is more dangerous than being too ready to admit a mistake" (1974: 1153). We should be thankful for every serious attempt to criticize our positions. Praise is of no intellectual value. Victories in debates are of no intellectual value. Yet if we can succeed even in getting a little clearer about our problems, we should be very happy with that intellectual achievement.

Although, over the years, I have met many interesting people who call themselves Popperians, my original expectations were disappointed. I usually cannot detect the difference between astronomy and astrology to which Bartley alludes in the work of philosophers who claim to follow Popper. Although Popperians stress the importance of Popper's ideas often and energetically, in practice their work usually isn't much different from that of other scholars. I have not been able to detect any radical differences between the eight or so Popper conferences I have attended and other academic conferences.

Another unsettling realization that came to me over the years was the frequent strikingly unPopperian behavior on the part of Popperians, including Popper himself. Ernest Gellner once referred good naturedly to Popper's great book as "The Open Society by One of Its Enemies." As Walter Weimer has put it: "An immediate complication arose when I studied what I have come to call the Popperian church – instead of a coherent philosophical position, one finds a lightly disguised squabble of alley cats" (1979: xi). Clearly, subscribing to the norms and views summarized above does not necessarily result in behavior that accords with them. It would be unreasonable to expect Popperians to be more than ordinary mortals. However, I have been struck by how little influence Popper's behavioral norms have had upon those who claim to subscribe to them.

Of course, if we reflect on Popperian norms, it should be clear how immensely difficult they are to practice. Debates and discussions in a genuine Popperian spirit are very rare. So is research conducted in a genuinely Popperian spirit. It is one thing to agree with Popperian norms. It is quite a different matter to be able to take these norms to heart and to practice them. For example, criticism, useful as it may be, can cause great emotional distress. It can be painful to live with open intellectual problems. Criticizing others can get us into trouble.

So, what is the point of all this? I guess the problem I want to end with is this: is it possible to do better by Popper's standards? Would it be possible to develop a tradition of inquiry in a genuine Popperian spirit, or will Popper's norms inevitably remain in the realm of unattainable utopia?

REFERENCES

Agassi, Joseph. 1982. "In search of rationality – A personal report." In Paul Levinson (ed.), *In Pursuit of Truth*. Atlantic Highlands, NJ: Humanities Press: 237–48.

Bartley, William Warren, III. 1982. "A Popperian harvest." In Paul Levinson (ed.), *In Pursuit of Truth*. Atlantic Highlands, NJ: Humanities Press: 249–89.

Popper, Karl R. 1965. "On the sources of knowledge and of ignorance." In *Conjectures and Refutations: The Growth of Scientific Knowledge*. New York: Harper & Row, esp. pp. 27–30.

—— 1966. *The Open Society and Its Enemies, vol. 2: The High Tide of Prophesy, Hegel and Marx*. Princeton, NJ: Princeton University Press.

—— 1974. "Replies to my critics." In Paul A. Schilpp (ed.), *The Philosophy of Karl Popper*, Part 2. La Salle, IL: Open Court, pp. 1153–9.

—— 1976a. "The logic of the social sciences." In Theodor W. Adorno, *et al.*, trans. Glyn Adey and David Frisby, *The Positivist Dispute in German Sociology*. London: Heinemann, pp. 87–104.

—— 1976b. "Reason or revolution." In Theodor W. Adorno, *et al.*, trans. Glyn Adey and David Frisby, *The Positivist Dispute in German Sociology*. London: Heinemann, pp. 288–300.

—— 1978. "Reflections on the prehistory of western universities and their present crisis," *Guelph University News Bulletin* 22 (39) (19 October 1978): 2.

Settle, Tom. 1982. "The standard bearer." In Paul Levinson (ed.), *In Pursuit of Truth*. Atlantic Highlands, NJ: Humanities Press: 109–25.

Weimer, Walter. 1979. *Notes on the Methodology of Scientific Research*. Hillsdale, NJ: Erlbaum [John Wiley].

SUBJECT INDEX

NAME INDEX

Adorno, T. 128 n.1
Agassi, J. 81 n.9, 105, 182, 184, 187, 189, 203
Aristotle 28, 46, 58, 200
Aron, R. 93
Atlas (Greek mythology) 49
Augustine, St. 187

Bacon, F. 189
Bakunin, M. 183, 190
Ballerowicz, L. 176 n.5
Balliol College 146
Bartley, W. 30 n.2, 204, 205
Bartnik, Father C. 163, 164
Bedford College 56
Beethoven, L. von 30
Bergson, H. 7
Bergson, P. 187; *see also* Hillel, Rabbi
Berlin, I. 12, 138, 171, 172, 173, 175, 176, 177, 178, 179
Bevin, E. 98
Bishop Pieronek *see* Pieronek, Bishop T.
Bishop of Rome 169
Bismarck, O. von 93
Black, M. 66
Blum, C. 86
Boolos, G. S. 62
Boyle, E. (Lord) 8, 97, 205
Bradley, F. H. 103
British Broadcasting Corporation (BBC) 17
British Library of Political and Economic Science 6 n.2
Brubaker, R. 94
Bryant, J. 90, 95
Buddha 143 n.5
Bunge, M. 84
Burke, E. 176 n.4
Butler, S. 87, 88

Canterbury 25
Carnap, R. 17, 47, 58, 64

Cartledge, P. 85
Charlemagne 99
Chmielewski, A. 10, 28
Chopin, F. 30
Christ, Jesus 86, 143, 153, 164
Cohn, N. 86
Colas, D. 91
Collingwood, R. 171
Comte, A. 201
Confucius 143
Constant, B. 91
Cook, M. 85
Copernicus, N. 117
Crone, P. 85
Crosland, A. 7
Crossman, R. 7

Danube area 89
Darwin, C. 105, 106, 199
Dawson, D. 85
De Valera, E. (Prime Minister of Ireland) 34
Democritus 102
Dewey, J. 25
Dummett, M. A. E. 66
Dworkin, R. 179

Eidlin, F. 13, 84
Einstein, A. 29, 30, 48, 106, 185, 198
Engel, P. 61
Engels, F. 148
Etchemendy, J. 62
Ewing, A. C. 66

Father Bartnik *see* Bartnik, Father
Father Piwowarski *see* Piwowarski, Father
Feyerabend, P. 102
Fichte, J. G. 89, 182
Field, H. 61, 62
Flis, A. 12
Franco, General F. 168